New Casebooks

COLERIDGE, KEATS
AND SHELLEY

New Casebooks

New Casebooks

COLERIDGE, KEATS AND SHELLEY

EDITED BY PETER J. KITSON

First published 1996 by
MACMILLAN PRESS LTD
Houndmills, Basingstoke, Hampshire RG21 6XS
and London
Companies and representatives
throughout the world

ISBN 0-333-60889–5 hardcover
ISBN 0-333-60890–9 paperback

A catalogue record for this book is available
from the British Library.

10   9   8   7   6   5   4   3   2   1
05   04   03   02   01   00   99   98   97   96

Printed in Hong Kong

Contents

v

Acknowledgements

The editor and publishers wish to thank the following for permission to use copyright material:

Andrew Bennett, for material from *Keats, Narrative and Audience: The Posthumous Life of Writing* (1994), by permission of Cambridge University Press; Susan Eilenberg, 'Voice and Ventriloquy in *The Rime of the Ancient Mariner*', from *Strange Power of Speech: Wordsworth, Coleridge and Literary Possession* (1992), by permission of Oxford University Press Inc.; Kelvin Everest, for '"Mechanism of a kind yet unattempted": The Dramatic Action of *Prometheus Unbound*', *Durham University Journal*, Special edition on Shelley, 85 (July 1993), by permission of the Durham University Journal; Frances Ferguson, for 'Shelley's *Mont Blanc*: What the Mountain Said', from *Romanticism and Language*, ed. Arden Reed (1984) Methuen & Co, by permission of Routledge; A. W. Phinney, for 'Keats in the Museum: Between Aesthetics and History', *Journal of English and Germanic Philology*, 90, 2 (1991). Copyright © 1991 by the Board of Trustees of the University of Illinois, by permission of the author and the University of Illinois Press; Nicholas Roe, for 'Keats's Lisping Sedition', *Essays in Criticism*, 42 (1992), by permission of Oxford University Press; Karen Swann, for 'Literary Gentlemen and Lovely Ladies: The Debate on the Character of *Christobel*', *English Literary History*, 52 (1985), by permission of Johns Hopkins University Press; William A. Ulmer, for '*Adonais* and the Death of Poetry', *Studies in Romanticism*, 32 (1993), by permission of the author; Kathleen M. Wheeler, for '"Kubla Khan" and Eighteenth-Century Aesthetic Theories', *The Wordsworth Circle*, 22 (1991), by permission of The Wordsworth Circle; Susan Wolfson, for 'Feminising Keats' from *Critical Essays on John Keats*, ed.

Hermione de Almeida (1990). Copyright © 1990 by Hermione de Almeida, by permission of G. K. Hall & Co, an imprint of Simon & Schuster Macmillan.

Every effort has been made to trace all the copyright holders but if any have been inadvertently overlooked the publishers will be pleased to make the necessary arrangement at the first opportunity.

General Editors' Preface

The purpose of this series of New Casebooks is to reveal some of the ways in which contemporary criticism has changed our understanding of commonly studied texts and writers and, indeed, of the nature of criticism itself. Central to the series is a concern with modern critical theory and its effect on current approaches to the study of literature. Each New Casebook editor has been asked to select a sequence of essays which will introduce the reader to the new critical approaches to the text or texts being discussed in the volume and also illuminate the rich interchange between critical theory and critical practice that characterises so much current writing about literature.

In this focus on modern critical thinking New Casebooks aim not only to inform but also to stimulate, with volumes seeking to reflect both the controversy and the excitement of current criticism. Because much of this criticism is difficult and often employs an unfamiliar critical language, editors have been asked to give the reader as much help as they feel is appropriate, but without simplifying the essays or the issues they raise. Again, editors have been asked to supply a list of further reading which will enable readers to follow up issues raised by the essays in the volume.

The project of New Casebooks, then, is to bring together in an illuminating way those critics who best illustrate the ways in which contemporary criticism has established new methods of analysing texts and who have reinvigorated the important debate about how we 'read' literature. The hope is, of course, that New Casebooks will not only open up this debate to a wider audience, but will also encourage students to extend their own ideas, and think afresh about their responses to the texts they are studying.

John Peck and Martin Coyle
University of Wales, Cardiff

Introduction

PETER J. KITSON

The stereotypical image of the inspired Romantic poet seeking out solitary and sublime landscapes as a subject for his song is one that persists in the popular mind. Yet if the last two decades of criticism of the Romantic poets has taught us anything, it has shown that we must be wary in our acceptance and use of such critical constructions as 'Romanticism' and 'Modernism' to define the culture of any given literary historical period. Editing a book of recent critical essays about the work of Coleridge, Keats and Shelley inescapably involves approaching the issue of 'Romanticism' as well as attempting to elucidate the relationship of these poets to the ideas and beliefs of their age. Certainly the canonical work of these three poets, along with their contemporaries Wordsworth, Blake and Byron, demonstrates the hallmarks of what has been traditionally known as Romanticism, revealing such traits as: the affirmation of the creative powers of the Imagination; a new feeling for the natural world (albeit the Keatsian version is somewhat suburban); the acceptance of an organic model for explaining human behaviour and the rejection of empiricist, materialistic and mechanistic philosophies to explain the world; a concern with the nature of the individual self; a belief in the possibilities of revolution and transformation whether in the moral or political sphere; an awareness of the limitations of language in describing reality; the possibilities of transcendence or 'unity of being' achieved through communion with nature; a preference for the sublime aspects of the natural world as a subject or setting for their art; a heightened view of the poet as variously sage, philosopher, prophet, political or religious saviour.[1] Indeed, until fairly recently scholars of Romanticism, with some notable exceptions, generally accepted René Wellek's classic formulation of their subject as 'Imagination for the view of poetry, nature for the view of the world, and symbol and myth for poetic style'.[2] For Wellek, Romanticism was a European phenomenon which manifested itself throughout the nineteenth century in Britain, Germany, France, Spain, the states of the Italian peninsula, as well as in America.

1

An early scepticism about the possibility of homogenising Romanticism as a movement in the European context was expressed by A. O. Lovejoy. After investigating the different manifestations of Romanticism in European countries he concluded with the view that 'the word "Romantic" has come to mean so many things that, by itself, it means nothing. It has ceased to perform the functions of a verbal sign'.[3] However, Lovejoy's more sceptical outlook on the subject has been held in critical abeyance until relatively recent times. Thus, for most critics, the Romantic period has generally been regarded as covering the years from c. 1790 up until around 1830 (or even up to 1850), while the word 'Romantic' has been used to describe a body of work using widely different techniques and styles but showing a number of shared characteristics or symptoms that have been used to justify such periodisation.

I

It is important to grasp the key point that those poets and writers who have been designated as 'Romantic' by later ages did not regard themselves as part of a movement, nor did they use the word 'Romantic' to designate their own work. When this word was used, for instance in Coleridge's discussion of his contributions to *Lyrical Ballads* (such as *The Rime of the Ancient Mariner*) in 1798, it was employed to indicate the action and modes of romance, suggesting that the contents of a work were exotic, idealised, marvellous, or supernatural.[4] The term was used in this period in the work of the German critics Friedrich and August W. Schlegel, but in their application it functioned as a way of discriminating classical or ancient literature from that of the modern age, and the modern age included medieval and Renaissance literature. For the Schlegel brothers, Shakespeare was the supreme Romantic artist. This more theoretical usage of the term was not widely available until the translation of the Schlegels' lectures in 1815, although Coleridge was aware of it as early as 1803.[5] It is salutary to understand that the Romantic poets did not regard themselves as belonging to a unified movement, and were very much divided among themselves on political and religious, as well as artistic, lines. If anything, the poets were viewed by the periodical press as forming three distinct groups: the 'Lake School' including Wordsworth and Coleridge; the 'Satanic School' of Byron and Shelley; and the 'Cockney School' of Keats and his associates. Ironically, the sixth canonical Romantic poet, William Blake, was so obscure to his contemporaries that he was hardly regarded by anyone as a significant literary figure.

So how did these six poets composing their work in the late eighteenth and early nineteenth century come to be regarded as exhibiting similar enough characteristics to justify their grouping as a literary movement? The process of literary canonisation for the Romantics was a long and complicated affair. Often it involved determined attempts by friends, relations or disciples to establish the literary reputation of their idols. Thus Mary Shelley devoted the years after her husband's death to the task of enhancing his reputation, and James Henry Leigh Hunt anthologised and marketed Keats's verse for an early Victorian audience, stressing its spontaneity, passion and sincerity. The roles of John Stuart Mill and Matthew Arnold in establishing the reputation of Wordsworth as a poet who preached the therapeutic powers of feeling, and who demonstrated inwardly perceived standards of 'tact' and quality, were crucial, as was the championing of the hitherto very obscure artist and poet William Blake by Algernon Swinburne and his late-Victorian Pre-Raphaelite friends. Equally significant was the anthologising of the poets of the period in such popular collections as F. T. Palgrave's *Golden Treasury* (1861–88) which allocated the Romantics as much space as the entire remainder of the body of English poetry,[6] and the creation of 'Romanticism' as a distinct historical object of study in university lectures and texts at the end of the nineteenth and during the early years of the twentieth century.[7] One result of this long and complicated process was the establishment of Wordsworth as the most significant and representative voice of Romanticism in the period, a view that, if measured by the amount of editorial and critical labour devoted to producing and interpreting his texts, is as true of today's scholarship as it was of the literary criticism of Arnold and his later Victorian and Edwardian successors. Later estimations of the true worth of the 'great' poets of the period contrast markedly with the estimations of Wordsworth's contemporaries who regarded Sir Walter Scott and Lord Byron as their age's most culturally epiphanic writers. It is also true to say that at the time only Scott and Byron had European reputations. The success of Wordsworth's poetry owes a great deal to Coleridge's championing of his friend's poetic genius (and concomitantly of his own critical genius) in his *Biographia Literaria* (1817), most of the second volume of which is allocated to establishing and criticising Wordsworth's poetry. Coleridge's own artistic values (his high claims for the powers of Imagination over Fancy, and his espousal of the organic analogy as a way of understanding art and society) were profoundly influential on critics of later years, such as Matthew Arnold, Thomas Carlyle and F. D. Maurice, as well as being crucial in the formation of an aesthetic theory of 'high' Romanticism.

One consequence of Coleridge's championing of Wordsworth as a poet of feeling, imagination and unity was a downplaying of the dramatic and ironic aspects of Wordsworth's art (most accessibly glimpsed in the *Lyrical Ballads*). Similarly the sceptical, ironic and self-doubting voice of Byron's poetry was soft-pedalled in establishing a dominant mode of typifying the best poetry of the period. It is this very ironic, urbane and sceptical voice which much recent deconstructive and historicist criticism has attempted to recover, a Romanticism which is deeply suspicious of the transcendental claims of the philosophy of Coleridge and the German Idealist philosophers. It is also fair to say that the concern with the sceptical voice of Romanticism has shown itself much more strongly in American than in British criticism of the subject. Nor must it be assumed that the distinction between Coleridgean idealism and Byronic irony is in any way a hard and fast binary opposition. Both tendencies are operative in all the sophisticated writers of the period, but in different ways and with differing emphases.

II

The most influential twentieth-century view of Romanticism has probably been that established by the comparativist criticism of A. O. Lovejoy, René Wellek, Harold Bloom, M. H. Abrams and others. In this body of criticism Romanticism is very much defined as a European phenomenon. René Wellek, as I noted above, argued for Romanticism as a 'system of norms', stressing imagination, myth, symbol and nature. The most influential comparative criticism of Romanticism must, however, be that of M. H. Abrams, whose two monumental studies of the subject, *The Mirror and the Lamp* (1953) and *Natural Supernaturalism* (1971), redefined Romantic thought for a generation of scholars.[8] Marshalling an enormous range of learning and reading, Abrams' work fully affirmed Romantic values and argued for their importance in the founding of modern consciousness. Abrams believed that Romanticism marked a distinct break from eighteenth-century Neo-classical ways of looking at the world – a movement from a mimetic or mirroring of objective social reality to an expressive projection of the mind's aspirations. Although troubled by many aspects of Wordsworth's early poetry, Abrams held that there was a distinct Romantic theory and criticism which typified the work of the artists of the period.

In *Natural Supernaturalism* (1971) Abrams further argued that Romanticism constituted 'the Spirit of the Age' (borrowing the phrase from the Romantic critic William Hazlitt) and that it responded directly to the political events of the American and French Revolutions. Abrams identified early Romantic thought with Enlightenment notions of democracy and the rights of man which became spiritually transformed in the work of the major Romantic poets. He claimed that the most typical of Romantic poems are structured by the figure of the circuitous journey from innocence to experience and from this state to a higher form of innocence. This internalised quest begins with the child's unconscious conviction of a primal unity between itself and the natural world but subsequently demonstrates a fall from that communion with nature into an experience of alienation, division and isolation. This fall, like the fall of Adam and Eve in Milton's *Paradise Lost* is, however, fortunate because it enables the individual to confront and utilise the higher powers of consciousness. Like the Wedding Guest in *The Rime of the Ancient Mariner*, the poet becomes 'a sadder and a wiser man'. A higher state of consciousness, possibly at times verging upon transcendence, is thus attained as the poet comes to know the ultimate harmony that exists between the workings of nature and those of his own mind. For Abrams, Romantic poetry secularises and humanises the Judaeo-Christian myth of innocence, sin, fall and redemption that has dominated Western culture for 2000 years. Central to Abrams' argument is the notion that the Romantics, such as Wordsworth and Coleridge, turned away from their early involvement in radical politics and their support of the French Revolution and relocated their political aspirations in the realm of art and imagination instead, finding, like Adam and Even at the close of *Paradise Lost*, 'a paradise within ... happier far'. Collective political transformation thus gives way to imaginative and individual redemption.

III

The Abrams reading of Romanticism, which is still available in many excellent works of traditional scholarship, has been criticised from three main directions which the essays in this collection to some extent represent. These are what we may call the poststructuralist, the historicist, and the feminist.

Poststructuralist accounts of literature have taken on the insights of the Swiss linguist Ferdinand de Saussure and the French philosopher Jacques Derrida which stress the arbitrariness and instability of language in determining meaning. Romantic poetry, with its stress on the transcendent vision of the poet, has proved a fertile ground for the major deconstructive critics, suspicious of the high claims such poetry makes. The work of Paul de Man has been typical of this tendency. De Man, in such impressively rigorous deconstructive works as *Blindness and Insight* (1971) and *Allegories of Reading* (1979), has questioned the assumptions about language and subjectivity which underpin the Romantic concern with sublime moments of vision.[9] In his important article 'Intentional Structure of the Romantic Image' de Man argued that the Romantic poets attempted to discover a natural language where words contained the same original meaning as the things that they described but that this attempt only resulted in an endless quest for an illusory singleness:

> For it is the essence of language to be capable of origination, but of never achieving the absolute identity with itself that exists in the natural object. Poetic language can do nothing but originate anew over and over again; it is always constitutive, able to posit regardless of presence but, by the same token, unable to give a foundation to what it posits except as an intent of consciousness. The word is always a free presence to the mind, the means by which the permanence of natural entities can be put into question and this negated, time and again, in the endlessly widening spiral of the dialectic.[10]

It is by no means immediately obvious what de Man is saying here, but he appears to imply that where moments of vision occur, they do so in language as 'acts of consciousness', and as such they are subject to doubts and questionings, and that they are incapable of providing the kind of transcendental security the Romantics sought for. Such moments are thus, inevitably, moments of failure.

De Man's best known essay on Romanticism is probably 'The Rhetoric of Temporality' in which he challenged the common assumption (in the work of Abrams, Wellek and elsewhere) that Romanticism was committed to the symbol as its most authentic and expressive kind of figurative language. Coleridge had argued that allegory was a mechanical and decorative style vastly inferior to the unifying and organic figure of the symbol which was always a part of the whole it represented rather than a mere additional ornamentation. In his essay de Man overturned this hierarchy of literary value, between words and their signifiers, positing the notion that, in fact, early nineteenth-century literature presents not symbolic but rather allegorical structures which expose the split between the origin and the meaning of the sign. What de Man is getting at here is an undermining of the idea that it is possible for a figurative language, such as symbolism, to stand independently as an image of the true reality of which it is a part. Instead he shows how language is always reliant on other language.[11]

Of the British Romantic poets, Wordsworth has been the chief subject for de Man's analysis, but he also wrote a celebrated essay, 'Shelley Disfigured', on that poet's uncompleted last poem, 'The Triumph of Life'. In this essay de Man claimed that Shelley's poem 'warns us that nothing, whether deed, word, thought, or text, ever happens to us in relation, positive or negative, to anything that precedes, follows, or exists elsewhere, but only as a random event whose power, like the power of death, is due to the randomness of its occurrence'.[12] The nature of Shelley's poetry with its ethereal imagery and hectic strain has made it especially conducive to the deconstructive analysis practised by de Man, an analysis that emphasises the free play and the randomness of language. Two of the essays in this volume on Shelley's verse (those by Frances Ferguson and William A. Ulmer) approach their subject from this methodological standpoint and several others are informed by de Man's influential writings.

The criticism of Geoffrey Hartman has been in some ways analogous to that of de Man, though it has been much more concerned with the actual texts than de Man's, as in his substantial and brilliant book *Wordsworth's Poetry 1787–1814*, a collection of essays on Wordsworth's poetry. Unlike Abrams and Wellek, Hartman was not all that interested in the view of Wordsworth as organic poet and healer of the divided subject, but instead concentrated on the ways in which consciousness is represented in Romantic poetry. In the essay 'Romanticism and Anti-Self-Consciousness' Hartman argues that what makes Romantic poetry modern is its mission to do without the role of a mediator, such as religion or literary tradition. The Romantic period witnessed an attempt by art to free itself from its subordination to religion. In Romantic art the traditional scheme of Eden, Fall and Redemption is merged with 'a new triad of Nature, Self-Consciousness, and Imagination'.[13] It is the Romantics' awareness of their self-consciousness and their wish to find a way of transcending this overpowering sense of self which marks out their work as modern. Rather than seeing the Romantic poets as poets of nature, Hartman sees them more properly as poets of imagination. He is also keenly aware of the errors and disjunction in their work, rather than celebrating them as prophets of unity and harmony. Although Hartman's major work has primarily been concerned with Wordsworth, his criticism is wide-ranging and superbly erudite. He has also contributed a famous essay on Keats entitled 'Poem and Ideology: A Study of Keats's "To Autumn"', which argues that Keats's ode is a very English kind of poetry in which the author avoids the rapt invocation to the Gods of the oriental 'epiphanic' verse. In depicting the mysterious picture of Autumn rather than a mystery itself, Keats demonstrates a new kind of consciousness that is Romantic as well as English.[14]

Related to the work of Hartman and de Man but on a very different track is the criticism of Harold Bloom, who applied the notion of the Freudian 'family romance' (the son's desire to possess the mother and to kill and replace the father) to the canon of the great poets. Bloom argues that since Milton, the first truly great 'subjective' poet, later poets have suffered an awareness of their late-coming and unoriginality, fearing that their poetic fathers have used up all the available poetic inspiration. They thus have a hatred of the poet-father and a desperate desire to deny paternity. Bloom argues that this leads the later poet to adopt a series of defensive strategies whereby he (and for Bloom it always is a 'he') 'misreads' the work of his predecessor poet and rewrites the prior poem as he believes it should be written. Bloom developed a rather involved critical vocabulary to describe this process derived from mystical Cabbalistic writing, arguing that the 'strong' poet grapples with his predecessor poet by first taking a new look at his work (*limitation*), then replacing one form of the work with another (*substitution*), and finally restoring the 'true' meaning of the poem (*representation*).[15] Bloom has found the Romantic poets to be a fertile area for applying this reading, especially in the crisis poems of the four 'strong poets' Blake, Wordsworth, Shelley and Keats in which each poet struggles creatively to misread his predecessor's work. What Bloom does, more effectively than most, is to provide a reason why the Romantic poets should be so obsessed by prior figures, such as Milton, although few critics have taken up his idiosyncratic terminology and method.

More straightforward psychoanalytical readings of the Romantics based on the work of Freud and his successors and revisers have been frequent. The Romantic concern with the psychology of the self has made them suitable cases for interpretation if not treatment. Indeed, the term 'psychoanalytical' itself was coined by Coleridge. Usually such writing presents the subject (the poet, the speaker, the 'I' in the poem) as impaired and needing to confess its own anxieties. More complex have been studies based on the writings of the psychoanalytical theorist Jacques Lacan. Lacanian thought is notoriously complex and difficult (and few would claim to have fully understood it), yet perhaps the reason for its application in Romantic studies is relatively easy to comprehend. Lacan regards human subjects as passing from an infantile phase in which there is no division between the self and the world (a phase Lacan calls the realm of the 'Imaginary') and entering into a pre-existing system of signifiers or language (which he describes as the 'symbolic' order). Language is thus always something other than the self, yet it is only through language that the self can attempt to express its desires, an attempt which is constantly subverted by the pressure of the unconscious.[16] Despite the difficulties of some of Lacan's ideas, it should be easily seen how the Romantic desire to penetrate through and beyond language to some ultimate reality which transcends both self and nature is conducive to explanation in Lacan's terminology. Lacanian thought provides a suggestive commentary on the typical desire of the speaker in a Romantic poem (for instance, Wordsworth in *The Prelude*, Coleridge in 'Frost at Midnight', Keats in 'Ode to a Nightingale', Shelley in 'Ode to the West Wind') to go beyond the world and by penetrating it to arrive at either some point of single harmony or, alternatively, to experience a complete dissolution of the self into others. The poetry of both Wordsworth and Shelley, in particular, has attracted this kind of analysis, which stresses how both the ideas of desire and search in Romantic poetry and its need to escape beyond language and recover the primal unity of the 'Imaginary' realm – always itself an impossibility – are an essential human aspiration.[17] In glossing the ideas of Lacan this way I have tended to flatten and systematise this very suggestive and open-ended thought, the application of which to Romantic studies has brought fresh interpretations to the poetry, although many have criticised its tendency to develop readings of the poems which appear distant and unrelated to the actual subjects of the poetry.

IV

The second major challenge to the Abrams reading of Romanticism has come from historically based approaches. Since the 1980s Romantic studies has been newly invigorated by a body of historical criticism which has provided fresh and original rereadings of both the poetry and the period. Such readings have been refreshingly sceptical of M. H. Abrams' notion that Romantic poetry transforms contemporary political thought into an apocalyptic politics of the imagination. In many ways this kind of criticism has returned to Byron's scathing attack on the 'Lake School' in the Dedication to *Don Juan* which accuses Wordsworth and Coleridge of simply dressing up their political treachery in the garb of mysticism. One distinction about historicist studies of the area, however, does need to be made. A number of critics have analysed Romantic texts in reference to the known and intended political sympathies and beliefs of their subjects, seeing their poetry as intervening in the political debates of the time. Such works as E. P. Thompson's essay 'Disenchantment or Default: A Lay Sermon', Nicholas Roe's *Wordsworth and Coleridge: The Radical Years* (1988), P. M. S. Dawson's *Shelley and Politics: The Unacknowledged Legislator* (1980), and the collection of essays 'Keats and Politics' edited by Susan J. Wolfson and published as a special number of the important subject area journal *Studies in Romanticism* (25 [1986]), are attempts to reveal and elucidate the relationship between the politics and the poetry (see Further Reading at the end of this volume). Nicholas Roe's 'Keats's Lisping Sedition' (essay 5) is an excellent example of the ways Keats's stylistic singularities can be read in political terms.

Roe's work in many ways represents a traditional kind of historically based literary criticism dependent on substantial knowledge of, and research into, the events and ideas of the age in which the

Romantic poets lived. His criticism makes specific connections between the poetry and the events of the times, finding the early poetry of Wordsworth and Coleridge to be very much involved in the political debates of the revolutionary period the poets lived through. The term 'New Historicism', however, has been coined to denote a different kind of historicist criticism which has departed from this more traditional scholarship. This term is loosely used to designate the work of a series of historicist critics of Romanticism, most famously Jerome J. McGann, Marjorie Levinson and Marilyn Butler, who have admonished those such as Abrams for too readily accepting the Romantic view of the world on its own terms. The publication in 1983 of Jerome McGann's *The Romantic Ideology* challenged both Abrams' paradigm of Romanticism as well as the evasion of historical meaning in the language-based accounts of the poststructuralists. McGann argues that Romanticists have slavishly accepted the critical concepts and vocabulary of their subject. They have failed to understand that the Romantic theorists were, in fact, a part of a particular class of British society whose artistic values and ideas were a reflection of their own class interests. McGann argued that only by critically detaching ourselves from such Romantic notions of art can we begin to understand their 'Romantic Ideology' or false consciousness.

McGann insists on the importance of making a clear distinction between cultural formations, such as 'Romanticism', 'Modernism' or 'Postmodernism', and the historical frameworks within which they have developed, that is between the 'Romanticism' and the 'Romantic Period'. McGann's earlier work was chiefly on the poetry of Byron, and his later criticism is informed by a sense that Byron has been excluded from the classic formulations of Romantic thought – as he notes, 'as Coleridge and Wordsworth gradually came to define the "centre" of English Romanticism in twentieth-century critical thinking, Byron slipped further from view'.[18] The work of Byron has certainly always been difficult to place in the Romantic context. Although the most Romantic personality among the six canonical poets, famed for his unconventional lifestyle, morality, and commitment to liberal causes, such as the independence of Greece (which cost him his life), Byron, in fact, was artistically the most un-Romantic of the poets. His ideal was the great exemplar of eighteenth-century Neo-classicism, Alexander Pope. Indeed, he confided to his publisher John Murray his anxieties 'that we are upon a wrong revolutionary poetical system – or systems –

not worth a damn in itself & from which none but Rogers and Crabbe are free – and that the present & next generations will finally be of this opinion'.[19] Byron dissented from the doctrines of Imagination and originality as preached by Coleridge and Wordsworth, and largely accepted (although in different ways) by Shelley, Keats and Blake. He commented that 'Imagination and Invention' were common qualities and that 'an Irish peasant with a little whisky in his head will imagine and invent more than would furnish forth a modern poem'.[20] Byron's subjects are as much cosmopolitan and social as natural and sublime, and his later style is more demotic and rhetorical than prophetic, mythic or symbolic, so that while it is easy to fit his work into the Romantic period, including it under 'Romanticism' poses important questions for the critic.

As well as bringing Byron back to the centre of the Romantic period, critics like McGann have reappraised the key Romantic texts, finding them to contain very different messages from those found by M. H. Abrams and his followers. As an example of how a New Historicist critic, such as McGann, approaches a Romantic text we can look at his article 'The Meaning of the Ancient Mariner'. Here McGann is not interested in arriving at any definitive conclusion regarding the poem's actual meaning, but rather he sees the wish to find the symbolic or allegorical meaning of the enigmatic tale of the wandering ancient seaman as reflecting the critic's acceptance of Coleridge's own critical strategies: 'for meaning, in a literary event, is a function not of "the poem itself" but of the poem's historical relations either to its readers and interpreters'. In revising, retitling and supplementing (particularly the addition of the marginal gloss) his poem between the years 1798 and 1828, Coleridge set up an interpretive model for understanding the poem which subsequent readers have worked within: 'For not until we see that our dominant interpretive tradition has been licensed and underwritten by Coleridge himself will we be able to understand the meaning of this tradition, and hence the meaning of the "Rime".' For McGann, then, the poem presents us with an example of the 'romantic ideology' which must be seen for what it is, 'a historical phenomenon of European culture', generated to save the 'traditional concepts, schemes and values of Christian heritage'.[21]

McGann is thus concerned less with any patterns of meaning that emerge from the text, such as the movement from innocence to experience and alienation, followed by possible redemption, than he is with the transmission and reception of the text in literary history. Significantly, McGann has recently edited *The New Oxford Book of Romantic Period Verse* (1993) which attempts to select work from the Romantic period rather than the work of the Romantic movement (he has elsewhere preferred the term Regency literature to Romantic). In this collection he elects to include only those works which had been printed or distributed at the time, so that, for example, Wordsworth's most quintessentially Romantic poem *The Prelude* (published posthumously in 1850) is not represented. McGann's collection is also ordered not by poet but by year, further effacing the notion of the six great Romantic poets, and it includes many non-canonical (hitherto minor) male and female writers.

The work of the British historicist critic Marilyn Butler has shown itself to be similarly revisionary. Butler, whose earlier work was concerned with Maria Edgeworth and the Romantic novel, has found the notion of Romanticism to be a particularly unhelpful one. In her *Romantics, Rebels, and Reactionaries* (1982) Butler challenges the relationship between Romanticism and Revolution so current in scholarship, arguing that the 'first wave of European Romanticism' should more properly be linked with the conservative cause than with radicalism. She claims this occurred in England from 1792 onwards and that much of what we regard as characteristically 'Romantic' work is, in fact, grounded on the central tenets of Neo-classicism. For her this is true of Blake's work and, indeed, of the early work of Wordsworth: 'Both are taken to be inaugurating a new artistic tradition, rather than joining an established one. Yet the fact is that Wordsworth was brought up in the mainstream of Enlightenment culture, and he realises its potential better than anywhere, with the possible exception of Goethe.'[22] Coleridge's *Ancient Mariner* and the rest of the poems in *Lyrical Ballads* for Butler are thus not experiments but extensions of Neo-classical theory, the fundamental tenet of which is that art should 'imitate Nature – not sophisticated life, not life refracted though literature, but human existence in its simple, essential forms'.[23] Butler argues against viewing Romanticism as a monolithic movement. She brings out the tensions and disagreements in the period, arguing that Wordsworth and Coleridge after turning their back on the French Revolution became writers of the counter-revolution against whom the more liberal second generation of Romantic poets, Byron, Shelley and Keats, struggled.

The question of canon formation is also raised in Butler's account of the period. In a recent essay she makes the case for restoring excluded voices to the literary canon:

> What kind of critical difference would it make to study actual literary communities as they functioned within their larger communities in time and place? I propose that the poets we have installed as canonical look more interesting individually, and far more understandable as groups when we restore some of their lost peers.[24]

She believes that any discussion of the Romantic period must take into consideration the prominent novelists, philosophers, and political writers of the time as well as those poets, such as Robert Burns, Robert Southey, John Clare, Thomas Chatterton, George Crabbe, and Sir Walter Scott who have been excluded from the canon for various reasons. The exclusion of Scott and Southey from discussions of Romanticism has particularly troubled Butler.

Much more theoretical in language and method are Marjorie Levinson's new-historicist discussions of Wordsworth and Keats. Her early book on Wordsworth attacked his poem 'Lines composed a few miles above Tintern Abbey' for its picturing of the poet as calmly reflecting on a very artificially composed landscape and its failure to mention the historical crises of 1793 and 1798 (significant dates for the poem) as well as the homeless unemployed camped in the Abbey ground.[25] Levinson finds much fault with Wordsworth for evading these issues in the poem which, she argues, constitute a kind of 'absent presence' (a favourite phrase of the New Historicists). In her book *Keats's Life of Allegory: The Origins of a Style* (1988), Levinson argues that Keats's characteristically sensuous style and the hostile reception it aroused in the reviewers were both in fact related to his status as someone aspiring to the middle class. In a difficult and complex argument, Levinson links the Keatsian style of writing poetry to the class position of the poet, who desires the cultural heritage of the past that men like Wordsworth and Byron are able to take for granted. Keats's characteristic obsessions with the themes of fulfilment and anticipation, demonstrated in 'The Eve of St Agnes' and the great odes, are class obsessions of a section of the middle class itself wanting to arrive at power and dominance. Levinson regards the plots and imagery of Keats's romances as ultimately commenting on their own connections with the modes of production and exchange of the literary marketplace that they both delineate and try to resist:

To those early 'readers' Keats was the allegory of a man belonging to a certain class and aspiring, as that entire class was felt to do, to another: a man with particular but typical ambitions and with particular but typical ways of realising them. A world of difference separates this hermeneutic from the 'poignantly allegorical life', an adventure in soul-making, which has become today's John Keats.[26]

Just briefly surveying the work of a few critics we can see the very exciting and contentious debates that exist within the area of historicist criticism, from Nicholas Roe's attempt to reclaim the Romantics for the left to the new-historicist project's desire to reveal the Romantics' complicity with the establishment. These varying strands of historicist criticism have been vital and crucial in bringing the poetry back into its political and historical context, including the great contemporary political debates about the rights of man (and of woman) and the meaning of the French Revolution. More than this, historically oriented criticism has reminded readers of Romantic poetry how literary studies can open up a range of new contextual concerns, such as the social, political and gendered inflections of poetic style, the histories of the poetry's publication and reception, and can transform biographical studies. This strand of criticism remains exciting and current; indeed, the latest book to appear on the poetry of John Keats, at the time of the writing of this introduction, is a collection of essays edited by Nicholas Roe, *Keats and History* (1995), which contains invigorating critical essays approaching their subject from the fields of politics, social history, feminism, economics, stylistics, and aesthetics.[27]

V

The third main strand of recent criticism of Coleridge, Shelley, and especially Keats, and of Romanticism in general is that which has been written from a feminist standpoint. The major impetus for restoring and examining women's writing has come from feminist studies of scholars such as Sandra Gilbert and Susan Gubar, Mary Poovey, Margaret Homans, Mary Jacobus, Susan Wolfson, Anne K. Mellor, Susan Levin, Jane Aaron and others (see Further Reading). Certainly it is true to say that most recent critics have found the exclusion of women from the canon of Romantic writers to be very troubling. Most older anthologies of poetry of the period do not include female poets of the period, such as Anna Laetitia

Barbauld, Felicia Hemans, Laetitia Elizabeth Landon, Hannah More, Mary Robinson, Anna Seward, Charlotte Smith, Jane Taylor, Mary Tighe, Ann Yearsley and Helen Maria Williams. After Byron the most successful poet of the age in terms of sales was Felicia Hemans and the most significant dramatist of the period was Joanna Baillie (whose call for a return to a simple language for poetry pre-empts that in Wordsworth's 'Preface' to *Lyrical Ballads*). Recent anthologies of Romantic poetry including McGann's *The New Oxford Book of Romantic Period Verse* (1993) and Duncan Wu's *Romanticism:An Anthology* (1994) as well as Jennifer Breen's *Women Romantic Poets* (1992) have redressed this balance to some extent. Oxford University Press has recently committed itself to publishing six texts by women Romantic writers and the first in the series, Stuart Curran's edition of *The Poems of Charlotte Smith* (1993), has already appeared.

However, it is fair to say that scholars of Romanticism have only recently begun to pay attention to the role of women writers within the period. As Stuart Curran points out in his important essay 'The "I" Altered', there were in actual fact thousands of women writing between 1780 and 1830 and it was these women writers who dominated the world of prose fiction, the essay and the theatre. It is also becoming apparent that with the rise of the novel as a genre in this period, poetry was becoming marked out as the preserve of male poets, which required birth and breeding as well as a common education and certain exclusive standards of shared taste.[28] This would seem to be the case with the epic which became a form associated with the male poet's artistic career. Those women who did attempt to become poets generally stuck to the form of romance and the sonnet. Indeed the Romantic revival of the sonnet form often attributed to Coleridge and Wordsworth was actually occasioned by the publication of Charlotte Smith's very fine *Elegiac Sonnets* which achieved a high degree of popularity and were much admired by Wordsworth and others.

Women writers were, though, chiefly working in the form of the novel which arguably became the female genre of the period, or at least became a 'feminised genre' in the same way that the epic became a 'masculinised' form. This is not to say that men did not write novels, but the novels written by Sir Walter Scott and William Godwin, for instance, were serious historical or philosophical works far removed from the domestic subject matter of Jane Austen's novels.

As Stuart Curran and others have pointed out, the women writers celebrated not the achievements of the imagination nor the spontaneous overflow of powerful feelings but the workings of the rational mind in both male and female. They stressed not so much the alienated self of the male writer but instead showed a concern with family and community care and attendant practical responsibilities (what Curran describes as the 'quotidian'). Curran's essay demands that we rethink of reassess our assumptions about gender and genre, the gendered nature of the Romantic visionary experience (which seems to be available only to males), Romantic notions of feeling and sensibility, and Romantic irony. This gendered difference in outlook between the masculine sublime and the female 'quotidian' has led Anne K. Mellor to argue in her recent book *Romanticism and Gender* (1993) that there are two kinds of Romanticism in the period, one 'masculine' and the other 'feminine". This for her is a gender bias and not a biological distinction. She argues, for instance, that Keats works within and struggles against a feminine Romantic aesthetic and that Emily Brontë's *Wuthering Heights* (1848) is a work of 'masculine' Romanticism. More than this, Mellor argues that the 'masculine' Romantic poets have attempted to assimilate those qualities which could be described as feminine into their own male egos:

> When we focus on the role that gender plays in masculine Romanticism, we often see the poet appropriating whatever of the feminine he deems valuable and then consigning the rest either to silence or to the category of evil. The female, certainly not the only, but always an inevitable other, becomes whatever the male poet does not wish to be. The male imagination speaks for female nature; the male lover casts the beloved as a female version of himself, the male poet cannibalises the feminine emotions of mercy, pity, love, he even becomes a mother giving birth to his own children poems.[29]

Thus, Mellor argues, the male Romantic poet appropriates those qualities gendered as feminine in the period and excludes women altogether, usurping female creativity by giving birth himself. Mellor claims that female figures in male Romantic poetry are silenced and that not one of the male Romantics is capable of imagining a Utopia where 'women exist as independent, autonomous, *different* – but equally powerful and respected – authors and legislators of the world'.[30] When women do appear in Romantic poetry as independent and wilful they are often demonised as in the case of the leprous figure of 'Nightmare Life-in-Death' or the ambiguous Geraldine of Coleridge's *Ancient Mariner* and *Christabel*. Mellor argues that if we give equal weight to the female poets of the period a paradigm shift in our understanding of Romanticism results.

Mellor, however, like Marjorie Levinson, identifies Keats as something of a special case, whose particular form of art is in some ways subversive of our established notions of Romanticism. A number of feminist critics have commented on the ways in which Keats has been associated with the 'unmanly' and 'effeminate' by critics of his own time and subsequently. The tone of such inquiries was set by Susan J. Wolfson's pioneering discussion ('Feminising Keats' [1990]), extracts from which are included in this collection (essay 4). Wolfson points to Keats's, at times anxious, perception of himself as an androgynously passive poet as well as the views of his contemporaries, such as Byron and Hazlitt, who regarded him as a precious and delicate writer. Shelley himself was also responsible for this perception of Keats by his popularising of the fiction that the poet's death was due to a viciously cutting review of his early poem *Endymion*.

Wolfson combines a scrupulous historicist account of the reception of Keats's poetry from the Romantic age to that of contemporary criticism and focuses on the critical obsession with Keats's masculinity. Keats's admirers have tended to defend his masculinity while his detractors have imputed an effeminacy of style and manner to his work. Wolfson points out that judgements of Keats as unmanly tend to coincide with more general cultural anxieties about the feminisation of men. For Wolfson, Keats becomes a site where the contradictions and ambiguities of gender definitions and discriminations are unveiled and opened to analysis. Other feminist critics have been less kind to Keats. Margaret Homans has argued that Keats, rather than being 'an honorary woman' evincing feminine characteristics, is instead a poet who equates his imaginative project with male sexual potency and who carries out a masculine appropriation of the feminine. For her Keats's position with regard to his female audience is a defensive one, conscious as he is that this audience has a power over him in terms of the literary marketplace.[31] For Anne Mellor, however, in *Romanticism and Gender*, Keats is an 'ideological cross-dresser' who embraces parts of feminine Romanticism although he is at times very uncomfortable with an assumption of ideas and feelings which could identify him too completely with the feminine.[32] Feminist criticism of poets and novelists from the period has thus been very wide-ranging in its scope, restoring neglected or excluded female writers as well as commenting on the gender implications of 'male Romanticism' and opening up the poetry to further analysis as we are obliged to rethink the implications of, for example, Keats's sensuous descriptions and Coleridge's demonic females and to re-appraise those discussions of Romantic poetry which have ignored the contributions of women writers.

VI

The essays collected in this volume, some of which have already been mentioned, are my attempt to provide a fairly representative selection of recent critical writing on the three poets and their most often discussed texts (detailed comment on the individual essays is given in the explanatory comment heading the endnotes to each piece). The first three essays treat three of Coleridge's poems: *The Rime of the Ancient Mariner*, 'Kubla Khan' and *Christabel*. Kathleen Wheeler's essay '"Kubla Khan" and Eighteenth-Century Aesthetic Theories' (essay 1) takes up some of the ideas first expressed in her important study *The Creative Mind in Coleridge's Poetry* (1981) and argues that the poetry composed between 1795 and 1798 exemplified Coleridge's adherence to the notion of the creativity of the mind in perception. As well as placing 'Kubla Khan' in the context of travel and garden literature, Wheeler demonstrates, through close reading, how the poem itself dramatis-es the very working of those creative artistic processes of which it is itself a finished product. This can be seen in the apparent 'flaw' or 'failure' of the poem in stanza iii. Susan Eilenberg's very impressive discussion of *The Rime of the Ancient Mariner* (essay 2) comes from her study of the poetry of Wordsworth and Coleridge, *Strange Power of Speech* (1992), and engages with the poem at the level of its formal qualities, its language, images and signs. Situating her discussion in the tradition of deconstructive reading established by Hartman and de Man, Eilenberg believes that it is language that tells the tale rather than the mariner, who, by contrast, appears as one possessed by a 'strange power of speech'.

The final Coleridge essay (3) by Karen Swann, 'Literary Gentlemen and Lovely Ladies', is on Coleridge's disturbing Gothic poem *Christabel*, and it attempts to explain why the poem was so exasperating and shocking to contemporary readers. Swann's work combines feminist perception with psychoanalysis, in particular in the ways she conveys the playfulness of desire as well as the defensiveness of the ways the masculine self attempts to construct itself.[33] Like the other critics on Coleridge represented in this section, Swann's work opens up the poetry to new perspectives and ideas that allow us to reread it in fresh and interesting ways.

Historicist and feminist writers have transformed criticism of Keats's poetry. As Nicholas Roe puts it, 'Keats has formed an important and rewarding focus for the newly-invigorated historical criticism that has flourished since the 1980s'.[34] After Jerome McGann's attack, in an essay of 1979, on the dominant aesthetic traditions of Keats criticism, it is no longer possible to regard the poet as an unworldy person living his life in an almost entirely literary context.[35] My selection of essays on Keats's work begins thus fittingly with Susan Wolfson's feminist discussion (essay 4) of Keats's preoccupation with gender and the ways subsequent criticism has been informed by such preoccupations. Nicholas Roe's 'Keats's Lisping Sedition' (essay 5) is very current in its attempt to relocate the poetry in a political context. Roe shows how the response to Keats's early poetry was occasioned by social and political prejudice and he argues that Keats's actual verse was thoroughly politicised. A. W. Phinney's account of Keats's 'Ode on a Grecian Urn', 'Keats in the Museum' (essay 6), takes on the arguments of new historicist critics, like Jerome McGann, arguing that Keats's poem had in fact pre-empted such discussions of the relationship between art and history, and that Keats himself was very aware of the 'paradoxes of writing for the future'.

Andrew Bennett's reading of Keats's poem 'To Autumn' (essay 7) takes what appears to be a work resistant to the political and discusses how this resistance both implies and at the same time represses a political reading of the poem. Bennett's essay is fully informed by recent developments in literary theory but he is particularly concerned with theories of reading and especially the Romantics' concern with a future audience: 'a reception infinitely but undecidably deferred to the future'. Bennett examines Keats's 'To Autumn' in the light of agrarian economics in the early nineteenth century, suggesting that recent political and historicist readings are both figured in the text and disrupted by it. As in the other essays, we are thus offered a different Keats from that of traditional criticism, a Keats who is politically aware and (in his own way) engaged and committed to the liberal and progressive cause. We are

presented with a poet who is intensely aware of the pressures of
history and the problems of gender and who is able to represent
such tensions in his most individualistic sensuously descriptive style.
No less important perhaps, the essays leave us with a set of superb
poems made all the more problematic and challenging in their
implications than traditional criticism allowed for.

Percy Bysshe Shelley's poetry has always been more tractable to
deconstructive and poststructuralist readings than that of Coleridge
and this is represented in my selection of recent writing on three of
his major works, *Mont Blanc*, *Prometheus Unbound* and *Adonais*.
The first of these, by Frances Ferguson (essay 8), playfully reads
Shelley's complex poem in poststructuralist terms as concerned with
the process of signification, where both the perceiving mind of the
subject and the objective world of nature are contained within the
language system of the poem. Kelvin Everest (essay 9) presents a
more traditional and materialistic brand of criticism focusing on the
crucial third scene of the second act of *Prometheus Unbound* and
demonstrating the substantial intellectual demand placed upon the
reader by the poet. Everest shows how older views of Shelley (chiefly
those of Matthew Arnold and F. R. Leavis) as an ethereal, vague and
ineffective poet are woefully inadequate in representing his thought-
ful, learned and achieved verse. Fittingly, the final essay (10) in the
volume is an extract from William A. Ulmer's difficult but impressive
deconstructive reading of Shelley's lament for Keats, *Adonais*. For
Ulmer, metaphor is the main means by which the poet attempts to
escape the problems exemplified by the death of Keats, and by which
he tries to validate his own hopes for literary immortality against his
pressing disillusionments and anxieties. As with the other two essays,
Ulmer's writing is intensively engaged with the language of Shelley's
poetry and the implications it has for our understanding of this most
assured and complex of poets. Shelley's rapid thought processes, his
ever-changing imagistic patterns, and his obsessive desire to break
through barriers, moral, political and aesthetic, have made him a
fertile site for an enormous variety of critical approaches from the
historicist to the psychoanalytical. Above all, however, recent criticism of Shelley has given us a poet who is vitally aware of the power
of language as well as of its limitations.

The ten essays collected here, along with the other books and
essays I have mentioned elsewhere in this Introduction, are merely
like the tip of a massive iceberg of contemporary critical endeavour.
New readings of the poets and their texts proliferate, pushing

forward fresh and challenging ideas and theories. All three of the major strands of Romantic criticism which I have identified, the poststructural, the historicist, and the feminist, are currently flourishing and producing much invigorating and contentious writing. We have come a long way from the traditional critical certainties about the Romantic movement, with their depiction of the archetypal rebellious poet challenging the dominant cultural and political mores in his attempt to achieve transcendence and unity through communion with sublime nature. Although subsequent criticism has problematised such notions in its various attempts to de-mystify the Romantic achievement, it has shown a compulsive delight in reinterpreting these fascinating texts and viewing them from new perspectives and against fresh contexts. The interest in Coleridge, Keats and Shelley, and the other writers of the period shows no sign of abating as new directions are, at this moment, being explored and new progress is being made. What the latest directions are it is difficult to say with any certainty. Clearly feminist studies of the period have only just begun and many historicist critics are turning their attention to such issues as orientalism (how the East is represented in the poems), colonialism and Romantic attitudes to the slave trade. However future critics develop and pursue their individual critical projects it is certain that the works of the Romantic poets and their contemporaries will provide scope for many more books and collections of essays such as this one.

NOTES

1. See, for instance, M. H. Abrams' definition 'Neoclassic and Romantic', in *A Glossary of Literary Terms* (1941; 4th edn, New York, 1981), pp. 113–17.

2. René Wellek, 'The Concept of Romanticism in Literary History', in *Concepts of Criticism* (New Haven, CT, 1963), p. 161.

3. A. O. Lovejoy, 'On the Discrimination of Romanticisms', in *English Romantic Poets*, ed. M. H. Abrams (1960; 2nd edn, New York, 1975), pp. 3–12 (p. 6).

4. Marilyn Butler, *Romantics, Rebels and Reactionaries: English Literature and its Background 1760–1830* (Oxford, 1982), pp. 1–2.

5. David Perkins, 'The Construction of "The Romantic Movement" as a Literary Classification', *Nineteenth-Century Literature*, 45 (1990), 130–1.

6. David Simpson, 'Romanticism, Criticism and Theory' in *The Cambridge Companion to British Romanticism*, ed. Stuart Curran (Cambridge, 1993), pp. 1–24 (6–7), Jerome McGann, 'Rethinking Romanticism', *ELH*, 59 (1992), 735–54 (743–6).

7. Chris Baldick, *The Social Mission of English Criticism* (Oxford, 1987), pp. 59–85.

8. M. H. Abrams, *The Mirror and the Lamp: Romantic Theory and Critical Tradition* (New York, 1953), *Natural Supernaturalism: Tradition and Revolution in Romantic Literature* (New York, 1971).

9. Paul de Man, *Blindness and Insight: Essays in the Rhetoric of Contemporary Criticism* (rev. edn London, 1983); *Allegories of Reading: Figural Language in Rousseau, Nietzsche, Rilke, and Proust* (New Haven, CT, 1979).

10. Paul de Man, *The Rhetoric of Romanticism* (New York, 1984), p. 6.

11. Paul de Man, 'The Rhetoric of Temporality', in *Blindness and Insight*, pp. 208–9, 222.

12. Paul de Man, 'Shelley Disfigured', in *The Rhetoric of Romanticism*, (New York, 1984), p. 122.

13. Geoffrey Hartman, *Wordsworth's Poetry 1787–1814* (1964; reprinted New Haven, CT, 1970).

14. Geoffrey Hartman, 'Poem and Ideology: A Study of Keats's "To Autumn"', in *The Fate of Reading* (Chicago, 1975); 124–46.

15. Harold Bloom, *The Anxiety of Influence: A Theory of Poetry* (Oxford, 1973); *A Map of Misreading* (Oxford, 1975).

16. Jacques Lacan, *Ecrits: A Selection*. Trans. A. Sheridan (London, 1977).

17. For instance, Laura Claridge, *Romantic Potency: The Paradox of Desire* (New York, 1992); Barbara Charlesworth Gelpi, *Shelley's Goddess; Maternity, Language, Subjectivity* (Oxford, 1992).

18. Jerome J. McGann, *The Romantic Ideology* (Chicago, 1983), 'Rethinking Romanticism', pp. 735, 736.

19. Byron to John Murray, 15 September 1817, *Byron's Letters and Journals*, ed. Leslie A. Marchand, 12 vols (Cambridge, MA, 1973–82), V, 265.

20. Cited in Sir Maurice Bowra, *The Romantic Imagination* (Oxford, 1950), p. 1.

21. Jerome J. McGann, 'The Meaning of the Ancient Mariner', *Critical Inquiry*. Reprinted in G. A. Rosso and Daniel P. Watkins (eds), *Spirits*

of Fire: English Romantic Writers and Contemporary Historical Method (London, 1990).

22. Butler, *Romantics, Rebels and Reactionaries*, p. 57.

23. Ibid., p. 59.

24. Marilyn Butler, 'Repossessing the Past: the Case for an Open Literary History', in Marjorie Levinson, Marilyn Butler, Jerome McGann and Paul Hamilton, *Rethinking Historicism: Critical Readings in Romantic History* (Oxford, 1989), p. 72.

25. Marjorie Levinson, *Wordsworth's Great Period Poems* (Cambridge, 1986).

26. Marjorie Levinson, *Keats's Life of Allegory* (Oxford, 1988), pp. 1–28, 36–7.

27. Nicholas Roe (ed.), *Keats and History* (Cambridge, 1995).

28. Stuart Curran, 'The "I" Altered', in *Romanticism and Feminism*, ed. Anne K. Mellor (Indiana, 1988), pp. 185–207.

29. Anne K. Mellor, *Romanticism and Gender* (London, 1993), p. 27.

30. Ibid., p. 28

31. Margaret Homans, 'Keats Reading Women, Women Reading Keats', *Studies in Romanticism*, 29 (1990), 341–70.

32. Mellor, *Romanticism and Gender*, pp. 171–86.

33. This is the second of two notable essays written by Swann on Coleridge's *Christabel*. In the first she argues that Coleridge's supernatural tale both dramatises hysteria as well as provoking it in the reader, largely through its use of a narrative which leaves it unclear as to whether there are one or two narrators. Swann points out that all the characters in the poem appear to be seized with hysteria in some form or another and they manufacture characteristically appropriate defence stratagems to deal with it. The indeterminacy of the genre of the poem (ironic tale or tale of terror) similarly occasions this sense of readerly hysteria. The poem 'mockingly and dreamily informs us that hysteria is the condition of all subjects in discourse, and the attribution of this condition to feminine bodies is a conventional, hysterical response'. Karen Swann, '"Christabel": The Wandering Mother and the Enigma of Form', *Studies in Romanticism*, 23 (1984).

34. Nicholas Roe (ed.), *Keats and History*, p. 5.

35. Jerome McGann, 'Keats and the Historical Method in Literary Criticism', *Modern Language Notes*, 94 (1979), reprinted in *The Beauty of Inflections: Literary Investigations in Historical Method and Theory* (Oxford, 1985).

1

'Kubla Khan' and Eighteenth-Century Aesthetic Theories

KATHLEEN M. WHEELER

Few poems of classic status in the English literary corpus seem more exotic to the modern reader than 'Kubla Khan'. Coleridge's tantalising account of its origins combines with the Oriental imagery to tend to disassociate the poem from its literary tradition. The perhaps surprising conclusion persists however that if ever a poem reflected the concerns and interests of its age, 'Kubla Khan' is that poem. Yet the work on sources has acted both to obscure and to reveal the exemplary nature of the poem. For it has located many coincidences of idea, imagery and phrase in travelogues, histories, religious myths, and Oriental literature generally, without emphasising sufficiently (to overcome the strangeness to a modern reader) the extent to which much of this material had already been assimilated into the English literary tradition in the eighteenth century, and already constituted exciting and well-known speculations of the day.

For Coleridge's own adept use of prefaces (and glosses) mimics often ironically the technique of authors' and translators' prefaces of many of the collections of Oriental Tales or English adaptations; he also realised how effective these techniques were in intensifying poetic illusion by projecting the origin and authorship of the tale into some distant and unknown time and country, or into some unusual state of mind. He wove a framework technique into the verse structure of his own poems, either explicitly as in 'The Ancient Mariner', or in the form of a radical change in the narrative perspective, as in stanza iv of 'Kubla Khan', thus imitating the Chinese-box structure of many tales. He thereby drew attention to the role of the story-teller in both poems, as was done so effectively in *Arabian Nights*. He also often made unity of apparently disconnected images an explicit issue, as in the preface to 'Kubla Khan'. And he preserved the action of the poems well outside the realm of reality or possibility (as he ironically owned to Mrs. Barbauld[1]). This Coleridgean kind of supernaturalism became moreover the direct mode of displaying imaginative symbol-making, or what we call 'figuration' (the production of figures of speech) at its most universally representative, that is, in its form most free from any dogmatic or didactic purposes and consequently effective for instruction in the way appropriate to art, that is by means of delight. Finally, as will be discussed below, Coleridge showed how exotic and even extravagant imagery could be used in the service of that 'educt of the imagination', the symbol, in order to direct the mind, first, towards the idea and the intelligential in and through the use of the sensuous, and, second, towards a self-consciousness about the mind's own processes and nature, which for Coleridge always constituted the genuine *unity* of a work of art.

The exploration of such a 'unifying idea' as self-conscious awareness of the importance of figuration, toward which the imagery of 'Kubla Khan' leads, can also be considered in the light of the less literary and more theoretical background of the aesthetic controversies raging in the eighteenth century. Dryden, Pope, Locke, Edmund Burke, John Baillie, Johnson and others contributed to the issues which were hotly debated, such as the relative value of painting and poetry, the nature of the sublime, the distinction between copy and imitation, the nature of genius, the analysis of language as literal or inherently metaphorical, and the role of rhetoric and emotion in poetry. This more theoretical direction is best approached by means of a brief excursus into the image of the garden in its eighteenth-century context.

In addition to reflecting the interest in travels, foreign (and especially Oriental) cultures, fantastic speculations about the Nile, the cosmos, origins of man, the first language, and mysterious eastern cults of wisdom and religion (all of which were topics popular throughout the late seventeenth and eighteenth centuries), 'Kubla Khan' also explicitly reflects the widespread interest in gardens, and particularly the oriental or 'Chinese Garden' whose design was actually imported into the grounds of stately homes throughout England. However strange it may seem to the modern reader or poet, gardening was a subject worthy of discourses and poems by the most eminent writers, and was eagerly read about by an interested reading public. Sir Thomas Browne (one of Coleridge's favourite writers), Sir William Temple, Walpole, and Pope exploited the symbolic significance of the garden as an example of earthly paradise and of culture generally. Nor did Spenser, Sidney, or Milton fail to take advantage of the symbolic ramifications of the garden as a metaphor for civilisation, art and the human soul. ...

The movement of 'Kubla Khan' from the formal geometric garden of the seventeenth century to the suggestions of a more natural garden towards the end of stanza i ('forests ancient as the hills', and so on), and finally towards the wild and natural scene of stanza ii, seems to chart this gradual change in interest throughout the previous century and a half. It had of course its symbolic counterpart in the eighteenth-century dispute of the nature of genius as dominated by a reasoning, measuring, analytical faculty or, alternatively, guided by a faculty of intuition, which was mysterious and acted according to its own, unknown, internal principles. Thus the garden symbol had its application in a theory of aesthetics as well as in a religious or moral sphere. Artifice was set up against inspiration, conscious against unconscious, and the mechanical against the organic. It was perhaps in the light of these eighteenth-century controversies that Wordsworth formulated his theory of a return to natural feeling and the language of the common man. ...

The garden, then, can be interpreted as a symbol of the controversy about the true nature of the activity of the mind's faculties, and particularly, about genius. Hobbes and Locke had set the terms of the dispute when they insisted that, essentially, the mind could only repeat the external world known to it through the senses. For them, the mind could not create new entities; it could only manipulate and aggregate the already known 'atoms' or simple elements of experience. However different Locke's 'representative theory of perception' from Hobbes's simple materialism, both still remained within the circle of thinkers who viewed the mind as essentially passive and receptive, even if for Locke the senses did add all of the secondary qualities of experience to a primary real base, with a faculty of understanding manipulating those qualities. Locke seemed to have a corresponding dualistic view of language as, first, built up into complex concepts by aggregations of simple atoms, and second, as containing a base structure and a layer of ornamentation, which included all tropes such as metaphors, similes, and irony, and which obscured the expression of truth by vitiating the pure rigour and directness of the base literal language of rationality. Later, Horne Tooke was to continue this strictly literalist view of language.

The dispute about whether the mind was passive (as Locke and Hobbes essentially maintained, though, of course, their arguments were different) or was active in its construction of experience, forms the basis of a number of related aesthetic arguments. Most relevant to the discussion here are such issues as, first, the nature of genius, second, the relative value of poetry to painting (and subsidiary arguments as to the purposes of poetry as 'representational'), third, the dispute about the meaning of imitation as opposed to mere copying, and finally, the role of metaphor in language. All four of these issues can be profitably related to the discussion of the use and developing function of imagery in 'Kubla Khan', as it sifts and shapes these aesthetic issues into poetic forms. ...

The Burkean notion of poetry as valuable primarily for arousing the feelings was also being challenged by other eighteenth-century theorists in the form of a theory of metaphor and its role in language. Hobbes, Locke, Thomas Spratt, Isaac Watts and many others had insisted that metaphors and all poetic tropes were mere fanciful ornamentation to a logical, rational language which had a literal base. According to them, this literal base was the language of science and truth. Ornamentation, while pleasing and gratifying, tended to lead the mind into error by distancing it from the firm, factual basis needed for knowledge. Other theorists, however, such as Vico in *Scienza Nuova* (1725) and Thomas Blackewell in *Enquiry into Homer* (1735), began by means of their speculations into the origins and development of language, to view metaphor, and figuration generally, as deeply rooted in, and an inherent part of language. That is, the notion of a literal base was seen as an illusion fostered by the way in which phrases and words once recognised as metaphorical, became so familiar that they were mistaken as literal. Language was not essentially logical, but also rhetorical – logic was a kind of rhetoric. (This is an indirect challenge to the senses–intellect dichotomy, that 'barren dualism'.) Such writers as Hugh Blair, in *Lectures on Rhetoric and Belles Lettres* (1783), basing themselves on the mid-century work of Robert Lowth and others, were maintaining that even if metaphor erupts from passionate feelings, as many earlier theorists had asserted, it can still be understood as essential to all language, not just to emotive or poetic language. For language itself may be to a significant extent a product of *passion*, in the fullest sense of the word. Coleridge clarified the argument by showing that thought and feeling, while distinguishable, were not essentially divisible; the highest language of truth, whether of poetry or philosophy, was a fusion of thought and feeling, expressive of the whole nature of man and of all his faculties. This language of fusion he frequently referred to as the language of passion, of which metaphor was a basic element.[2] Thus, if metaphor and figuration were not just ornamentation, poetry could not be understood as merely pleasing either, or as an ornament of thought. It too could act as a source of knowledge and truth, both about relatively inherent formal properties of language and mind, and as a 'picture', not of course of the 'surface' or appearance either of nature or of man (his thought, judgement, emotions and feelings), but rather of genuine principles or formal relations which organise those appearances.

In England, then, it was Coleridge, and later Shelley, who most convincingly brought together these issues into one central focus of the mind as essentially creative in both the related activities of perception (the senses) and of art (the 'higher' faculties), and of language as essentially metaphoric, not logical, both in scientific discourse and in poetry. For example, to Coleridge genius was not an aggregative power, nor a power which gained knowledge only by analysing complexities into simples. Distinction and reduction were only the preliminary acts of knowledge. Reassimilation of parts into new wholes and patterns was the more important function of genius. These wholes, in terms of their truth and power, exceeded the mere aggregative sum of parts or what was analysable from them. Secondly, the object of none of the arts, not even painting, was explained according to Coleridge by a representational, descriptive, or picture theory of copying the surface of nature or mind. It is hardly surprising that Plato condemned this type of 'art' as a third remove from reality. The genuine object of poetry, and of all other art including painting, was for Coleridge (as it was for Plato) ultimately symbolic, in the sense that the external and sensuous are valuable as means towards the intelligential and the ideal. The image must be made to work in the service of the idea. This image/idea distinction was not adequately made by eighteenth-century theorists, especially Locke,[3] and upon it could be said to turn the solution to the prominent aesthetic disputes. From Coleridge's clear perception of the necessity for the distinction grew the concept of the *symbol* as that which could embody the relatively universal (the idea) in the individual (the image), or the representative and general in the particular. Too often the image, the means, was mistaken for the idea, the relative end, and the result in religion was idolatory and in poetry degenerate art, in philosophy materialism, and in personal experience selfishness.

Coleridge concluded (consistent with his theory of mind as essentially creative and of art as symbolic in the above sense) that language was inherently metaphorical, and that metaphor was the only vehicle for truth. The notion of a basis of *literal* language of truth *ornamented* by tropes was only another aspect of the delusion of the mind as passive in perception and experience. For Coleridge, all acts of the mind degenerate through custom, habit and familiarity – whether they be language, metaphor, or art – into the literal. The literal (and logical) is merely the result of the metaphoric no longer perceived as such. Imagination, that faculty reconciling the barren duality of reason (logic) and sense, can, according to Coleridge and to Shelley, renew degenerate, literal language by revealing or reinventing connections which once informed language as metaphor, as figuration, or by creating fresh metaphors and figures, and thereby fresh truth. All knowledge, then, is metaphorical, and articulated by figurative, not literal language.

'Kubla Khan' can be seen to illustrate these solutions of Coleridge's to the eighteenth-century aesthetic and philosophic controversies in a very specific way. The enigmatic transition in the poem from stanza ii to stanzas iii and iv, and the relation of stanza iv to the rest of the poem suggest the solutions discussed above by means, first, of a careful transition in the function of the imagery, and second, in the change in narrative technique or perspective. Stanza iii has often been seen as a problematic and disruptive portion of the poem in several ways. For example, it tends to disrupt the otherwise neat Pseudo-(Cowleian) Pindaric Ode form. Stanza i as strophe, ii as antistrophe, and iv as epode answer to the form of the ode, with the turning about and contrasting character of the antistrophe, and with the 'after-song', incantatory nature of the final stanza. Stanza iii is disruptive at other levels, too, of, for example, metre, tantalising numerological interpretations, and also of imagery. Not only does it introduce new and unassimilated entities, such as the 'shadow' and the 'rare device', or even the 'mingled measure'. It also disrupts the landscape: the caves and fountain, beginning and end point of the river, are now so close to each other that there is hardly room for the river to meander, however crookedly, for five miles. Like the less obvious uncertainty of the topography of the Khan's garden in stanza i (whether the walls enclose the ancient forest or not, and where the chasm is), image and landscape disruption seem to prevent externalisation, that is, the picturing in the mind's eye of a coherent and unproblematic landscape. This disruption of stanza iii, however, and the resulting separateness from the first thirty lines of the poem of the visions of stanzas iii and iv especially, is not disruption without a purpose, nor does it mar the poem. This disruption strives rather to portray the conflicts about the nature of genius, the role of figuration in knowledge, language and poetry as metaphorical, the use of imagery and the purposes of poetic language as representational, emotive, or other, and, finally, the nature of aesthetic unity as aggregative and mechanical or as organic and integral.

Stanza iii has particularly puzzled readers and critics as it introduces new and perplexing imagery into the poem, and departs from the primarily descriptive and landscape imagery of the first thirty lines. Clearly the imagery of lines 1–30 also functions figuratively or metaphorically (symbolically, to use Coleridge's preferred term)[4] as innumerable critics have shown. But the rather new perspective and role of stanza iii is best described as a self-conscious, witty mimesis, or effort to draw the reader's attention to the way in which the language, rhythm, and imagery of lines 1–30 have so far functioned aesthetically. In stanza iii the poet seems openly to play with the techniques of poetic language used unobtrusively in stanzas i and ii: he forges in front of our eyes new and playful images out of the previous materials. Those new elements which arise from the fusion of old material do not genuinely add either to the landscape of the Khan's garden or to the romantic cavern at a surface level. But they do add a new 'odic' dimension, in so far as they constitute a 'turning about' and a contemplation upon the way in which the images in lines 1–30 ought to function not only representationally, but also as metaphors and figures of speech to enrich the symbolic content of the poem. For these new elements of stanza iii which do not seem to cohere in any important way to the previous imagery, are themselves playful metaphors, wittily instancing the way an image, through the synthesis of oppositions or differences, leads to a metaphoric meaning. They do not indeed work well as representational images, as the images of lines 1–30 do (the incoherence of these images has been noticed by numerous critics), but as metaphors, or as examples of the *form* or figuration of metaphor, they are exemplary. They fuse apparently opposite or irreconcilable elements, and show that crucial 'similarity in difference', the classic definition of metaphor. They also show how the image takes on metaphorical significance when its connection with an apparently dissimilar element is discovered.

Two examples of this enriching of the image by the discovery of its metaphorical implications illustrate the mimetic technique of stanza iii. First, the caves and the dome belong to two apparently contrasting worlds in the poem, one to the world of nature, the other to the world of human culture. By fusing these two in stanza iii ('sunny pleasure-dome, with caves of ice') we gain an image which fails as a representation (that is, in no sense is it a convincing natural or 'real' unity), but which acts perfectly as a metaphor for the idea that art is a product of the unity of the natural and human. In other appropriate terms, aesthetic productions, true works of art, those 'miracles of rare device', that is, result only from the synthesis of the spontaneous, instinctive impulse with the measuring, conscious planning and decreeing exemplified by the Khan. Thus, a theoretical gesture seems to be made in stanza iii, by means of images which fail at a literal, landscape level, but which mimic the aesthetic processes involved in understanding the previous images by acting as exemplary metaphors of the process of image-making or 'figuration' – the process of imagining and creating beautiful figures of speech.

The second example of stanza iii displaying the proper functioning of the imagery of the first thirty lines is the use of the 'shadow of the dome of pleasure'. The metaphysical implications of shadow and substance will be discussed later, but here this new image, taken as a model of form, can suggest that each image of the previous lines may have a 'shadow' which enriches its content. Unlike the above example, this related shadow-element, this 'absence', may not be presented in the poem explicitly, but might in part at least be derivable from the literary tradition, or from experience generally. Thus the dome might be enriched by sexual connotations. Or the garden might be recognised as a metaphor for the cultivation of genius (perhaps the most important image in the poem with respect to its structural unity). The river might be interpretable as consciousness, life, or language. The chasm might be a metaphor for the subconscious and the unknown, and the fountain and fragments for the production of imagination. All of these shadowy metaphors or traditional associations enrich the poem's imagery, and create issues which the poem as a whole may seek to resolve, or only represent. But the discovery of such relations and their import for questioning the nature of the meaning in poetic language as itself a kind of 'absence', is essential to a greater appreciation of the beauty or unity of the poem. Stanza iii emphasises precisely this process of the discovery of relations, the synthesis or fusion of different elements into an idea, and the nature of metaphor as opening out to (rather than closing in on) meaning, as allegory does. Many other oppositions in the poem, such as the Khan and the visionary, the visionary and the damsel, nature and culture, garden and wild, and so on, indicate that the poem proceeds in part by the relating of oppositions and the discovery of identities and solutions through these conflicts, whether implicit, as in the second example, or explicit as in the first. Each of the elements of stanza iii presses the importance of opposition, or similarity in difference, as shadow and substance, fountain and cave, and sun and ice, or dome and cave can be seen as oppositions with, nevertheless, essential connections.

The (only relative) 'failure' of these images of stanza iii to participate integrally in the rest of the poem (or to be convincing representational or descriptive unities in themselves), serves not only to signify the shift away from the predominant 'descriptive' or landscape (eighteenth-century) mode of the surface structure of lines 1–30 (whatever the depth symbolism); it serves also to capture a quality inherent in metaphor, namely the apparent 'flaw', the 'missing' element, or the apparent 'failure' of connection or relation, the gap, fragment, or disunity which is unresolved by the discursive understanding, but which is acceptable and meaningful even in the 'flawedness' to the faculty which apprehends relations, whether we call it the imagination, *nous*, intuition, or wit. Wit seems to be the word which many eighteenth-century theorists used for this faculty (corresponding to the *Witz* of German aestheticians somewhat later), and it is instructive for grasping the way in which the 'flawed' element may function in aesthetic experience. For the essence in wit is to bring two disparate elements into unfamiliar and daring, but not absolute, proximity; for a space is left. In the case of the joke, the listeners must apprehend the missing relation with their own 'wit', or they will 'miss' the point. Nothing is so tiresome as to have to explain a joke, if it is even possible to do so, and nothing robs it of its inherent power to delight so much as to have to attempt to explain the meaning.

The images of stanza iii are in large part contrived and unconvincing unities at least at the surface of representational function. But as soon as their function is seen as mimetic of the making of metaphors, they become models of effective stimulation to an awareness of aesthetic techniques. The phrase 'miracle of rare device' may help to emphasise the role of these contrived unities, for it makes claim to a miraculous unity and coherence which is entirely unwarranted in view of the questionable unity of the image of, for example, 'a sunny pleasure-dome with caves of ice'. Nor does such an image anywhere fit into the previously established landscape and architecture of stanzas i and ii. Indeed it seems to confuse and contradict the layout of the landscape already charted. Thus it fails to function adequately at *this* level. But with respect to its form, it exquisitely displays the structure of metaphor and the design of the poem generally, which relies on structures of opposition both at the level of imagery, rhythm, and stanza, as well as of narrative voice and poetic unity of the whole.

Another of the elements of stanza iii further suggests the changing role of imagery from representation of externals to embodiment of ideas and mimesis of creative figuration, or, rather, the transition of the poem to a new level of mimesis and aesthetic consciousness about the production and function of the images of the previous two stanzas. The phrase, 'Mingled measure/From the fountain and the caves', also makes use of opposition and, in this case, of explicit synthesis, which at first may even seem convincing. The image further theorises by punning upon the musicality of the poem and its subtle changes in rhythm and assonance in the words 'mingled measure', with its use of four and three-four accent lines against the five accent line of stanza ii. Mimesis at the level of 'music' or assonance and accent has been anticipated earlier in the poem, as in line 25, 'Five *m*iles *m*eandering with a *m*azy *m*otion', or line 20, with the final accent on 'forced' and 'burst', or lines 5 and 13 on 'down'. It is played upon in line 6 by 'twice *five* miles' which described the extent of the garden, and the rhythm then moves into *five* accent lines for lines 7–11. But none of these occurrences function predominantly as mimetic of figuration, as 'mingled measure' does in stanza iii. This is once again an illustration of the transition in the poem; *aesthetic* events which occurred in the first two stanzas are now being reflected upon and explicitly exhibited. 'Measure' of course also puns as the double meaning of music and also the meaning: 'a division of a metrical line in poetry'. The flaw in the image has also been pointed out by critics, however; an inconsistent proximity of fountain and cave is forced, so that the river's five miles of meandering becomes completely impossible if its origin, the fountain, and its end point, the cave, are as close together as this image suggests. But even if the image is thought to fail as an external representation it delightfully illustrates that element so necessary to wit and figuration, namely the surprising (but not too great!) proximity of two apparently distant or unrelated elements. Spaciousness is also essential. The 'mingled measure', as a result of this unexpected relation, seems to suggest that music and poetry depend upon precisely such metaphoric junctions through apparent disjunction.

Nor indeed is the other synthetic image of the third stanza straightforward. The shadow, a product of the dome and (unmentioned) light on waves, has no apparently significant function in the rest of the poem at the explicit level of representational imagery. It is also unclear how the adverb 'midway' should be taken. But the idea of shadow has certain symbolic associations which point to a level of reflection about reality, and about illusion. First, the platonic contrast between the phenomenal and the noumenal world is set up, and lines 1–30 can be partly interpreted as a picture of this phenomenal world. If the River Alph is interpreted as an allegory of consciousness, then the shadow of the dome also invites comparison with the duality of experience, in which the consciousness comes into contact initially, at the surface, only with the 'shadow' of the 'thing-in-itself'. Shadow – or substance – opposition is also suggestive of the illusion-versus-reality and absence-versus-presence dichotomy, which intimately involves artistic products. In *Biographia Literaria* (1817) Chapter Thirteen Coleridge had described the power of this shadow-substance opposition:

> In short, what I had supposed substances were thinned away into shadows, while everywhere shadows were deepened into substances: 'if substance may be call'd what shadow seem'd, /For each seem'd either!' MILTON. Yet after all, I could not but repeat the lines which you had quoted from a MS. poem of your own in the FRIEND, and applied to a work of Mr Wordsworth's though with a few of the words altered:

'----An orphic tale indeed,
A tale obscure of high and passionate thoughts
To a strange music chaunted!'
                    (*BL*, I, xiii, 199–200)

The implied exchange of value between shadow and substance reinforces the idea that the metaphors (shadows) implied by the images (substances) of lines 1–30, may be at least as important as the images taken literally: stanza iii has one further significant complication, and that is the ambivalent referent of the pronoun 'it' in line 35. The pronoun ought by progression and continuity to refer to the 'shadow of the dome of pleasure'. But the continuation into line 36 shifts the force of the referent to 'A sunny pleasure-dome with caves of ice'. The 'miracle of rare device' itself floats between these two images, and the uncertainty as to which is the miracle unifies the shadow with the final image in another daring stroke of identification or synthesis, which seems to confuse at the level of imagery, but which continues the game of mimesis at the level of self-referring poetic commentary. Thus the 'miracles of rare device' are metaphors, symbols, and images embodying ideas, as well as whole works of art. Stanza iii has forced us to a recognition of the nature of relationship at the expense of sensible content in poetic tropes. But this is precisely the direction necessary for the gradual transition from representative language and description to symbolic and relational language expressive of ideas, especially the idea of the nature of human creativity as figuration, or the making of figures of speech. And of the idea that figures of speech are meaningful through resonance and expansion of possible relations – by radiation – rather than meaningful only by enclosing or 'comprehension'. Hence the significance of the notion of the 'illuminating' intellect. Shelley's predilection for radiating imagery of Star, flower, song, and light in general, for example, contrasts with the linear mode of the discursive intellect.

The sacrifice of 'traditional' content for the purpose of emphasising relation and, ultimately, ideas and figures is consistent with Coleridge's tireless distinction between the image and the idea and the necessity of always making the sense and images serve something higher than mere descriptive representation.[5] He had sharply criticised Locke in his well-known Locke–Descartes letters for failing to make the distinction, which is crucial to a theory of mind as active and constructive of experience, as opposed to the passive, materialist, or associationist theory. 'Kubla Khan' makes the indirect claim, then, that the image divorced from the idea, and correspondingly, poetic language used merely for description, copying, and representation, and not for the embodiment of the intuition, language or figuration, the intellectual relations of thought, the union of thought and feeling, and self-conscious reflection about the nature of creative activity, would mean idolatry and degenerate art, just as the Reason divorced from the senses leads to degenerate philosophising. 'Kubla Khan' depicts precisely and self-consciously the necessity for the image and the senses to work in the service of the idea and the imagination, and vice versa, through the medium of metaphor and symbol. This is not to say, however, that the first thirty lines are merely representational and imagistic. They are not; for they are enriched with innumerable metaphorical implications. But they do not mimetically or *explicitly* illustrate this aspect of language and truth as metaphorical or figurative as stanza iii does. Stanza iii, through its 'self-referring' commentary of mimesis, is an account of how the previous 30 lines ought to be enriched and brought to a fullness of meaning by exploring the symbolic figurative possibilities. This is why stanza iii seems to disrupt and even contradict the landscape and architecture of the earlier verse. It marks a turning away to a new dimension of reflection about the processes of figuration which made the previous lines possible and which give them an elegant complexity of meaning which exceeds their surface beauty.

Stanza iv is an advance upon stanza iii, which had acted primarily as a transition to a new mode of expression. First, it daringly introduces completely new elements – the damsel (the Abyssinian maid), the song of Mt Abora, the music, and the wild-eyed youth. The challenge of stanza iv is how to integrate these elements into the structure of the poem. In fact, they will not integrate at the level of imagery, and this failure forces a reorientation of the structure, according to the 'directions' or 'instructions' of stanza iii. These directions lead the reader, we said earlier, to look upon imagery as functioning in a new way, as symbols working more complexly, and less simply representationally, in the service of ideas than the previous images. The structural incoherence of stanza iv at the level of naïve imagery is, like the previous 'flaws' in the imagery in stanza iii, often purposive and not necessarily marring. It shifts the aesthetic action to a level of new significance, which now goes beyond that of stanza iii. For in stanza iii the shift leads to a contemplation of how imagery and other poetic techniques such as musicality can work for the idea *via* symbols and metaphors, and this is essentially a concern for the medium of expression, poetic language. But in stanza iv the concern is no longer only the language and mimetic displays of how metaphors and symbols are made, and their nature, structure, and role. It is now the origins of this language, its agency and production which are being contemplated and indeed displayed in and through that contemplation. That is, the nature of inspiration itself, or imagination, and not only the music or products of imagination which is poetry, are self-consciously contemplated by the visionary Poet. Theoretical gestures are evident, as the poet sets up the elements of this reflection and reveals the extremely problematic nature of their interrelations. That is, in what way is his vision of the maid related to the dome he will build, or to the music which will inspire it? How would a revival become possible: what would be the conditions for it? And how would it be understood by his audience? Whether we allegorically equate the damsel, her song, or the revived music with imagination, or the dome in air with an artifact, such as this poem, the elements of the complex situation of creativity are all there; no strict *allegories* for these various elements are desired to see the metaphor of the poet's (*and reader's*) situation which is being portrayed. In some ways the images of stanza iv may be seen to integrate with those of i and ii by contrast, even at a very literal level. For the visionary and the Khan are related through their respective dome in air and pleasure dome. This suggests the theoretical gesture of contrasting talent with genius, or the measuring and decreeing conscious will of the Khan with the inspiration and visionary Power of the youth. But the youth's success is dependent upon the intermediary figure of the maid, which is beyond his conscious control and will. For Coleridge, the imagination was described precisely as that:

> reconciling and mediatory Power, which incorporating the Reason in Images of the Sense, and organizing (as it were) the flux of the Senses by the permanence and self-circling energies of the Reason, gives birth to a system of symbols, harmonious in themselves, and consubstantial with the truths, of which they are the *conductors*.
> (*Statesman's Manual: Lay Sermons*, 29)

The change of the narrative voice from the distance and omniscience of the first two stanzas, to the uncertain voice of stanza iii, and finally to the clear first-person narrative of iv reflects a metaphor of progression from unconscious creative activity: first, to a contemplation about the products or medium of that activity, namely, figuration, and finally to a consciousness and reflection about the activity itself, its origins and its relation to the ego and the 'now'. This self-conscious, detached glance back over, firstly, one's artistic products and, secondly, imaginative activity or agency itself, built into the design of the whole, is precisely the touch which most effectively finishes the poem; ironically, it is also the touch which at a merely surface level of representational or descriptive imagery makes the poem seem disunified and fragmentary. The final word, 'Paradise', illustrates the way in which the poem comes full circle back upon itself, leading back to the man-made paradise-garden of Xanadu. But this paradise in stanza iv, while it may have important religious connections with the garden image of the Khan in stanza i, is also its opposite: for it is the Paradise which is Genius itself, and not a sensible or purely sensuous, fallen world (a world devoid of imagination) as in stanza i. This idea, that paradise is genius itself, and not something existing in space-time, seems to have emerged only at the end of the poem. Yet it was also an aspect of the garden seen metaphorically at the beginning of the poem. For, as we said earlier, the garden image as a metaphor for genius was indeed a familiar 'trope' in eighteenth century literature. This familiar metaphor of garden as genius and genius as paradise is one of the most powerful inducements to the interpretation of stanzas iii and iv as mimetic and self-conscious of the process of figuration evident in the first two stanzas. For this discovery at the end of the poem combined with the initial implicit but predominant metaphor of the *garden as genius* at the beginning reveals one of the major unifying themes of the poem, the idea that *genius is paradise*, which the imagery served to elucidate. And it reveals the form of the poem as progressing through differences and oppositions towards similarity, and finally oneness or unity, both at the level of specific concrete imagery, and at the level of the use of imagery, from descriptive, to metaphorical, and finally to the sensuously imaginative. 'Kubla Khan' thus seems to illustrate Coleridge's account of the purpose of all poems and of imagination itself:

> to convert a *series* into a *Whole*: to make those events, which in real or imagined History move on in a *straight* Line, assume to our Understanding a *circular* motion the snake with its Tail in its Mouth.
>
> (*Letters*, IV, 545)

To express this idea of *genius as paradise*, no representational imagery is adequate, a point which the poem seems to make by transcending to a new level of aesthetic endeavour from that engaged in stanzas i and ii, or even in stanza iii. For in stanza iv there reigns over the verse a 'pure imaginativeness' which occurs nowhere else in the poem, as representative landscape imagery is deliberately sacrificed for the idea of relation and figuration, and not imagery, description or objectification, as paramount to the experience of imagination. Coleridge had spoken of this 'pure imaginativeness' which frees the mind from the constraints of space, time and causality (all categories of the discursive under-standing) in relation to the *Fairie Queene* and the *Arabian Nights*, as well as to his own 'supernatural Poetry'.[6] He seems to mean by the phrase an atmosphere in which images function most freely in the service of metaphors, symbols, and ideas, with as little descriptive, representational, or externalising effect as possible. Paradoxically, imagery of this sort seems to be stripped of natural referents, or of context value, and succeeds primarily in creating an unfamiliar atmosphere or effect, as do nearly all of the images of stanza iv. The dulcimer, the adjective 'Abyssinian', the singing about Mount Abora, and even the dome in the air or the final images of milk and honey seem almost exclusively to create an atmosphere of strangeness, removing the reader from the familiar realm of ordinary consciousness into a realm of imaginativeness which knows no bounds. Thus these images can be tremendously effective without any source-work or any awareness of their con-nections with the world of geography, history, religion, or other areas. The predominant function of these images is as symbols of aesthetic processes and faculties, which were also a concern of stanza i and ii, but only at an indirect level. Thus dogmatic or overt moralising inhibits the free play of imagination, as does any other form of allegorising.[7]

If 'Kubla Khan' had ended at line 30 or had had no preface, it might have seemed more superficially organised and unified, but it would have been a poem of infinitely less richness than in its present form. The development of the use of imagery and the theor-etical gestures, which are made both in the last 24 lines and in the preface, complete the poem by adding that level of self-conscious reflection both about the instrument of expression, language, about figuration, and about the agent, the mind, and its faculty of imag-ination. The same self-referring level of 'commentary' is evident in numerous other poems, such as 'This Lime-Tree Bower My Prison', beginning at line 43, or in the Wedding Guest framework of 'The Ancient Mariner'. 'The Eolian Harp' (for example lines 20–5), and *Christabel* (Conclusion to Part I) share this extraordinary, airy incorporeality. The gradual transition in the use of imagery in 'Kubla Khan' (which concisely expresses so many of the aesthetic issues of the eighteenth century about the purposes of poetry as compared to painting, the nature of genius, and the language of truth as opposed to that of beauty, a dichotomy which all the Romantic poets rejected), from a traditional descriptive, representational function in stanza i to self-conscious representational function and to representation with metaphorical complexity in stanza ii, then contemplation about the medium of poetic language in stanza iii and, finally, self-consciousness about the agency, or imagination itself, can best be described in Coleridge's own terms as the process of 'humanizing nature'. 'Kubla Khan' more than almost any other poem of classic stature has suffered from the 'confounding mechanical regularity with organic form ... The organic form ... is innate; it shapes as it develops itself from within, and the fullness of its development is one and the same with the perfection of its outward form. Such is the life, such the form', as Coleridge says in *Shakespearean Criticism*.[8]

In conclusion, to speak of the metaphor of genius as paradise is to say something about the nature of imagination, namely, that Coleridge's concept of imagination is almost indistinguishable from Blake's and Shelley's. That is, it (first) 'incorporates the Reason in images of the Senses' and, second, correlatively, it 'organizes the flux of the Senses by the permanence and selfcircling energies of the Reason'. Not only is the concept of imagination the means whereby that 'barren dualism' of much of Western philosophy is overcome. In Coleridge's distinction between the primary and secondary imagination we see this reconciliation radically pursued and effected.

Primary imagination is basic, 'sensuous' perception itself. But it is the senses at work constructively, actively, and creatively. Put another way, the senses are 'imbued with Reason'. Coleridge remarked that it is wonderful how close the senses and the reason are. Hence, 'intuition', as Kant aptly called sensuous perception, is no contrary to the reason, but reason itself. Relatedly, Blake argued that to the eye of the man of imagination, nature is all imagination itself. Further, Blake insisted in a related insight that the body is the soul's perception of itself through the five senses.

Secondary imagination, or artistic creation, is an echo of primary perception, of primary imagination. Artistic creation is a re-creation which renews, restores, and refreshes the familiar, the no longer strange, the merely customary, or that habitual world which has degenerated, because literalised, and now, like 'La Belle Dame', is an unrecognisable world (whether of nature, of language, or of art), a world of primary imagination estranged into the familiar by time and repetition, a world of duality where the senses have become dissociated from the reason.

We may need to distinguish if we are to achieve greater understanding, but we must not divide. The reason we must not divide from the senses. The imagination conceived of both as primary (intelligent perception) and secondary (artistic creation) is that power of reunifying elements (results of reflection) such as the faculties of mind. Imagination is a 'self-circling energy' capable of converting elements of a 'series into a whole', it encircles the senses in the reason and vice versa, and transforms reason's series into a sensuous whole.

The senses are not separate from the intellect or reason; these are figures of speech only, constructs of reflection. The senses are imbued with reason, with intellect, with intelligence. We do not just see, we see intelligently and imaginatively. The 'reason', that figure of speech, is not superadded to a material which the senses (that other figure of speech) supply us with. Reason is in them, even as the senses are in reason. Hence the Kantian idea of 'sensuous intuition' – that direct beholding – is truly a contradiction in terms for any dualistic philosophy.

Kant was, for Coleridge, 'no metaphysician', for he lost hold of his own best insight (arrived at in the Logic) namely, of rejecting the notion of a sensuous manifold outside reason. Coleridge recovered and restored Kant's earlier insight in his Blakean concept of imagination as a fusion of those figures of speech, the reason and the senses, into a unity constituting the very basis of perception. Mind and world are reunified, seen as metaphors only, or functions of each other since products of reflection and thought, and not traits of some higher reality.

Coleridge's definition of symbol, his theory of imagination, and his insistence on using imagery in the service of ideas are concepts realised in 'Kubla Khan' in such a way that the dichotomy between the senses (the so-called concrete, the 'essence' of poetry) is overcome. The senses are intellectual, the intellect is sensual. As in Blake and Shelley, imagination bridges and reconciles opposites, including that most terrible opposition of all, life and death. Paradise is no after-life, occurring after death. Paradise is Genius, for it is in acts of the imagination that life and death, self and other, 'I am and it is', are reconciled. This is, no doubt, a terrifying Christianity, but nonetheless authentic for its terror, which left as courageous a soul as Kierkegaard in fear and trembling.

From *The Wordsworth Circle*, 22 (1991), 15–24.

NOTES

[In this opening essay Kathleen Wheeler looks again at many of the issues which have been at the centre of traditional Coleridge scholarship, including Coleridge's theories of the mind, of imagination, metaphor, language, and symbol. Wheeler shows how, for Coleridge, the mind is creative in perceiving knowledge and making art. She compares Coleridge's Romantic theories of mind and art to those of seventeenth- and eighteenth-century thinkers, such as Thomas Hobbes and John Locke (who argued that the mind is passive in perception and that poetry is merely a decorative ornamentation of the language of science and truth). Wheeler shows how the garden can be used as a symbol for the mind's activities and she relates Coleridge's visionary poem 'Kubla Khan' to this debate. She is most original in her awareness of the disruptions and sudden transitions in the poem which she ingeniously connects with Coleridge's desire to acquaint us with the process of figuration itself, preventing our understanding of the poem descending to the merely literal. Most of the essay is included but some contextual material concerning the use of gardens as a metaphor for genius has been cut. Ed.]

1. S. T. Coleridge, *Table Talk*, ed. Carl Woodring (Princeton, NJ, 1990), 31 May 1830.

2. The meaning of 'passion' as almost equivalent to imagination is discussed in S. T. Coleridge, *Collected Letters*, ed. E. L. Griggs (Oxford, 1966–71), III, 361; *The Notebooks of Samuel Taylor Coleridge*, ed. Kathleen Coburn (New York and London, 1957–90), III, 3615, 3611 and in S. T. Coleridge, *Biographia Literaria*, ed. J. Shawcross (Oxford, 1907), II, xviii.
    [Further references to these texts will be by the short titles, *Letters*, *Notebooks* and *Biographia Literaria*.]

3. Note *Letters*, II, 678–702, the letters to Josiah Wedgewood, which include an account of the indebtedness of Locke to Descartes and the inadequacy of the empiricist dogma.

4. The distinction between metaphor and symbol is not always easy to maintain; in this discussion it is not crucial to do so. Coleridge seems to have used 'symbol' the way Shelley used 'metaphor', both important pre-eminently as distinct from allegory. For example, note the *Statesman's Manual* in S. T. Coleridge's *Lay Sermons*, ed. R. J. White (London and Princeton, NJ, 1972), p. 30 and compare *Notebook*, III, 4503.

5. The image/idea distinction is treated in *Letters*, II, 678–703; S. T. Coleridge, *The Friend*, ed. Barbara Rooke (London and Princeton, NJ, 1969), I, 464–5; *Lay Sermons*, p. 101; and *Notebooks*, I, 1842.

6. Compare, for example, *Notebooks*, III, 4501.

7. Compare *Table Talk* 31 May 1830, and *Letters*, II, 864 for Coleridge's criticism of Bowles's inappropriate moralising of nature in his poetry. Elsewhere he maintains that the only legitimate mode of instruction for the poet is delight (*Biographia*, II, 105), for it is not by precepts and by dogmas, but by seeing and experiencing the best possible that we become the best possible.

8. S. T. Coleridge, *Shakespearean Criticism*, ed. T. M. Raysor (London, 1960), I, 198.

2

Voice and Ventriloquy in *The Rime of the Ancient Mariner*

SUSAN EILENBERG

The ordinary tale of the supernatural is like the magician's trick of pulling a rabbit out of a hat. It depends upon a false bottom, an illusion of sourcelessness. Bad metaphysics, it exploits our confusion about the relationship between cause and effect, appearance and reality, body and soul. The supernatural of *The Rime of the Ancient Mariner* pulls not rabbits out of hats but voices out of voices. It makes its home in the space between speaker and spoken, motivation and action, intention and meaning. Instead of pretending there is no source, it pretends there is one, that behind the mariner-as-dummy there is a ventriloquist, a figure or language or system of meanings in the context of which the tale that comes out of the Mariner's mouth makes sense.

The *Rime* evades the question any reader asks upon opening to this first poem in the originally anonymous *Lyrical Ballads*: 'Whose voice is this?' The *Rime*, one of the most deeply and elaborately anonymous poems ever written, comes to speech through the medium of an alien voice – archaic, inhuman, uncanny – in response to an impossible demand. 'What manner man art thou?' the Hermit cries out in horror at the speaking corpse. It is a question derived anagrammatically from the answer the corpse is unable to give: man < manner < Mariner. The question contains the fragments of the word that, fleeing into anonymity, the Mariner leaves behind. 'I am an Ancient Mariner' becomes 'There was a ship'. It is the first in a series of dislocations – translations, displacements, metonymies – that spring from the Mariner's refusal of his own name. It is a revelation of the anonymity whose power calls into being both the *Rime* and the collaborative project – the *Lyrical Ballads* – that the *Rime* inaugurates.

The impropriety of the *Rime's* language, suited neither to the expression of anything we would regard as sound character nor to the evocation of any familiar system of reference, dares its audience to make sense of it.[1] We respond by talking about madness and the supernatural, notions that convert the failure of signification into evidence of significance and allow us to defer the unwelcome recognition of our interpretive helplessness. We sacrifice our belief in the Mariner's sanity on the altar of 'character' or admit the possibility that spirits and demons cause the effects we cannot otherwise explain. Thus we attempt to rescue a purely ideal propriety.

Why can the Mariner not name himself? Perhaps because, as Wordsworth, obtusely accurate, seems to have been the first to notice, he is a man without 'distinct character, either in his profession of Mariner, or as a human being'.[2] He has no name because he has no identity. Ignorant of who he is, unable to recognise his fears and desires as his own or distinguish himself from his surroundings, and practically devoid of conscious intention and affect, the Mariner apprehends the contents of his own psyche as alien and inexplicable, perceptible only in the forms of an unnatural nature, frightened and hostile men, and spirits. Everywhere he looks he sees with no recognition versions of himself, the human and natural worlds he moves in functioning as agents of his psyche,[3] their energies and actions displacements of his own.[4]

The Mariner's empty world is crowded with what he cannot own, cannot distinguish, and therefore cannot name; anonymity is the common linguistic condition of people and things in his tale. There are strangely few proper names here; the Mariner identifies almost no one, and names even of simple abstractions elude him. Despite the excesses of his later speech, his relation to language is, like that of so many of Wordsworth's early protagonists, that almost of an aphasic. With the single exception of his painful exclamation at the sight of the spectre ship, 'A sail! a sail!', the Mariner seems to say nothing during the length of his voyage. When he does speak, he speaks like a man suffering from what Roman Jakobson describes as a similarity disorder.[5] How appropriate that the

Mariner's cry should trope Coleridge's own standard example of synecdoche.[6] 'A sail' for 'a ship' whose sails have rotted away.[7]

The Mariner's difficulties with language and his reluctance to abstract judgements from the mass of discrete observations he presents may signal intellectual deficiency, but they could also indicate the impossibility of such identifications and judgements as we are accustomed to expect. We cannot discount the possibility that what look like distortions of language and logic in the Mariner's rendition reflect truly the incoherence of the world he has passed through.

> The Sun came up upon the left,
> Out of the Sea came he;
> And he shone bright, and on the right
> Went down into the Sea.
>
> Higher and higher every day,
> Till over the mast at noon –[8]

Unlike the Wedding Guest, who beats his breast in an agony of impatience, we may recognise in the Mariner's somewhat pedantic attention to days and directions an attempt to defend against cosmic derangement. But readerly dependence upon the Mariner – an obviously unreliable narrator – limits our ability to distinguish with any degree of certainty between psychological or linguistic and physical or metaphysical effects; we have a hard time deciding how much the tale's oddity has to do with the oddity of its teller and how much it has to do with the oddity of its material. Ultimately, however, the tale dissociates itself from both teller and theme and takes its place *en abyme*, generating its own linguistic origins and constituting itself as the object of its own signification.

As Arden Reed remarks, the Mariner is 'more the effect of the "Rime" than its cause', 'the by-product of a text that wills its own repetition'.[9] The Mariner's relation to his tale is tautological, at once totally arbitrary and totally determined. The Mariner tells his tale to explain that he is the man who tells the tale in order to explain what manner man he is. It is only after the end of his marine adventures, when the Hermit questions him, that the Mariner becomes aware of the unnaturalness of his relation to the story he tells:

> Forthwith this frame of mine was wrench'd
> With a woeful agony,
> Which forc'd me to begin my tale

And then it left me free.

Since then at an uncertain hour,
Now ofttimes and now fewer,
That anguish comes and makes me tell
My ghastly aventure.

(ll. 611–18)

A 'strange power of speech' forces him out of silence. His aphasia violently reverses itself as language steps into the role of persecutor left vacant by the avenging *genii loci*, vestigial guardians of the proprieties the Mariner has violated.[10] An alien spirit thus comes to inhabit the body of the Mariner's speech, which, endlessly iterated and claiming no source in the Mariner's will, must be regarded as enclosed in invisible quotation marks. The tale that comes out of his mouth is not his. Prophet rather than source, the Mariner is only the perpetual, helplessly uncomprehending audience to the tale that speaks itself through him.

Clearly, the Mariner's recital is no mere history. He does not choose his words; he suffers them, reliving what he tells. Who can tell whether he does not relive even his impulse to kill?

'God save thee, ancyent Marinere!
'From the fiends that plague thee thus –
'Why look'st thou so?' – with my cross bow
I shot the Albatross

(ll. 77–80)

The fiends that plague him may be simultaneously those of bitter remorse and those that tormented him at the time of his original violence: the penitential representation comes very close to repeating the crime the Mariner is trying to expiate. No wonder the penance must be repeated so often. As Homer Brown puts it, 'The tale that repeats the crime "repeats" it in a double sense: it tells the story which identifies the self-assertion of the crime with the self-assertion of the telling – the killing of the albatross with the usurpation of the Wedding Guest'.[11] In the words of Jonathan Arac, 'Repetition solicits repetition'.[12] The effect is to implicate the ancient Mariner so deeply in the circumstances of his younger self as to discredit the authority of his final moral summing up: its lesson is either irrelevant or impermanent; it cannot save the Mariner from an endless repetition of his agony, from being possessed by the voice of the past.

But the Mariner is not the only victim of his voice. In this poem founded upon the power of quotation, quotation marks are strangely unreliable indices of the borders of speech. The Minstrel indicates when the Mariner is speaking with 'quoth he' and 'thus spake on that ancient man', and he consistently punctuates the openings of speeches by the Wedding Guest, the spirits, the Hermit, the Pilot, and the Boy. But he is not always careful to mark the end of a speech. To a reader careless of the convention – not observed in every poem in this volume – that places a quotation mark in front of every line in a quoted speech and one last mark at the end of the final line, one voice may seem suddenly to become two.

> He holds him with his skinny hand,
> Quoth he, there was a Ship –
> 'Now get thee hence, thou grey-beard Loon!
> 'Or my Staff shall make thee skip.
>
> He holds him with his glittering eye –
> The wedding guest stood still
> And listens like a three year's child;
> The Marinere hath his will.
>
> (ll. 13–20)

A punctuational lapse, the absence of a closing quotation mark, allows the reader also to hear the two voices as one and so to perceive the dialogue as monologue. The story dissolves the distinction between the roles of speaker and audience: both here are equally in thrall to the tale, the Wedding Guest no more capable of closing his ears against the tale than the Mariner is of closing his mouth against it.

It hardly seems to matter who speaks the words the tale requires; for the purposes of vocalisation, one character is as good as another. Characters confuse their own identities and voices with those of others, and so, in matters of revision, does Coleridge. In 1798, for example, the Mariner and the reanimated body of his nephew are pulling together at one rope when the Mariner's horror of zombies suddenly becomes a horror of himself:

> The body and I pull'd at one rope,
> But he said nought to me –
> And I quak'd to think of my own voice
> How frightful it would be!
>
> The day-light dawn'd – they dropp'd their arms,
> And cluster'd round the mast:

Sweet sounds rose slowly thro' their mouths
And from their bodies pass'd.
(ll. 335–42)

In 1800 the nephew remains silent. But instead of the Mariner's fears, we get the Wedding Guest's:

'I fear thee, ancient Mariner'
Be calm thou Wedding-Guest!
'Twas not those souls who fled in pain
Which to their corses came again,
But a troop of spirits blest:
(ll. 345–9)

Fearing at that uncanny moment the sound of his own voice, lest it *not* be his, the Mariner hears instead the Wedding Guest's, whose ventriloquy gives voice and fulfilment to the Mariner's fears. Taken by itself, the 1800 text provides reassurance for the reader who, with the Wedding Guest, fears that the Mariner might be a ghoul; the Mariner's reply to the Wedding Guest[13] allays his suspicions. But the relationship between the revised and the original text lends support to the possibility that the words of 1800 deny. As the spirits bless'd work through the bodies of the crew, so the spirit of the Mariner speaks through the Wedding Guest. Both men become functions of the tale whose telling they must endure and to whose impersonal power they must bear witness.

Having begun by crossing the boundaries of speech and character ordinarily marked by punctuation, the anonymous voice of this self-propagating tale develops into full-scale ventriloquism. What we register as a linguistic problem, however, the tale's characters register as a demonological one; they see the Mariner himself, and not the tale that he tells and that they enter, as the problem. Instrument rather than author of the tale he tells, the Mariner appears to them a dead man possessed by a demon of loquacity.

To the Hermit, the Pilot, and the Pilot's boy, who assume that the body they draw from the sea at the sinking of the ship is that of a corpse, the sight – or sound – of the Mariner's attempt to speak is uncanny:

Stunn'd by that loud and dreadful sound,
Which sky and ocean smote:
Like one that hath been seven days drown'd
My body lay afloat:

> But, swift as dreams, myself I found
> Within the Pilot's boat.
> ....
> I mov'd my lips: the Pilot shriek'd
> And fell down in a fit.
> The holy Hermit rais'd his eyes
> And pray'd where he did sit.
> (ll. 583–8, 593–6)

They do not recover from their horror when he takes the oars. They do not react with relief that one they mistook for dead should prove still to be alive. Nothing the Mariner does convinces them that he is a living man. And although the Wedding Guest, not having seen him rise from the waters, is not as immediately or as forcibly affected as they are, he also soon becomes uneasy. Something, presumably, in the Mariner's manner – his mesmeric power, the unnatural concentration of vitality in his glittering eye and his unstoppable mouth, perhaps – causes the Wedding Guest to wonder what sort of creature he has before him. Nor can he believe that the tale the Mariner tells can be told by a living man. Hence his fear that he may be talking to a zombie. Hence too the question that calls forth the tale.

By giving the Mariner the air of a zombie, the poem forces the reader to confront a radical split between speaker and speech, both of which seem haunted. The connection between possession and ventriloquy is made explicit late in the poem, when the spirits that have been inhabiting the dead bodies of the crew take the form of embodied imitative voice:

> The day-light dawn'd – they dropp'd their arms,
> And cluster'd round the mast:
> Sweet sounds rose slowly thro' their mouths
> And from their bodies pass'd.
>
> Around, around, flew each sweet sound,
> Then darted to the sun:
> Slowly the sounds came back again
> Now mix'd, now one by one.
> (ll. 339–46)

It would be a display of exquisitely acrobatic voice-throwing if the voices had an origin to be thrown from, but the circumstances forbid us to locate the source of voice in its apparent speakers; these voices no more belong to the crew out of whose mouths they pass than the tale belongs to the Mariner.

Were it not for the fact that the Mariner is but the first victim of the tale's compulsive repetitions, we might attribute his behaviour to hysteria. But he is not the tale's only teller; his story is enclosed and repeated by others over whom the Mariner (as opposed to the tale) has no influence. That the later narrators are even more deeply anonymous than the Mariner himself (whose appearance, social demeanour, and history we know) is, of course, a problem; their retellings can neither authorise the truth of the original tale nor enable us to sort out its errors. But unless we decide that everyone who tells or retells the tale is mad in precisely the same way, we cannot read the tale's peculiarities as symptoms of pathology either psychological or ethical. Indeed, the framing of the tale calls into question the very notion of character upon which considerations of psychology and ethics – and hence, of course, propriety – depend.

The reduction of the poem's characters to reflections and echoes of the tale-ridden Mariner could, one imagines, be the work of the minstrel who narrates the tale that the antiquarian would gloss. But the tale's curse is not so easily explained; it exercises its power on figures whom one would like to assume stand beyond its reach, outside its fictional space – on those figures precisely who determine the boundaries of the tale. Both minstrel and antiquarian are absorbed into the mechanism of the tale's telling. With no punctuation distinguishing the minstrel's voice from the Mariner's, both voices seem to emanate from the same source, and the poor minstrel, his independence thus undermined, transmits to the antiquarian (not yet, in 1798, brought into being) the compulsion to repeat.

The poem's strange power to bring itself to voice against the knowledge or will of its sometimes arbitrary subjects is something other than a simple fiction: it affects Coleridge too.[14] As the Mariner is subject to a 'strange power of speech' that forces him to repeat his tale endlessly, so the poet himself lay under a similar though more limited compulsion to repeat himself, revising the poem in 1800 and again in 1817, when he doubled it with a prose gloss in the style of a learned seventeenth-century antiquarian. 'Each revision', writes Homer Brown, 'is an apparent attempt to define and control the wandering meaning – in a sense the reading – of the poem ... And each version of this tale is allegorical in relationship to the one prior to it.'[15] The gloss attempts to prop up the original narrative, making explicit what the Mariner either left implicit or, perhaps, missed. The brief 'Argument', though tracing little more than the ship's movements and holding out the bare lure of 'strange things that befell', does in little what the gloss does in full. Both repeat to rationalise or explain – to reclaim sense from apparent nonsense. But an uncanny motive behind the retellings gives itself away; rationalisation reveals itself as an attempt to conceal the nature of the Mariner's story.

For the reader who accepts the authority of the gloss and the connections the gloss makes, the commentary is the completion of an otherwise incomplete structure. Walter Jackson Bate speaks for these readers when he asserts that Coleridge added 'the beautiful gloss in order to flesh out the otherwise skeletal bones of the supernatural machinery and also to help smooth the flow of the narrative.'[16] If we can take Bate's words more seriously than he meant them, the gloss humanises the supernatural, animates the dead – worthy aims both, from the Wordsworthian perspective. But Bate's image suggests an unwitting interpretive necromancy, for the literary critical raising of bones merely repeats one of the *Ancient Mariner's* objectionable wonders. The gloss does to the poem what the spirits do to the bodies of the crew, and what the spirits do to the crew the tale does to its explicators. A structure of nested quotations, the poem behaves in linguistic terms like its own ventriloquist, appropriated by and taking possession of one voice after another: the Mariner's, the minstrel's, the antiquarian's, the critic's. Acknowledging no author, the tale dominates its speakers. To encounter it is to be infected.

The *Rime's* ventriloquisms are both fictions and realities. When the Wedding Guest, preternaturally sensitive to the presence of linguistic demons, realises that the voice that has been telling him about the strange death of the crew could not belong to the terrifying body whose glittering eye and rigid hand have immobilised him, we should listen carefully:

> 'I fear thee, ancyent Marinere!
> 'I fear thy skinny hand;
> 'And thou art long and lank and brown
> 'As is the ribb'd Sea-sand.

> 'I fear thee and thy glittering eye
> 'And thy skinny hand, so brown –
> Fear not, fear not, thou wedding guest!
> This body dropt not down.
> (ll. 216–23)

It is the body, and particularly the hand, that terrifies the Wedding Guest, and it is about the body, though not the hand, that the Mariner tries to reassure him. But he says nothing about the voice. In fact, there is an alien voice, and even an alien hand, in the vicinity; it belongs, as Coleridge points out in a note appended in 1817, to Wordsworth, who contributed the lines about the Mariner's ghoulish appearance. Coleridge's uneasiness about the Wordsworthian lines he uses finds expression in the Wedding Guest's cry of apprehension; the Wedding Guest – or is it Wordsworth? – serves as ventriloquist to voice Coleridge's fears of ventriloquy. But if Wordsworth is the ventriloquist here, he is only the nearest to hand; there are others behind him.

The voice that repeats the *Rime* is strange not only because it is mysteriously motivated, and not only because it fails to explain anything more than its frame or the reason it is being told, but also because it is archaic, as indeed is the language of the entire poem. The style of the *Rime* seems strange because its familiarity goes too far back for us to recognise it. 'A Dutch attempt at German sublimity', Southey called it,[17] his desire to poke fun accidentally leading him the direction of a truth. An earlier English style[18] has returned sounding almost foreign.

So carefully did Coleridge set about archaising the vocabularies of the poem and establishing plausibility of the historical details that scholars can guess with fair assurance when the voyage was supposed to have been undertaken,[19] when the minstrel was supposed to have made the Rime,[20] and when the commentator was supposed to have written the gloss.[21] But Coleridge's scholarly success worked against him. His contemporaries, responding not to the authenticity of the details but to the fact of their unfamiliarity and their suggestion of stylistic ventriloquism, reacted to the poet the way the Hermit reacted to the Mariner: with deep suspicion about the source of so obviously unnatural an utterance. Speaking anonymously for the *Critical Review*, Southey objected to what he regarded as the inauthenticity of the poem:

> We are tolerably conversant with the early English poets; and can discover no resemblance whatever, except in antiquated spelling and a few obsolete words. This piece appears to us perfectly original in style as well as in story.[22]

Others took exception to the diction while appreciating the overall style. An anonymous critic for *The British Critic* wrote,

The author ... is not correctly versed in the old language, which he undertakes to employ. 'Noises of a *swound* ... and 'broad as a *weft*' ... are both nonsensical; but the ancient style is so well imitated, while the antiquated words are so very few, that the latter might with advantage be entirely removed without any detriment to the effect of the Poem.[23]

When he revised the poem in 1800, Coleridge did change the phrases to which critics had raised particular objections.[24]

Perhaps one reason for the critics' displeasure at the language of the *Ancient Mariner* as it appeared in 1798 is that others before Coleridge had drawn so heavily upon archaic and pseudo-archaic English as to have given the public a disgust for the style. During the 1780s and 1790s sophisticated writers of 'ballads of simplicity' had their productions 'encrusted with a patina spuriously induced by consonants doubled at random and superfluous *e*'s' in order to make them seem older than they really were.[25] The fraud was not always so transparent. Lowes remarks that

> nine out of ten of the archaisms which went into the earliest version of 'The Ancient Mariner' had already imparted a would-be romantic flavour to the pages of Chatterton, and Shenstone, and Thomson, and of such smaller fry as Mickle, and Wilkie, and William Thompson, and Moses Mendez, and Gilbert West.[26]

Some readers were tired of antiquity. Others had never had a taste for it. Charles Burney, speaking for the eighteenth-century generally,[27] expressed uneasiness about poetic regression:

> Would it not be degrading poetry, as well as the English language, to go back to the barbarous and uncouth numbers of Chaucer? Suppose, instead of modernising the old bard, that the sweet and polished measures, on lofty subjects, of Dryden, Pope, and Gray, were to transmuted into the dialect and versification of the XIVth century? Should we be gainers by the retrogradation? *Rust* is a necessary quality to a counterfeit old medal: but, to give artificial rust to modern poetry, in order to render it similar to that of three or four hundred years ago, can have no better title to merit and admiration than may be claimed by any ingenious forgery.[28]

Yet the style of the *Ancient Mariner* would fool no reader into thinking the poem ancient. Even the 1798 version, its archaic words and spellings not yet removed, would have looked odd to a sixteenth-century reader, for, despite its curiosities of diction, the basis of the poem is the English of 1798. To use Coleridge's own distinction,[29] his poem was meant to imitate and not copy ancient poetic language. It seems to have been this mixture of the strange and the familiar, more than the strangeness itself, that disturbed contemporary readers.

Coleridge himself may have been uneasy about the unnaturalness of his imitation-antique language. He disparaged badly managed archaisms in others' poems, expressing particular dislike for 'their inverted sentences, their quaint phrases, and incongruous mixture of obsolete and spenserian words'.[30] Praising the ballad in Monk Lewis's *Castle Spectre*, a work he otherwise disparaged as 'a mere patchwork of plagiarisms', he wrote,

> The simplicity & naturalness is his own, & not imitated; for it is made to subsist in contiguity with a language perfectly modern – the language of his own times, in the same way that the language of the writer of 'Sir Cauline' was the language of *his* times. This, I think, a rare merit: at least, *I* cannot attain this innocent nakedness, except by *assumption* – I resemble the Dutchess [sic] of Kingston, who masqueraded in the character of 'Eve before the Fall' in flesh-coloured Silk.[31]

If to copy 'innocent nakedness' is lascivious, to copy primitive language is sophisticated. In both cases the imitation offends because it pretends to imitate what is valued precisely for its freedom – as object and as subject – from the taint of imitation. It offends because it acts out of awareness of that which must be unconscious.

But the objects of the *Rime's* mimetic intentions are hardly innocent victims. Deeply and consciously involved in echoes and ventriloquies, the *Rime* derives from, or echoes, sources that are themselves perplexed. It is not simply the echoic structure that denaturalises the language; the earlier voices are no more natural than those they haunt. There was never a first time the Mariner recited his *Rime*. From the outset the tale was a repetition – of the experience itself, which the Mariner relives as he retells it, of the words in which he retells it, and of the other words, with which Coleridge and Wordsworth had been telling or trying to tell other tales during the last half-dozen years. The poem's obvious and exotic anachronisms cover more recent and more local influences, particularly 'The Wanderings of Cain' and 'Salisbury Plain'.

The *Rime* was the result of two separate collaborative failures. It was meant to be a joint project, like the *Lyrical Ballads* to which it gave rise. As Wordsworth told Isabella Fenwick the story of the poem's inception and early development, he, Dorothy, and Coleridge were on a walk when they decided to write a poem in order to finance a tour. Parts of the idea for it came from the dream of a Mr Cruikshank; other parts, such as the shooting of the albatross, the navigation of the ship by the dead men, and the spirits' revenge, were suggested by Wordsworth, who also contributed a few lines. But 'as we endeavoured to proceed conjointly (I speak of the same evening) our respective manners proved so widely different that it would have been presumptuous in me to do anything but separate from an undertaking upon which I could only have been a clog.'³² Thus even before the poem took definite shape it was already a conversation turned monologue; years before the gloss was written there were voices other than the narrator's telling versions of parts of the same tale. The final form recapitulates what would otherwise seem to be irrelevant facts about its production.

The plan Wordsworth tells about was already a repetition of, or substitution for, an earlier plan. In his 'Prefatory Note' to the fragmentary 'Wanderings of Cain', Coleridge writes:

> The work was to have been written in concert with another [Wordsworth], whose name is too venerable within the precincts of genius to be unnecessarily brought into connection with such a trifle, and who was then residing at a small distance from Nether Stowey. The title and subject were suggested by myself, who likewise drew out the scheme and contents for each of the three books or cantos, of which the work was to consist, and which, the reader is to be informed, was to have been finished in one night! My partner undertook the first canto: I the second: and whichever had *done first*, was to set about the third. Almost thirty years have passed by; yet at this moment I cannot without something more than a smile moot the question which of the two things was the more impracticable, for a mind so eminently original to compose another man's thoughts and fancies, or for a taste so austerely pure and simple to imitate the Death of Abel? Methinks I see his grand and noble countenance as at the moment when having despatched my own portion of the task at full finger-speed, I hastened to him with my manuscript – that look of humorous despondency fixed on his almost blank sheet of paper, and then its silent mock piteous admission of failure struggling with the sense of the exceeding ridiculousness of the whole scheme – which broke up in a laugh: and the Ancient Mariner was written instead.³³

Coleridge's account of the poem's 'birth, parentage, and premature decease' (as he calls it) inadvertently suggests a parallel between the writing and the story being written. In stressing the absurdity of one man attempting to offer what is not his to offer, Coleridge's account cannot help but remind us that Abel the shepherd was killed because his offering of sheep was accepted while Cain the farmer's offering of grain – he had no sheep to sacrifice – was not. The brother poets proved unable to cooperate on a story centring around the fratricidal consequences of that unequally regarded sacrifice. It is no coincidence that so many of the poems on which Wordsworth and Coleridge tried to collaborate concern violence and envy.

As so often is the case, Coleridge's remarks on textual history provide a key to reading the text as an allegory of its own production. His remarks raise questions about the authenticity of expression that 'The Wanderings of Cain' and its successor will dramatise. Though it may be ridiculous for one man 'to compose another man's thoughts', Coleridge found the possibility of such an impersonation sufficiently intriguing to make it one of 'Cain''s major themes. Ventriloquism may be no proper source of poetry, but the *Rime*, 'Cain''s stepchild, depends on it, internalising the relationship that Coleridge now writes off.

'The Wanderings of Cain' matters to a reading of the *Rime* because of the relationships among its history, its subject, and its formal structure – if one can call a text so confused, so nonsensical, either formal or structured. In 'The Wanderings of Cain' as in the *Rime*, different voices and different versions of the same story compete with one another. The relationship among the introductory verse stanza Coleridge claimed to have reconstructed from memory ('Encinctured with a twine of leaves', etc.), the prose version of canto II, and the 'rough draft of a continuation or alternative version ... found among Coleridge's papers'[34] is not clear. It is hard to say whether we are dealing with different versions of the same events or with different, although perhaps similar, events – a problem the reader of the *Rime* and its gloss should recognise.

Though the plot of 'The Wanderings of Cain' is too baffling to recount, it is – happily – not as a narrative but as a collection of themes, images, and questions about representation that 'The Wanderings of Cain' finds its way into the *Rime*. 'The Wanderings of Cain' contains the raw materials for the *Rime*: killing, punishment by solitude, spirits, trances, the sacrifice of blood from an arm, and wandering. It contains passages that translate almost immediately into the words of the later poem. One such passage follows:

And Cain lifted up his voice and cried bitterly, and said, 'The Mighty One that persecuteth me is on this side and on that; he pursueth my soul like the wind, like the sand-blast he passeth through me; he is around me even as the air! O that I might be utterly no more! I desire to die – yes, the things that never had life, neither move they upon the earth – behold! they seem precious to mine eyes. O that a man might live without the breath of his nostrils. So I might abide in darkness, and blackness, and an empty space! ... For the torrent that roareth far off hath a voice· and the clouds in heaven look terribly on me; the Mighty One who is against me speaketh in the wind of the cedar grove; and in silence am I dried up.'

Cain's complaints resemble the Mariner's: he is persecuted by storm and by freakish winds; he wishes he could die; he learns to love the slimy things that crawl with legs upon the slimy sea; the bodies of the dead crew move with no breath in their nostrils; he is alone, alone, on a wide, wide sea; he can hear the winds roaring far off; drought silences him. Both Cain and the shape of Abel resemble the Mariner: Cain whose eye 'glared ... fierce and sullen and whose countenance told in a strange and terrible language of agonies that had been, and were, and were still to continue to be'; and the shape of Abel, who cries, 'Woe is me! woe is me! I must never die again, and yet I am perishing with thirst and hunger'. The Mariner is in part a composite of Cain and the delusive representation of the brother he murdered, uncertain what god or what spirits may have dominion over him now.

In neither poem it is apparent whether the cosmos *is* a cosmos, united under a single, benevolent God, or a place of warring and delusive spirits. We see the spirits and hear their reports, but are they reliable? The Mariner asserts the unity of God and the universality of His laws of love, but the evidence suggests that the shape of Abel may have spoken the truth when he talked of another God ruling over the nightmare world of sin and death. The 'Wanderings of Cain' articulates the heresy that the *Rime* rehearses to deny. ...

A summary of the *Rime*, a transcription of a recital of a repeatedly ventriloquised tale, might go, ""'"I" can't stop talking."""' The Mariner's compulsive self-quotation, which calls into question the self he quotes, expresses on the level of individual character a compulsion to repeat that constitutes not just the poem's psychology and genealogy but also its morphology. Stanzas, lines, phrases, and even individual words reveal the same penchant for repetition and self-quotation as do the poem's ancestors, inhabitants, and redactors.

Echoes and patterns of imagistic repetition ordinarily invite comparisons: we take them as indices – straight or ironic – of continuity, coherence, or analogy. Some of the *Rime*'s echoes – verbal, imagistic, and structural – behave as we expect them to; others do not. As Arden Reed points out,

> The process of doubling the 'Ancient Mariner' operates in two directions. One is the creation of resemblance or identity out of difference, when the poem demonstrates how two things that seem unrelated or even opposite can come to mirror each other. ... But ... the poem is also engaged in splitting identity (the presence of the word to itself, for instance) into differences, in turning the singular 'rime' into two meanings that are not necessarily commensurate. This second process may be related to a more general fragmentation that marks the entire poem. Both of these operations, the making and unmaking of congruence, take place throughout the text and are woven together; but they do not form any regular, much less any dialectical pattern.[35]

Through much of the poem, the tendency to repeat disguises itself as balladic repetition:

> Water, water, every where,
> And all the boards did shrink;
> Water, water, every where,
> Nor any drop to drink.
> (ll. 115–18)

Traditional balladic repetitions depend for their effect either upon their rhythmic value alone or upon their ability to unfold an irony or a revelation. *The Rime*'s repetitions sometimes seem to function the same way, as forms of punctuation laden at once with musical and with thematic value. One of the more accessible of such clusters involves interruption. The 'loud bassoon' that announces the entrance of the bride into the hall interrupts the Mariner's tale just when the ship has reached the equator, where twice later its voyage will be interrupted. The voyage is interrupted first by a deadly calm that brings the spectre ship bearing Life-in-Death, whose appearance parodies the bride's. It is interrupted again by the changing of the spirit-guard that makes the ship pause and rock and lunge. The 'roaring wind' that approaches the becalmed ship makes 'the upper air burst into life' and sets 'fire-flags sheen' and stars dancing in a fashion that anticipates the conclusion of the wedding, when 'what loud uproar bursts from that door!' at the singing of the bride and her maids. These echoes hint at a relationship of inverse analogy between the Mariner's journey and the wedding that his tale prevents the Wedding Guest from celebrating.

Clusters such as this one, much favoured by those who insist upon the organic unity and Christian implications of the poem, lend themselves to analysis into categories of life and death, vitality and stasis, love and hate, good and evil. Taken themselves, these patternings seem to set human life and love into the context of universal life and love, giving cosmic overtones to the wedding and affirming the universality of the human moral and epistemological codes. They suggest that what happens in the middle of the ocean remains comparable to what happens in ordinary English villages and remains interpretable by terrestrial rules. But of course the analogy can work the other way around as well, suggesting that what happens in the villages is properly interpretable only in terms of what happens to unlucky mariners at sea. It is disturbing thought, but when – as here – the alternative is total unreadability, even a sinister interpretation may be better than none at all.

Most of the *Rime*'s repetitions are neither unmeaning 'hey nonny noes' nor clues whose meaning will become clear by the end of the poem but passages in which the mere mechanism or materiality of language seems almost – but not quite – to deny the possibility of sense. 'Alone, alone, all all alone, / Alone on a wide wide Sea', laments the Mariner. The cry approaches the condition of a wordless moan. At the same time, it dramatises a solitude that seems to imply its absoluteness by verbal necessity. The line resembles both a stutter, mere sound haunted by its own terrifyingly arbitrary and disparate possibilities, and an oxymoron, 'all' being an unfinished 'alone', 'alone' being a portmanteau of 'all' and 'lone' or 'one'. The barely articulate wail contains its own comfort and the germ of one of Coleridge's favourite intellectual convictions, that the 'all' and the 'one' could be reconciled. But little other than wistful thinking holds the line's paradoxical echoes together; and even so it is unclear whether the wistful thinking is the critic's or the Mariner's.

Many of the *Rime*'s apparent echoes and symmetries resemble accidents rather than analogies. These repetitions, instances of what one might call the *instance de la lettre*, suggest primarily the power of images to recur and the powerlessness of the Mariner or the narrator to dispose of them. They seem not merely the objects of obsession but agents of contagion, infecting those who behold them. Their metonymy exercises a metaphoric, even metamorphic, effect. For this reason both looking and speaking can be dangerous activities.

In the *Rime* you become what you meet. This principle dictates the poem's structure and plot. The hypnotic power the Mariner exercises over the Wedding Guest he has absorbed, painfully, from the dead crew, who, having met Death and Life-in-Death, experience the meaning of the first and enact the meaning of the second:

> All stood together on the deck,
> For a charnel-dungeon fitter:
> All fix'd on me their stony eyes
> That in the moon did glitter.
>
> The pang, the curse, with which they died,
> Had never pass'd away:
> I could not draw my een from theirs
> Ne turn them up to pray.
>   (ll. 439–46)

The Mariner's ship displays a similar vulnerability during its transformation into an image of the two things it encounters at sea, the albatross and the spectre ship. By the time it returns to port, the Mariner's ship is inhabited by Death in the several persons of the crew and Life-in-Death in the person of the Ancient Mariner, an apparent corpse still capable of both speech and movement. The ship itself, says the Hermit, 'hath a fiendish look': 'The planks looked warped! and see those sails, / How thin they are and sere!' It has become a skeleton ship. Though it does not plunge and tack and veer, it does, like the spectre ship, move 'without a breeze, without a tide', powered by supernatural forces.[36] The wind that blows as it comes to land has no navigational use:

> But soon there breath'd a wind on me,
> Ne sound ne motion made:
> Its path was not upon the sea
> In ripple or in shade.
> ....
> Swiftly, swiftly flew the ship,
> Yet she sail'd softly too:
> Sweetly, sweetly blew the breeze –
> On me alone it blew.
>   (ll. 457–60, 465–8)

The ship shares too the fate of the albatross, whose behaviour foreshadows elements of the coming catastrophe. 'It ate the food it ne'er had eat', as the Mariner will shortly after, although perhaps a diet of blood is not strictly comparable to one of biscuit worms. The ship, doomed to go 'down like lead' when the Hermit approaches it in his boat singing 'godly hymns', suffers a fate not unlike that of the albatross, which falls into the sea at an 'unaware' blessing from the Mariner. The ship sinks to the sound of underwater thunder that 'split the bay'. Its sinking creates a whirlpool in which the Hermit's boat 'spun round and round'. Both ships together thus re-enact in a sinister fashion the scenes in which the playful albatross first comes to the frozen ship: 'round and round it flew: / The Ice did split with a Thunder fit; / The Helmsman steer'd us thro'' (ll. 66–8).[37]

It is not necessary, however, actually to encounter a physical object in order to feel its metamorphosing influence. Sometimes a merely verbal encounter is enough. Passing through the neighbourhood of a simile or even a submerged metaphor puts you (even, perhaps, you the reader) at risk; the words are capable of realising themselves at your expense. So the ship's very setting off is a sinking, as it 'drop[s] / Below the Kirk, below the Hill, / Below the Light-house top'; its final moments realise in literal terms the implications of its first ones. The cracking and growling and roaring and howling of the ice at the south pole, 'like noises of a swound', anticipate the trance in which the Mariner later hears two spirits discussing his past and his future. And the first hint that the Mariner is in trouble comes before the commission of the crime, when the Mariner compares the force of the storm that drives the ship south to the violence of persecution. In 1798 a fairly impersonal tempest 'play'd us freaks'. In 1817 the tempest became a hostile spirit:

> And now the STORM-BLAST came, and he
> Was tyrannous and strong;
> He struck us with o'ertaking wings,
> And chased us south along.

> With sloping masts and dipping prow,
> As who pursued with yell and blow
> Still treads the shadow of his foe
> And forwards bends his head,
> The ship drove fast, loud roared the blast,
> And southward aye we fled.[38]

When the albatross appears, as Paul Magnuson points out, 'the mariner unconsciously associates the albatross with the storm while he and the crew outwardly receive the bird as a member of their Christian community'.[39] The shooting of the Albatross, which most readers regard as the single event that produces the more dramatic misfortune that follows,[40] may have been a consequence of that unconscious association; alternatively, it may have been an attempt to produce belatedly a reason for what would otherwise lack explanation. A figure of the effect produces the reality of its own cause.

But to speak of before and after, anticipation and fulfilment, may be inappropriate here, where chronology is a blur, events are metalepses, and what drives the plot is the conversion of figures into literal realities and sometimes back into figures again. Chronology does not really apply to the events of this poem: its temporality is rhetorical. The same scenes – or at least the same figures – are always before our eyes, even if we cannot see them or understand what they represent. Things we never saw before are greeted like sudden recognitions, as if successful interpretation had called them into being. Thus the odd sense of familiarity at the appearance of the spectre ship:

> Alas! (thought I, and my heart beat loud)
> How fast she neres and neres!
> Are those *her* Sails that glance in the Sun
> Like restless gossameres?
> (ll. 173–6)

This itself echoes the gesture of recognition that opens the poem. 'It is an ancient Mariner', says the narrator, as if we had already seen 'it' and wanted to know what it was.[41] The lack of antecedent is no obstacle to recurrence in a poem like this, in which a figure may generate its own *etymon* and interpretation precedes its own object.

While the *Rime* deprives its declared and undeclared origins of originality, it also produces the image of a linguistic genesis of sorts. At the heart of the poem (if it can be said to have such a thing) one finds a passage in which the poem's principal obsessions and paradoxes converge. The appearance of the spectre ship, an emblem of what he is about to become, inspires the Mariner to invent a rash method of what the gloss calls 'free[ing] his speech from the bonds of thirst'.

> I bit my arm and suck'd the blood
> And cry'd, A sail! a sail!
> (ll. 152–3)

The lines intimate a close relation among naming, violence, and death. Bloodshed, after all, is bloodshed: with the killing of the albatross so recently past, the Mariner's desperate attempt to quench his thirst cannot help but suggest murder.[42] Even worse, the bloodsucking conjures up superstitions about how the dead prey upon the living. But although the poem elsewhere provides what may be evidence for such a reading, one need not think solely in terms of vampires and ghouls. Odysseus offered bloody oblations to the most respectable shades in Hades in order to release them from speechlessness. When he drinks his own blood, the Mariner puts himself in the position of one already dead, and this despite the fact that Death and Life-in-Death are only at that moment coming over the horizon. Whereas in Homer the dead drink blood so that they can address the living, the Mariner drinks blood in order to hail the dead.

The act is a parody of the archaic rite, itself a Hadean inversion of divine inspiration: drinking blood in the underworld is a necessary prelude to true speech, just as inhaling divine breath is – or was – the necessary prelude to true song. In either rite, one takes into oneself the essence of another's life or spirit. If the drinking of his own blood can be considered the Mariner's version of inspiration and not merely a novel way to clear his throat, then the source of his inspiration is not a higher being but himself. Paradoxically, the traditional gesture of poetic dependence has become an assertion of vocal and imaginative autonomy. It is the physiological equivalent of self-quotation and the literary equivalent of suicide.

This is not the first time the Mariner has been inspired by the blood he sheds. It was the killing of the albatross that first enabled him to identify himself, at least retrospectively, as an 'I'; it may have been what provided him with a self to refer to.[43] This second shedding of blood functions like the first, enabling the Mariner to identify an inchoate 'something' as a ship. It provides him too with the words that will prove to be the germ of his tale, the vocabulary (a literalisation of an earlier vehicle) with which he will later try to answer the Hermit's question about his own identity. 'A sail! a sail!' becomes the first line of the Mariner's autobiography: 'There was a Ship'.

The moment that brings into view that incarnation of the principle of uncanniness, Life-in-Death, brings also the mind's recognition of its own originary power. What answers to the Mariner's cry is an engine of autonomy and the first violation of the laws of nature. The spectre ship moves without wind, without indeed any apparent motive power at all – as fits the instrument of retribution for a motiveless crime. When the Mariner's ship becomes spectral itself, it moves the same way, powered by the absence of wind, which in this case is something other than mere stillness.

> And soon I heard a roaring wind:
> It did not come anear;
> But with its sound it shook the sails,
> That were so thin and sere.
> ....
> The loud wind never reached the ship,
> Yet now the ship moved on!
> Beneath the lightning and the Moon
> The dead men gave a groan.
>
> They groaned, they stirred, they all uprose,
> Nor spake, nor moved their eyes:
> It had been strange, even in a dream,
> To have seen those dead men rise.
>
> The helmsman steered, the ship moved on;
> Yet never a breeze up-blew. ...
>   (ll. 309–12, 327–36, 1817 edn)[44]

Natural wind exists as a constant moving away from itself; its condition, like that of language, is differential. This wind, curiously independent of the movement of air, affects things not by presence, not by absence, but – so to speak – by the absence of that natural absence in which normal wind consists: only the sound or voice of its roaring ever reaches the ship. It behaves like metonymy of its own metonymic potential, a deconstructive metalepsis that leaves nature, causality, and identity behind. Its appearance amounts to a confession of allegory, voice that lives in despair of its object.

The association between wind and language is, of course, ancient and universal.[45] Traditionally, poetic wind, bearing the voice and breath of the muse into the very body of the human singer, guaranteed the truth of song: it testified to a metaphysics of presence. And so Coleridge was content to regard it until as late at least as 1795, when he imagined it sweeping, 'Plastic and vast, one intellectual breeze, / At once the Soul of each, and God of all', over a world of Eolian harps. A similar ideal, albeit expressed in the mode of despair, would behind the 'Dejection' ode, whose wind the poet imagines no longer as an ecstatic, impersonal power but now as the magical counterpart to his own blocked voice, capable not only of expressing all he cannot but also of reviving that lost state in which nature and consciousness were one. He wants, in Frost's words, not 'copy speech' but 'original response', neither inspiration nor an interpreter but an echo that reestablishes his dialogue with what now he only gazes at '– and with how blank an eye!' Though he argues that 'from the soul itself must there be sent / A sweet and potent voice, of its own birth', the priority of the internally generated voice is uncertain; the poet still yearns for the 'wonted impulse' of a storm that 'Might startle this dull pain, and make it move and live!' By the time the storm has risen and Coleridge has realised that he has recovered his voice, the wind has become his double, and it is impossible to locate the origin of the voice it represents.

The *Rime*'s uncanny wind, like those of the 'Eolian Harp' and the 'Dejection' ode, is allied with language and with spirit, but in uncomfortable ways. It is not life-giving, truthful, or cathartic, and the way it raises spirits is not cheering. Though it takes the form of spirits, it is not spiritual: insisting upon its independence, it usurps upon the souls and bodies of those it occupies, substituting voice for intentionality and turning those it inspires into zombies. It is a demonic version of the force the two conversation poems invoke, an allegory of influence, enacting the horrors against which those more traditional representations are meant to defend.

The *Rime*, like the Mariner, is obsessed with its need to talk about itself and its relation to speech but never quite manages to name its subject. The poem is filled with emblems and allegories of its history and constitution: the Mariner possessed by his 'strange power of speech' and the dead crew whose bodies house the spirits that sometimes sing and sometimes sail are working through aspects of inspiration, influence, and intertextuality. Just how terrifying these issues could seem to Coleridge we may see in a passage that appeared in the 1798 edition before being suppressed. The Mariner has just encountered the spectre ship. Life-in-Death whistles, and a wind responds by whistling back at her through Death:

A gust of wind sterte up behind
And whistled thro' his bones;

Thro' the holes of his eyes and the hole of his mouth
Half-whistles and half-groans.

(ll. 195–8)

It plays upon him as upon some ghastly Aeolian harp – a strange
power of speech indeed. These lines, along with some other details of
grossly Gothic character, were purged from the poem by 1800 in an
attempt to placate the critics,[46] whose voices, like so many others,
found lodging in Coleridge's text. But the mysterious behaviour of the
wind, something hostile critics pounced upon as 'absurd or unintelligi-
ble'[47] and even friendly readers found disturbing,[48] remained in place.

Like the wind, the *Rime* denies its origins: no original language,
no language of spirits, no motivation, no proper causes. It gives us
imitations, repetitions, representations – but no originals. It constitutes its own motivation; its telling demands the explanation its
retelling, like the re-enactment of Freudian transference, fails to
provide. Yet the surprising thing is not, finally, that the *Rime* feels
and fears the influence of outer or earlier voices, that its originality
is open to question, but that the poem works so hard to put itself in
second place, to confess and exhibit its secondariness. It shudders at
alien voices, but it shudders at its own voice – thoroughly haunted,
possessed, dispossessed, and characterless, and thereby most deeply
and characteristically Coleridgean – most of all.

Divided from himself as from other men, inhabiting a world of
baffling disjunction, and speaking a language neither whose motive
force nor whose meaning is apparent, the Mariner is in no position to
tell who he is. In a world where identity fails to coincide with character, where motivations are external and apparently autonomous, the
difficulty of naming himself would be enormous. Perhaps the *Rime*
really is the shortest answer to the Hermit's question, demonstrating
the difficulty of saying 'I am' in one's own voice.

From Susan Eilenberg, *Strange Power of Speech: Wordsworth,
Coleridge and Literary Possession* (Oxford, 1992), pp. 31–46,
49–59.

NOTES

[Eilenberg's book is informed by deconstructive and pyschoanalytical
thought, and is particularly influenced by the work of Bloom, de Man and
Hartman. It takes as its subject the relationship between tropes of literary

property and signification in the writings of Wordsworth and Coleridge. Eilenberg raises such deconstructive questions as, Who owns language? and Who controls meaning? and applies these to the texts of Wordsworth and Coleridge's early collaborations. In her ingenious discussion of *The Rime of The Ancient Mariner*, Eilenberg shows how the Mariner is an effect rather than a cause of the language of his tale. He is possessed as much by language as by the spirits of the poem. She demonstrates how the tale is structured by repetitions, even at the level of Coleridge's frequent revisions of, and additions to, the work, and she points out that a number of voices other than that of the poet and the mariner inhabit the work. Eilenberg shows how the text functions at times through metonymy, that is where signs listed sequentially begin to take on the characteristics of the things they are next to. This extract is from the second chapter of Eilenberg's book and is substantially complete: a brief discussion of Wordsworth's treatment of similar themes in his Salisbury Plain poems is excluded. Ed.]

1. 'The difficulty of the poem', writes Frances Ferguson, 'is that the possibility of learning from the Mariner's experience depends upon sorting that experience into a more linear and complete pattern than the poem ever agrees to do. For the poem seems almost as thorough a work of backwardness – or hysteron proteron – as we have.' See 'Coleridge and the Deluded Reader: "The Rime of the Ancient Mariner"' *Georgia Review*, 31 (1977), 617–35.

2. Wordsworth's remarks can be found in *Lyrical Ballads*: the text of the 1798 edition with the additional 1800 poems and the Prefaces, ed. R. L. Brett and A. R. Jones (London, 1963), p. 277.

3. In the best reading of this kind, Lawrence Kramer discusses the poem in terms of demonic imagination, which reveals itself 'as a kind of anti-self' or 'hostile other', 'the personification of an unconscious will to represent whatever aspects of the self that the self chooses to forget – the side of the self we can still call repressed, if we use the term loosely'. See 'That Other Will: The Daemonic in Coleridge and Wordsworth', *Philological Quarterly*, 58 (1979), 298–320. Anya Taylor reads the story as the product of psychological projection of dreams in *Magic and English Romanticism* (Athens, GA, 1979), p. 115. Richard Haven offers a perceptive reading of this 'history of an ego' in *Patterns of Consciousness: An Essay on Coleridge* (Amherst, MA, 1969), pp. 18–36. In a related version, the poem is supposed to be an allegory of epistemological categories. See for example, Irene Chayes, 'A Coleridgean Reading of "The Ancient Mariner"', *Studies in Romanticism*, 4 (1965), 81–103.

4. The Wedding Guest, whom Paul Magnuson has called 'a pyschological double of the mariner', is required to suffer (vicariously) what the Mariner suffered in his own person (Paul Magnuson, *Coleridge's Nightmare Poetry* [Charlottesville, VA, 1974], p. 84).

5. See 'Two Aspects of Language and Two Types of Aphasic Disturbances', in Roman Jakobson and Moris Halle, *Fundamentals of Language* (4th edn, New York, 1980).

6. S. T. Coleridge, *Miscellaneous Criticism*, ed. T. M. Raysor (London, 1936), p. 99.

7. His exclamation identifies the unnameable 'something in the Sky' that, when it 'took at last/A certain shape', proves to be not only an image of what the Mariner's ship will become but an emblem of the story they are living through: the very vehicle of contagion, metonymy turned literal.

8. Lines 29–34. Unless otherwise noted, all citations will be from the 1798 edition of the poem printed in *Lyrical Ballads* 1798, ed. W. J. B. Owen (2nd edn, Oxford, 1969).

9. Arden Reed, *Romantic Weather: The Climates of Coleridge and Baudelaire* (Hanover, 1983), p. 177.

10. Geoffrey Hartman, *Beyond Formalism: Literary Essays, 1958–1970* (New Haven, CT, 1970), p. 334.

11. Homer Obed Brown, 'The Art of Theology and the Theology of Art: Robert Penn Warren's Reading of *The Rime of the Ancient Mariner*', in William V. Spanos, Paul A. Bove, and Daniel O' Hara (eds), *The Question of Textuality: Strategies of Reading in Contemporary American Criticism* (Bloomington, IN, 1982), p. 254.

12. Jonathan Arac, 'Repetition and Exclusion: Coleridge and New Criticism Reconsidered', in Spanos et al., *The Question of Textuality*, p. 269.

13. It is a curiously shrewd reply, reinterpreting the Wedding Guest's exclamation at the possibility that he might be possessed as a question about the nature of the spirits inhabiting the bodies of others. His reassurance that the spirits are not the original inhabitants of the bodies is not really reassuring, however.

14. The mariner is something of a self-portrait of the poet, who was at the time of the poem's composition only slightly less odd than his creation. Coleridge was still a young man when he wrote the poem and, though a great talker, not yet the notorious glittery-eyed monologuist of the Highgate years. He did have a weakness for recycling his words; when the demands of correspondence became too great, he would repeat not only the same bits of news but the same wording, sometimes pages at a time, letter after letter. His penchant for reusing poetry and prose was still probably a matter of efficiency, not pathology. It was only later that Coleridge began drawing parallels between his experience and the Mariner's.

15. Brown, 'The Art of Theology', p. 249.

16. Water Jackson Bate, *Coleridge* (Cambridge, MA, 1968), pp. 56–7. What Frances Ferguson says of the gloss is true of any possible remark on the poem: 'In assuming that things must be significant and interpretable, [the gloss] finds significance and interpretability, but only by reading ahead of – or beyond – the main text' ('Coleridge and the Deluded Reader', p. 623).

17. *Critical Review*, October 1798; in John O. Hayden (ed.), *Romantic Bards and British Reviewers: A Selected Edition of the Contemporary Reviews of the Works of Wordsworth, Coleridge, Byron and Shelley* (Lincoln, NE, 1971), p. 4. In a letter written a decade later, Coleridge gets Southey's witticism interestingly wrong: '"over-polished in the diction with *Dutch* industry"' *Collected Letters*, III, 203).

18. Richard Payne has demonstrated that 'Coleridge was attempting, in the idiom of *The Ancient Mariner*, to recapture the lost natural idiom' of the 'elder poets' and that he succeeded in producing a 'quite authentic rendition of the idioms of a broad section of the British literary tradition' of the sixteenth and seventeenth centuries ('"The Style and Spirit of the Elder Poets": *The Ancient Mariner* and the English Literary Tradition', *Modern Philology*, 75 [1978], 368–84).

19. 'There is...enough historical evidence to date the imaginary voyage, very broadly, around 1500, a natural date for a late-medieval ballad, and consistent with the elaborately Catholic and medieval detail', writes George Watson (*Coleridge the Poet* [London, 1966], p. 90). See also Huntington Brown, 'The Gloss to *The Rime of the Ancient Mariner*', *Modern Language Quarterly*, 6 (1945), 319.

20. The purity and simplicity of the minstrel's language mark him as a medieval minstrel as opposed to one of the 'broadside journalists of Shakespeare's London', observes Huntington Brown, above, p. 319. Coleridge copied this particular ballad form keeping an eye on Percy's *Reliques*, particularly 'Sir Cauline' (*Collected Letters*, I, 379 note). John Livingston Lowes traces another large portion of *The Ancient Mariner*'s vocabulary to Chaucer, Spenser, William Taylor's translations of Burger's 'Lenore', Chatterton, Hakluyt, Purchas, Martens, and Harris (*The Road to Xanadu. A Study in the Ways of the Imagination* [Boston, 1927], pp. 296–308).

21. The writer of the gloss was an inhabitant of the seventeenth century. See Huntington Brown, 'The Gloss to *The Rime* ', pp. 322, 320.

22. Quoted in Hayden, *Romantic Bards and British Reviewers*, p. 4.

23. Ibid., p. 6

24. B. R. McElderry, Jr, 'Coleridge's Revision of "The Ancient Mariner"', *Studies in Philology*, 29 (1932), 71.

25. Albert Friedman, *The Ballad Revival: Studies in the Influence of Popular on Sophisticated Poetry* (Chicago, 1961), p. 269.

26. Lowes, *The Road to Xanadu*, p. 307.

27. Earl Wasserman explores the Neo-classicals' confusion about and ambivalence toward their forebears in *Elizabethan Poetry in the Eighteenth Century* (Urbana, IL, 1947).

28. Quoted in J. R. de J. Jackson (ed.), *Coleridge: The Critical Heritage* (London, 1970), p. 55. Burney's attitude was the kind that made writers of pseudo-antique poems into hoaxers. The poetry of Chatterton, for example, was valued, when it was valued largely for being a relic of an earlier age.

29. 'The composition of a poem is among the imitative arts; and...imitation, as opposed to copying, consists in the interfusion of the SAME throughout the radically DIFFERENT, or of the different thoughout a base radically the same' (*Biographia Literaria*, II, 72).

30. S. T. Coleridge, *Poetical Works*, ed. E. H. Coleridge (Oxford, 1979), II, 1139.

31. Letter 225 to William Wordsworth, 23 January 1798, in *Collected Letters*, I, 379.

32. *The Poetical Works of William Wordsworth*, ed. Ernest De Selincourt and Helen Darbishire (Oxford, 1940–7), I, 361.

33. Coleridge, *Poetical Works*, I, 285–7.

34. Ibid., p. 285.

35. Reed, *Romantic Weather*, p. 150.

36. Presumably now that the crew have absorbed the wind into themselves in the form of singing spirits they no longer need an external wind to sail the ship. The Mariner suggests that a spirit moves the ship from below.

37. From all this the reader bent on finding a certain kind of poetic unity might deduce a kind of poetic justice: as the albatross responds to the ship, so the ship responds to spirits who administer its doom. The Mariner's perception that the death of the crew was linked to the death of the albatross might support such a reading. But it does not take us far, partly because we see so little into the spirits' motivations, partly because the behaviour of a living albatross does not shed much light on the behaviour of a skeleton ship.

38. Lines 41–50. I am quoting here from the 1817 version printed in *Poetical Works*, I.

39. Magnuson, *Coleridge's Nightmare Poetry*, p. 58.

40. But see Lawrence Kramer, who argues that the appearance of the alba-
    tross means a respite from the nightmare of the ice and that by 'killing
    the albatross, therefore, the Mariner does not initiate his nightmare; he
    returns to it, and allows it to perpetuate itself' ('That Other Will',
    p. 307).

41. See Lawrence Lipking's remarks on the opening 'phantom reference' in
    'The Marginal Gloss', *Critical Inquiry*, 3 (1977), 615. It is curious to
    note that the first of the two spirits whose voices the Mariner hears in
    his trance begins in a similar manner: 'Is it he?' quoth one, 'Is this the
    man?'

42. Shipwrecked men were known to commit cannibalism in order to
    survive, however, and the maritime law made allowance for the fact.

43. See Richard Haven, *Patterns of Consciousness*, pp. 29–30, and Paul
    Magnuson, *Coleridge's Nightmare Poetry*, p. 62.

44. In 1798 the wind 'reach'd the ship... And dropp'd down, like a
    stone!'

45. In Sanskrit, Hebrew, Greek, Latin, Japanese and other languages, the
    word for 'wind' doubles as the word for 'spirit'. M. H. Abrams dis-
    cusses the ubiquity of the association and Coleridge's relationship to it
    in 'The Correspondent Breeze: A Romantic Metaphor' in *The
    Correspondent Breeze: Essays on English Romanticism* (New York,
    1984), pp. 37–54.

    Many critics have seen in the wind of the *Rime* a symbol of the
    mind or the creative impulse. See, for example, Maud Bodkin,
    Archetypal Patterns in Poetry: Pyschological Studies of Imagination
    (London, 1934), pp. 30, 34–5; Richard Harter Fogle, 'The Genre of
    The Ancient Mariner', *Tulane Studies in English*, 7 (1957), 123–4; and
    Robert Penn Warren, 'A Poem of Pure Imagination: An Experiment in
    Reading', in *Selected Essays* (New York, 1941; rpt, 1958), pp. 237–8.

46. B. R. McElderry, Jr, shows that Coleridge took his critics' criticisms
    seriously enough to follow whatever particular changes in diction they
    recommended and to work on passages that aroused special ire
    ('Coleridge's Revision of "The Ancient Mariner"', p. 71).

47. Robert Southey, quoted in Hayden, *Romantic Bards and British
    Reviewers*, p. 4.

48. For example, Lamb, in a letter to Southey intended as a defence of the
    poem, deplored a passage about the supernatural behaviour of the
    wind as 'fertile in unmeaning miracles'. See Jackson, *Coleridge:
    The Critical Heritage*, p. 60.

3

Literary Gentlemen and Lovely Ladies: The Debate on the Character of *Christabel*

KAREN SWANN

Often when Coleridge discusses *Christabel*, his poem becomes a lady whose character needs protecting or explaining. In April 1803, writing to Sara Coleridge from London, he boasts of Sotheby's interest in the poem:

> To day I dine again with Sotheby. He ha[s] informed me, that ten gentlemen, who have met me at his House, desired him to solicit me to finish the Christabel, & to permit them to publish it for me/they engaged that it should be in paper, printing, & decorations the most magnificent Thing that had hitherto appeared. – Of course, I declined it. The lovely Lady shan't come to that pass – Many times rather would I have it printed at Soulby's on the true Ballad Paper – .[1]

Refusing Sotheby and the ten gentlemen, Coleridge stands on his literary principles: a ballad is a popular form, and it would be politically and aesthetically inappropriate to publish one in a guinea volume. But with a shift symptomatic of his and his critics' writing on *Christabel*, he frames the genre question in the poem's own terms, playfully casting its *literary* character as a *feminine* character. Posing as a Baron-like protector of maiden innocence, he asserts

74

that his *Christabel* shall not become a Geraldine, making up in 'magnificence' for what she has lost in honest virtue.

The Baron is not the only role Coleridge plays here. His soliciting 'ten gentlemen' recall Geraldine's 'five ruffians', the anonymous and plural abductors who eventually deposit her under Christabel's tree. Like the story Geraldine tells to Christabel, Coleridge's tale is itself solicitation, an attempt to convince Sara that this latest flight from home has yielded professional if not financial returns. He simply plays his enchantress as a flirt – a heartless flirt, one might add, noticing the way he flaunts his power to attract monied gentlemen. He leads Sara to hope for his capitulation, then drops her flat with his protest that a lady's good character cannot be bought; he charms her with a glimpse of a world from which she is excluded – a world where gentlemen make deals and dine together, and where *he* is attractive because he possesses a certain 'lovely Lady'. Despite what he tells his wife about the lady's good character and his own honourable intentions, Coleridge is toying here with the unstable, charming character of *Christabel*.

This essay addresses the question of *Christabel's* generic status. Coleridge's letter to Sara Coleridge might seem at best a negative example of how to go about such an inquiry: defining the proper literary form of his poem, Coleridge quite improperly comes under the sway of its fictional content, conflating the poem with its 'lovely Lady', and incorporating that feminine character into the dramas of real life. This negative example, however, is also a good example of his and his contemporaries' habitual ways of writing about *Christabel*. When the poem was finally published in 1816, its reviewers attacked it on literary grounds, declaring it an improper *kind* of poem. Their terms, however, had more to do with gender than genre: the lady, they declared, was immodest and improper, and its author, not simply 'unmanly', but an 'enchanted virgin', a 'witch', and an 'old nurse'.

My analysis of the debate of *Christabel's* character will dwell on the poem's peripheries. The first two sections of this essay explore Coleridge's references to his poem's disturbingly ambiguous status and his reviewers' scandalised responses to the poem. I propose that men of letters reacted hysterically to *Christabel* because they saw the fantastic exchanges of Geraldine and Christabel as dramatising a range of problematically invested literary relations, including those between writers and other writers, and among authors, readers, and books. By feminising the problem, critical discourse on

Christabel both played out and displaced the excessive charges of these literary relations: it cast impropriety as *generic* impurity, and then identified this impurity with dangerously attractive feminine forms – the licentious body of Geraldine, and more generally, of the poem *Christabel*. The final sections of the essay argue that the feminisation of the terms of the debate on *Christabel* repeats, in an exemplary way, a strategy habitually adopted by high culture when defending its privileges. *Christabel* can be located in the context of Coleridge's writings on a variety of ghostly exchanges between observers or readers and representations. Coleridge's thinking about perception suggests that what is at stake in these exchanges is the identity and autonomy of the subject in relation to cultural forms; a footnote to the *Biographia Literaria* on circulating library fare indicates that it is ladies' literature – the derogated genres of romantic fiction – which conventionally represents this threat in the discourse of literary gentlemen. *Christabel's* connections with Gothic romance account for the conventionality of the critics' responses to the poem; its exposure of their hysterical defences accounts for its exemplary power among Coleridge's poems of the supernatural.

I

Perhaps Coleridge's only uncontroversial definition of *Christabel's* literary character is in Chapter 14 of the *Biographia Literaria*, where he classifies the poem with others whose 'incidents and agents were to be, in part at least, supernatural'.[2] But his intention here is to lay old controversies to rest, and his emphases are on harmony – disquietingly so. According to him, the idea of the *Lyrical Ballads* presented itself to two minds working as one – mutually possessed minds, if we care to edge his description toward the concerns of *Christabel*: 'The thought suggested itself (to which of us I do not recollect) that a series of poems might be composed of two sorts.' Describing his and Wordsworth's respective tasks, Coleridge implies that the difference between the two collaborators hardly amounts to more than an accident of light or shade: his poems were to give a 'semblance of truth' to supernatural incidents, while Wordsworth's would 'give the charm of novelty to things of every day' and thus 'excite a feeling analogous to the supernatural'. 'With this view', he continues, 'I wrote "The Ancient Mariner", and was preparing among other poems, "The Dark Ladie", and the "Christabel", in which I should have more nearly realized my ideal, than I had done in my first attempt.' If in the end his poems came to seem like 'heterogeneous' material, the reasons were purely circumstantial: 'But Mr Wordsworth's industry had proved so much more successful ... that my compositions, instead of forming a balance, appeared rather an interpolation of heterogeneous matter' (*BL*, II, p. 6).

Several chapters later, though, Coleridge hedges on *Christabel's* character and charges the poem with introducing discord into his life. Although professing surprise that a work which 'pretended to be nothing more than a common Faery Tale' should have excited such 'disproportionate' responses, he himself clearly attaches 'disproportionate' significance to *Christabel*. His account of the 'literary men' who '[took] liberties' with it before it went on 'common sale' but failed to defend it in 1816 identifies that date as a major divide: whereas in the past '[he] did not know or believe that [he] had an enemy in the world', now he must reproach himself 'for being too often disposed to ask, – Have I one friend?' (*BL*, II, pp. 210–11). Pointing to the date of *Christabel's* publication as a great rupture in his life, Coleridge plays a role he had created more than sixteen years before – the Baron, betrayed into solitude by 'whispering tongues [that] poison truth'.

Actually, from the very beginning Coleridge had difficulty keeping *Christabel* in proportion – or rather, he was always happy to exaggerate its proportions. Already by 1799 he was casting it as controversial, disruptive of generic categories and collaborative efforts alike. *Christabel* would be an 'improper opening poem' for that year's *Annual Register*, he explains to Southey:

> My reason is – it cannot be expected to please all / Those who dislike it will deem it extravagant Ravings, & go on thro' the rest of the Collection with the feeling of Disgust – & it is not impossible that were it liked by any, it would still not harmonize with the *real-life* Poems that follow.
>
> (*CL*, I, p. 545)

Whatever *Christabel's* character here, it is emphatically *not* the decorous, modest character of a 'true ballad', nor the 'common' character of a 'Faery Tale', nor yet the character of a poem of the supernatural, if the latter is meant to 'balance' with the poems of real life.

This hyperbolic account of the poem's reception is of course more indicative of Coleridge's extravagance than *Christabel's* – he is amusing Southey at the expense of an overnice reading public, and lightening with bluster a tacit admission that *Christabel* will not be ready in time for the *Annual Register*. His remarks were prophetic, however, not only of the poem's reception in 1816, but also, of Wordsworth's response to it in 1800, when after the second edition of the *Lyrical Ballads* had already gone to press he decided to pull *Christabel* from the volume.³ The *Biographia* account of the great collaborative project suppresses *Christabel's* role in its disintegration – *Christabel* was the poem that made Wordsworth realise that the poetry of real life and the poetry of the supernatural do not 'balance'. Explaining his decision to Longman & Rees, Wordsworth emphasises the 'impropriety' of including a poem that does not harmonise with the others: 'A Poem of Mr Coleridge's was to have concluded the Volumes; but upon mature deliberation, I found that the Style of this Poem was so discordant from my own that it could not be printed along with my poems with any propriety' (quoted in *CL*, I, p. 643). His words fulfil Coleridge's predictions of 1799, and contradict the *Biographia's* explanation of Coleridge's 'heterogeneity' – *quality*, not quantity, makes his work discordant.

Wordsworth's tone – his defensive or exasperated emphases on '*mature* deliberation', '*so* discordant', '*any* propriety' – hints at personal as well as literary differences between the two men; perhaps 1800, not 1816, was the year that *Christabel* was instrumental in sundering friendships. In contrast, Coleridge's account of the same event tempers personal discord. It also produces some strange, Christabellian effects. Writing to Josiah Wedgewood shortly after the decision, Coleridge seems to parrot Wordsworth's accusation of 'discordancy': *Christabel* was 'discordant in its character' with the *Lyrical Ballads*, he explains. At the same time, he bestows a character of generosity on his friend and vicarious praise on himself by passing on Wordsworth's extravagant appreciation of the poem's excellencies: 'My poem grew so long & in Wordsworth's opinion so impressive, that he rejected it from his volume as disproportionate both in size & merit' – sentiments so discordant with Wordsworth's letter to Longman that we suspect Wordsworth of speaking them under compulsion, or Coleridge of putting words into his friend's mouth (*CL*, I, p. 643).

Although Coleridge's claims about his poem generally address its literary improprieties, a measure of its extravagance would seem to be its capacity to disrupt the boundaries between literature, commentary, and real life. Asserting *Christabel's* problematic literary status, Coleridge conflates the poem with the extravagant, ambiguous Geraldine, the character *in* the poem who excites desire and disgust, and introduces discord into apparently harmonious circles; describing the poem's origin in a collaborative endeavour and its receptions in 1800 and 1816, he produces muted versions of *Christabel's* story of an uncanny exchange and a friendship 'rent asunder', and recreates, in the register of his own telling, the slippages of identity that mark the exchanges of Geraldine and Christabel. Reading Coleridge's accounts of *Christabel*, we begin to feel that all the characters involved – the 'literary gentlemen' through whom he ventriloquises his fluctuating, extravagant responses to his poem, the poem he employs as a go-between in his extravagant relations with other gentlemen, and the figure of the author, who appears by turns as the Baron and an enchantress – acquire the curious status of Geraldine, a figure from fantasy or dream who intrudes into daytime existence.[4]

Like all uncanny effects, Coleridge's apparent possession by *Christabel* is a motivated and gainful loss of control, allowing him to perform, domesticate, and manipulate the charged relations of his literary life. His strategy is most overtly one of domestication, of course, when he casts his poem as a woman – as a 'lovely Lady' whose character must be defended, as the 'other woman' in his sparring with Sara Coleridge, or as a doubtful character with whom gentlemen 'take liberties'. The lady becomes the locus of rhetorical and erotic play, when, disarmingly, Coleridge figures his lapses of authorial control as capitulations to extravagant femininity, or renders the exchanges of poems among literary gentlemen as the movements of a scandalous woman from man to man. *Christabel* circulates licentiously, captivating readers and tainting its author with its femininity. Flaunting his poem's impropriety, but coyly withholding it from 'common sale', he presents himself as both master and possessor of its charms.

Even Coleridge's more hysterical performances with *Christabel* figure and control the operations of fantasy in literary life. In an oddly explicit accession to the poem's femininity he becomes its mother, in 1801 producing the second part of *Christabel* with 'labour-pangs' in competition with Sara's delivery of Derwent: announcing the double event in a letter to James Tobin, he relegates his wife's labours to a postcript (*CL*, I, p. 623). Later, writing to De

Quincey, he associates his poem's publication, its 'embodiment in verse', with birth and death: *Christabel* 'fell almost dead-born from the Press' (*CL*, V, p. 162).[5] When he holds it in 'suspended animation', however, it has the virulent life of fantasy.[6] Repossessing the poem after Wordsworth rejected it in 1800, Coleridge enacted a possession as lurid and extreme as the enchantments of *Christabel* – an illness he dramatises in numerous letters to his friends as a hysterical pregnancy. It began with a symbolic castration, inflamed eyes and boils on the scrotum;[7] the next '9 dreary months' or more he passed with 'giddy head, sick stomach, & swoln knees', his left knee at one point '"*pregnant* with agony"' as Mr Dodsley says in one of his poems' (*CL*, II, pp. 745, 748). During one of his 'confinements', he reports, 'one ugly Sickeness has followed another, fast as phantoms before a vapourish Woman' (*CL*, II, pp. 729, 725).[8] Flirting now with actual madness, but still performing the woman for an audience of gentlemen, he figures his strange entanglement with literature as the apparent duplicity of the female body when it is pregnant with child or with the vapourish conception of the 'wandering mother' or womb. Inhabiting him as an alien, internal body, his poem constitutes him as a female hysteric who cannot 'tell', but can only enact the intrusion of fantasy into real life.

II

Christabel engaged the fantasy lives of more than a narrow circle of literary gentlemen. In 1799, Coleridge imagined his apparently 'extravagant Ravings' exciting the equally extravagant response of 'Disgust', which he predicted would cling to the reader even after he had finished reading the poem. Urging Coleridge to publish the poem in 1815, Byron attests to its excessive, clinging 'hold': '[the poem's details] took a hold on my imagination which I never shall wish to shake off' (quoted in *CL*, IV, p. 601). When the poem came out the next year the critics described it as 'ravings', hysterically assessing poem and author in a Christabellian vocabulary of dream and possession.[9] Frequently they attribute its strange, singular character to its author's wild confounding of genres, styles, and intentions. *Scourge*, for example, criticises the poem's blending of 'passages of exquisite harmony' with 'miserable doggrel'; in a similar vein, the *Augustan Review* complains that 'there are many fine things [in the poem] which cannot be extracted, being closely connected with the grossest absurdities' (*RR*, II, p. 866, I, p. 36). But the vocabulary of poetic decorum easily becomes the vocabulary of sexual, and particularly feminine, decorum: when *Christabel's* reviewers protest that 'poetry itself must show some modesty', or criticise the poem for merely 'affecting' simplicity, they capitalise on that play (*RR*, I, pp. 229–40). Like Coleridge, they hint that *Christabel's* extravagances are more than rhetorical, and have a peculiarly feminine character.

Moreover, just as in Coleridge's imagined scenes, the extravagant, sexual character of *Christabel* proves to be contagious. In the hands of the critics, the author's poetic licence becomes more-than-poetic 'licentiousness': 'In diction, in numbers, in thought, ... Mr Coleridge's licentiousness out-Herod's Herod', the *Champion* protests, while *Farrago* claims that 'on no occasion has Mr Coleridge appeared in so degraded and degenerate a light as in the present publication' (*RR*, I, p. 269, II, p. 546). Coleridge's breaches of decorum are not simply 'unmanly', they feminise him: his 'epithets of endearment, instead of breathing the accents of manly tenderness, are those of the nurse', charges *Scourge*; according to others, he tells an 'old woman's story', and is himself acting the part of an 'enchanted virgin' or a 'witch' (*RR*, II, p. 866, I, p. 214, I, p. 373, II, p. 531). Reading *Christabel* would seem to draw one into a charmed circle where all the participants have the taint of affected, licentious femininity. Even the poem's real-life readers are feminine, according to the *AntiJacobin* reviewer. Professing bewilderment at the poem's success despite the universally scathing reviews, he concludes that the ladies must be responsible: 'for what woman of fashion would not purchase a book recommended by Lord Byron' (*RR*, I, p. 23).

If, pursuing *Christabel's* character, we ask the critics why *Christabel* became the poem they loved to hate, we might choose William Hazlitt's review in the *Examiner* as our focus; one of the earliest, it set the tone for subsequent notices. From the very first lines of his essay, Hazlitt adopts a strategy of diminishment against *Christabel* and its author. The review begins with some biting comments on the 'mastiff bitch', regularly cited by critics as an example of the poem's 'doggrel'. Appealing to 'gentlemen' to share his contempt for her impotence ('Is she a sort of Cerberus to fright away the critics? But – gentlemen, she is toothless!'), he reduces the poem's impropriety to toothless naughtiness, its author to a buffoon (*RR*, II, pp. 530–1). Then, still on the subject of Coleridge's caprice, he makes a spectacle of withered femininity for a second time. Quoting the scene of Geraldine's undressing, he pauses to supply a missing line:

> The manuscript runs thus, or nearly thus: –
> 'Behold her bosom and half her side –
> *Hideous, deformed, and pale of hue.*'
> This line is necessary to make common sense of the first and second part. 'It is the keystone that makes up the arch.' For that reason Mr Coleridge left it out. Now this is a greater physiological curiosity than even the fragment of *Kubla Khan.*

The 'sight to dream of, not to tell' ought simply to be *told*, Hazlitt protests, deploring 'Mr Coleridge''s power play while trumping him with a line from his own manuscript. The reviewer's quarrel with the author is rendered as a battle for control of Geraldine: the author conceals her bosom from view, and the critic unveils it again. As when he made sport of the 'mastiff bitch', Hazlitt implicates poem and author in the fate of the impotent female, reducing the former's obscurity to a transparent mystery, and the latter's motives to a 'physiological curiosity', a deformity like Geraldine's.

So far, Hazlitt's tactics have been similar, not just to those he imputes to *his* 'Mr Coleridge', but also to those Coleridge adopts when he uses the poem's feminine subject to domesticate its impropriety, and then employs the poem as a third character in his relations with other literary gentlemen. In the last paragraph of the review, however, *Christabel* threatens to escape its bounds. Here, Hazlitt's description of *Christabel's* hold on the reader's mind recalls Byron's approbation of the 'hold' he 'never shall wish to shake off':

> In parts of *Christabel* there is a great deal of beauty, both of thought, imagery, and versification; but the effect of the general story is dim, obscure, and visionary. It is more like a dream than a reality. The mind, in reading it, is spell-bound. The sorceress seems to act without power – *Christabel* to yield without resistance. The faculties are thrown into a state of metaphysical suspense and theoretical imbecility.

Hazlitt implies that interpretive mastery involves locating a source of power and meaning in the text. *This* poem, however, is obscure in its treatment of volition, depicting sorceress and victim in mysterious communion. Disclosing a radical complicity between actor and yielder, good and evil, the exchanges between Christabel and Geraldine confound the logical and moral categories the reader attempts to bring to bear on the poem, throwing his faculties into a state of 'metaphysical suspense and theoretical imbecility'. Thwarted in his effort to interpret, he becomes 'bound' passively to imitate the relation between Christabel and Geraldine in his own relation to the story.

Continuing his final remarks about *Christabel*, though, Hazlitt rescues this hypothetical reader from impotence by providing him with a dual focus of moral outrage – an unnamed, unsavoury content, 'something disgusting at the bottom of the subject', and a wilful author at the bottom of it all:

> The poet, like the witch in *Spenser*, is evidently
> 'Busied about some wicked gin.' –
> But we do not foresee what he will make of it. There is something disgusting at the bottom of his subject, which is but ill glossed over by a veil of Della Cruscan sentiment and fine writing – like moonbeams playing on a charnel-house, or flowers strewed on a dead body. Mr Coleridge's style is essentially superficial, pretty, ornamental, and he has forced it into the service of a story which is petrific.

Many readers of this review, including Coleridge himself, have speculated that Hazlitt has 'something' specific in mind here – something he *could* tell, but won't. Rumour has identified him as the source of a scandalous report that Coleridge intended to unmask Geraldine as Christabel's male lover.[10] But significantly, at this point Hazlitt does not band with other 'gentlemen' to deride the poem's impropriety as sophomoric naughtiness, nor does he simply identify Geraldine's deformity as the suppressed 'keystone' of the poem. Rather, bursting into rhetorical flower at just the moment he purports to descry 'something ... at the bottom' of *Christabel*, he gives the impression that there is more to the poem than is in his or Coleridge's power to declare. In this Gothic scenario, Geraldine's body is not the 'keystone' to the poem's obscurity, but a figure of the problem: Hazlitt displaces her character onto both poet and poem, metaphorising the former as a 'witch', and the latter as a veiled, horrific site. 'Something' which cannot be figured is 'disgusting' or 'petrific' 'at the bottom' of that site, in the poem's nether regions – 'something' which ought to be well hidden, but is only 'ill glossed over'. Hazlitt's rhetoric suggests that he is now seeing the poem, not as a woman who has been or could be had, but as a potent figure of castration, a Medusa. His 'scandalous' rumour, then, is a subterfuge masking the *real* scandal of *Christabel* – that Geraldine is a woman.

But Hazlitt, who put down these clues, may have prepared a trap. Certainly, the movement of the whole paragraph suggests that this melodramatic scene of a horrific, buried 'something' is a feint. For it follows an acknowledgement that there is *nothing* 'at the bottom' of *Christabel* – no single source of power or significance: 'The sorceress seems to act without power; *Christabel* to yield without resistance.' This 'nothing' is not the lack psychoanalysis allots to women, but a strange overdetermination which creates disturbances in the register of metaphysics as well as sexuality. Hazlitt suggests that the obscure and compelling logic of *Christabel*, effecting displacements of identity and power which reveal the affinity of apparent opposites, is the logic of dream or fantasy; that the danger of this 'dim, obscure, and visionary' poem is that it threatens to hold the reader as if it were his *own* dream or fantasy. He holds this imagined experience of complete surrender to *Christabel* within bounds, however, by almost immediately transforming the poem's unsettling, uncentred power into a disgusting 'something' obscurely visible behind a veil of language and sentiment, thus reducing to its sexual content power he has just described as having philosophical as well as erotic dimensions: he contains this power in the 'bottom' and invites us to declare it female. Although it suggests that *Christabel* is potent and horrific, Hazlitt's melodrama, which associates the poem with a derided genre (the Gothic) and gender (the feminine), actually reduces it as fully as did his play with the 'mastiff bitch'.[11]

Like Coleridge, Hazlitt cannot or will not 'tell' what is enchanting or distressing about *Christabel*. Instead he objectifies the poem as a feminine body, in a move which allows him to disentangle matters of intellect from matters of desire to some extent; admitting the pull of, and stridently defending himself against, this body, he charges his writing with the libidinal possibilities he has contained. *Christabel* has subterfuges of its own, however. In a sense it is the poem which contains its critics, whose two responses to it – a spellbound accession to play and a petrified and petrifying refusal of exchange – are figured in the text. When Hazlitt asserts manly judgement against a feminised author and poem at the close of his essay, he only substitutes one form of impotency for another, shedding the role of a mute, enthralled Christabel to become the Baron, whose world is a 'world of death'.[12]

Turning now to Coleridge's writing on perception, on circulating library literature, and on the poetry of the supernatural, we see him exploring, in a range of situations, how individuals and culture produce 'bodies' – hallucinated 'realities', but also literary genres, bodies of literature. *Christabel* figures the responses it elicits because in the poetry of the supernatural, Coleridge is dramatising and manipulating a conventional or 'bound' relation between certain kinds of figures and certain kinds of responses; particularly, he is examining the way certain bodies conventionally function to objectify a problematic response to representation.

III

'Disgust' is the response Coleridge and his reviewers most frequently attached to *Christabel*. When at the end of his review Hazlitt attempts to shake off the poem's hold, he locates 'something disgusting' – something like a body or a corpse – under its decorative surface. His gesture is dismissive: the disgusting body is elsewhere. During the years 1799–1801 Coleridge was already predicting that his poem would inspire 'disgust', but the investigations would have prompted him to insist on the complicity of mind and body, and self and elsewhere, in disgusted response. 'Define Disgust in philosophical Language – . – Is it not, speaking as a materialist, always a stomach-sensation conjoined with an idea?' he asks, and answers, Humphry Davy in January 1800: the object of disgust is 'always' an already-internalised 'idea' (*CL*, I, p. 557). Just a day later, writing to Thomas Wedgewood about a similar sensation, he implies an even more thorough entanglement of physiological and ideational entities and processes in certain responses: 'Life were so flat a thing without Enthusiasm – that if for a moment it leave me, I have a sort of stomach-sensation attached to all my Thoughts, like those which succeed to the pleasurable operation of a dose of Opium' (*CL*, I, p. 558). In this description of the conjoined response, Coleridge's analogy to the 'dose' implies that even a terminological distinction between 'sensation' and 'idea' may distort: perhaps the very 'sensation' of difference between mind and body is one stage in a self-perpetuating economy of desire. 'Disgust' is not the mind's critical pronouncement on a body (although it may masquerade as such), but a symptom of the subject's mourning or revulsion for the lost, mutual pleasures of mind and body. ...

The second part of the poem was conceived after a 'dose' that peopled 'barrenness' according to its author, who then imagines it as infinitely reproducible ('I would rather have written Ruth, and Nature's Lady than a million such poems', he confesses to Davy after *Christabel* was rejected from the *Lyrical Ballads* [*CL*, I, pp. 643, 632]); he isn't sure how to classify *Christabel* but knows to exclude it from the category of 'real-life' poems, a genus whose boundaries he suggests it has the capacity to disturb. Its readers responded to it with hysterical attacks of the sort burlesqued in Coleridge's note. Almost all of them connected the poem's disturbing character to its licentious femininity, one even going so far as to suggest it appeals only to the devotees of Lord Byron. To suggest that these terms and postures are conventional does not answer the question of why *Christabel* excited the response it did, but perhaps helps to explain the coincidence between Coleridge's perception of the poem and the way it was received: he must have suspected that *Christabel* would be regarded as belonging to a tainted category of literary endeavour.

Christabel, then, is not just a ghost story, but also the 'ghost' of literature: men of letters perceive it as belonging to a body of literary products which figure the possibility that books are fantastic representations exercising a dangerous attraction for the subject. We should not imagine that the typical man of letters' relation to this category of goods is straightforwardly defensive, however. For the scenario of the *camera obscura* translates the energy of systems that drive the subject into libidinal energy, which circulates back to 'one man', and, eventually, to the man of letters and the body of his text. The scene encysts a state of pleasurable indeterminacy, where representations transmit 'doses' of fantasy from devotee to languid devotee, whose 'hundred [feminine] brains' are loosely but gratifyingly oriented toward the potentate who 'peoples [their] barrenness'. The speaker closes off this circle from 'time' and his literary life, and then by his self-ironic admission of his complicity in it charges his own discourse with libidinal possibility: this is not 'real' literature, and yet literature and literary men are always flirting with the dangerous and heady attractions of fantasy. And surely, both Hazlitt and Coleridge seem at their most seductively interesting to the critic when by hysterically charged attack or coy self-betrayal they reveal their attraction to a charmed circle, whether that represented by Christabel in the arms of Geraldine, or that of the circulating library.

Modulated just a little, Coleridge's attack on lending library culture becomes the famous account of his role in the *Lyrical Ballads*, an experiment he is anxious to legitimise in the *Biographia Literaria*:

> [M]y endeavors should be directed to persons and characters super-natural, or at least romantic; yet so as to transfer from our inward nature a human interest and a semblance of truth sufficient to procure for these shadows of imagination that willing suspension of disbelief for the moment, which constitutes poetic faith.
>
> *(BL*, II, p. 5)

The terms he used earlier to protest the devotees' absorption are here employed to describe the ideal reader's generosity: if successful, he will procure 'for the moment' ('pro tempore') the reader's 'suspension of disbelief' (a 'suspension of all common sense') for his 'shadows of the imagination' ('phantasms'). But as a formerly excluded experi-ence of books is admitted to the genus 'reading', a new category, actual madness, is produced as a figure of that which is at once other than literature and literature's internal possibilities and limit. If readers are deluded by the 'shadows' of his poetry, Coleridge implies, it may be because in real life they have actually confounded shadow and substance and come under the spell of hallucinated realities: 'And real in *this* sense [supernatural incidents] have been to every human being who, from whatever source of delusion, has at any time believed himself under supernatural agency.' 'For a moment' the reader of supernatural poetry may touch the perimeters of madness. The experience is not limited to one genre; even Wordsworth, Coleridge's writer of real-life poems, 'for short spaces of time' plays with shadows, as any good poet might. Describing the figure of the poet in the 1802 preface to the *Lyrical Ballads*, Wordsworth suggests he must be something of a madman – and something of a Christabel: 'Nay, for short spaces of time perhaps, [the poet might] let himself slip into an entire delusion, and even confound and identify his own feelings with [those of his characters].'[13]

In moments of imaginative generosity, of voluntary relinquish-ments of self to fictions, writers and readers flirt with the possibility of going too far – of losing their 'Substance' to a 'ghost', of 'letting themselves slip' into delusions which could become difficult to

escape, of acceding to 'holds' they might 'never – wish to shake off'.
In these moments the subject touches a perpetually bracketed, continually displaced representation of literature's fantastic appeal, a
'moving phantasm' of Coleridge's discourse and a discourse about
literature in which he participates.

Coleridge's poems of the supernatural illustrate mental states,
including states where the mind comes under the sway of a hallucinated 'reality'. When 'for the moment' a reader of these poems sus-
pends disbelief and gives himself over to representations, he touches
madness – doubling, in his own relation to fiction, the very condition the poem dramatises. But although *all* the poems of the supernatural are intended to produce this effect in the reader, it is
Christabel which most alarms its public. Coleridge's account in the
camera obscura footnote of the circulating library devotees casts
the pleasure one takes in certain kinds of books as a feminine pleasure: the implicit message is that to read is to behave like a woman,
an axiom the man of culture might find both alarming and alluring
to contemplate. I would propose that Coleridge explores the relation between cultural processes and (fantasised) feminine erotic
experience in *Christabel*, a poem which dramatises hysteria, conventionally figured as the flights of a 'wandering mother', which
alienates female subjects from their own speech. To 'tell' the story
of *Christabel*, a narrator or narrators – we cannot tell if we hear
one voice or two – resurrect the ghosts of genres as apparently disparate as Spenserian romance and pulp fiction; they re-enact and
tumble into the exchanges of Christabel and Geraldine, and suggest
that the subject's relation to cultural forms is hysterical.[14] It may be
a measure of the poem's success that many of its contemporary
readers responded to it like hysterics who 'cannot tell' what ails
them – who could only repeat its effects in the manner of Byron,
Scott, and a host of other imitators and parodists of the poem, or,
like Hazlitt, resist its effect by hysterical defence.

From *English Literary History*, 52 (1985), 397–418.

NOTES

[This is the second of Karen Swann's articles on Coleridge's *Christabel* (see
note 33 to the Introduction for further details of Swann's essay exploring
hysteria in the poem). In this piece, Swann attempts to explain the review-

ers' scandalised response to the poem in terms of the ways the central characters in the poem, Christabel and Geraldine, act out the literary relations between the poet and his readers. For Swann, the poem has a capacity to disrupt the boundaries between literature, commentary, and real life. Using William Hazlitt's famously hostile review of the poem, Swann shows how the reviewer is drawn into the poem in a way that imitates the relation between Christabel and Geraldine, thwarting Hazlitt's efforts at interpretation. Swann's work is fully informed by an awareness of the gender implications of the critical debate on *Christabel*: the first reviewers imputed femininity to the form of the text (as Gothic romance) and to the poet himself, but in recent criticism these imputed weaknesses have been reversed. Critics have found a source of energy and interest in the disruptions to familiar forms of male authority, rationality and coherence. This extract is substantially complete, but Swann's discussion of the relationship between disgust and representation, including material from Coleridge's *Letters* and *Notebooks,* has been omitted. Ed.]

1. S. T. Coleridge, *Collected Letters,* ed. E. L. Griggs (Oxford, 1966–71), II, 941 (hereafter cited as *CL*).

2. S. T. Coleridge, *Biographia Literaria,* ed. J. Shawcross (Oxford, 1907), II, 5 (hereafter cited as *BL*).

3. This episode is discussed by Marilyn Katz in 'Early Dissent Between Wordsworth and Coleridge: Preface Deletion of October, 1800', and by James Kissane in '"Michael", "Christabel", and the *Lyrical Ballads* of 1800'. Both articles appeared in *The Wordsworth Circle,* 9:1 (1978).

4. My reading of Christabel's capacity to disturb and to influence Coleridge's literary relationships is indebted to Reeve Parker's essay, '"O could you hear his voice!" Wordsworth, Coleridge, and Ventriloquism', in *Romanticism and Language,* ed. Arden Reed (Ithaca, NY, 1984).

5. In 1801, Coleridge was also thinking of the poem's 'birth' as a death: he marked Christabel's and Derwent's simultaneous appearance with a spate of notebook entries about dead or dying children which have interesting connections with his post-partum feelings about *Christabel* as well as with his sickly child: in one, he recalls a local woman's expression of relief at parting with a 'little Babe one had had 9 months in one's arms'; in another, he quotes from the *Star* a derscription of a drowned infant, 'a spectacle &c' whose 'flesh was more yielding to the touch than is either necessary or agreeable to describe'–a 'sight to dream of, not to tell' (*Notebooks*, I, 814, 809; hereafter cited as *N*).

6. Coleridge's descriptions of his relation to the poem come from the preface to *Christabel:*

Since the latter date[1800], my poetic powers have been, till very lately, in a state of suspended animation. But as, in my first conception of the tale, I had the whole present to my mind, with the wholeness no less than the loveliness, of a vision; I trust that I shall yet be able to embody in verse the three parts yet to come.

In Coleridge's account it is the author's 'powers', not the poem, which have existed 'in a state of suspended animation'; but my shift is, if not excused, at least precedented by his own.

7. See, for example, Coleridge's letter to Davy, 11 January 1801 (*CL*, II, 662–3).

8. See also *CL*, II, 731–2, 735–6, 739. For a more extended discussion of this period and these letters, see Jerome Christensen, *Coleridge's Blessed Machine of Language* (Ithaca, NY, 1981), pp. 76–81. Christensen focuses on the grandiose philosophical claims that appear in the letters I have been quoting, relating them to attempts, described in *The Notebooks of Samuel Taylor Coleridge*, ed. Kathleen Coburn (New York and London, 1957–90) to derive knowledge and perception from infantile experience of the mother.

9. Variously, they liken it to 'a strange fantasy', 'a nightmare', a 'symptom' of madness, and the 'ravings of insanity'. These reviews are printed in *The Romantics Reviewed*, ed. Donald H. Reiman (New York, 1972). I have just quoted from I, 239; II, 470, and I, 36 (hereafter cited as *RR*).

10. For Coleridge's speculations, see *CL*, IV, 917–18. This rumour found its boldest public expression in a parody printed in 1818, which took up the story of Christabel nine months after Geraldine's first visit, with the heroine in the advanced stages of pregnancy (*Christabel*, by 'Morgan O'Doherty', published in *Blackwood's Edinburgh Magazine*, 5 April–September 1819, 286–91).

11. This strategy – of reducing the poem to just a Gothic tale of terror – repeats tactics conventionally used on the Gothic itself. In 'The Character in the Veil: Imagery of the Surface in the Gothic Novel' (*PMLA*, 96[1981], 255–70), Eve Kosofsky Sedgwick describes a prevalent critical tendency to read the Gothic as a literature of 'depth and the depths', and argues that this reading is blind to the Gothic novel's thematic insistence on surfaces as 'quasi-linguistic' carriers of sexuality: to see the Gothic in terms of a convention of surfaces and depths is to repress the possibility that (one's own) identity and responses are conventional. Coleridge's and Hazlitt's readings of *Christabel* suggest that one movement – itself highly conventionalised – in this repressive strategy is an imagined access to the logic of contaminative linguistic experiences; the glimpse of this threat to the self's autonomy becomes a pretext for hyping-up of an attack on the (supremely conventional) literature of buried things.

12. Like the Baron, who in a moment of confusion imagines himself separating 'souls/From the bodies and forms of men', and like Perseus, Hazlitt takes cutting measures to reassert the implicitly hierarchical categories of thought that allow one to 'tell': he dissevers surface from 'bottom', decoration from content, and life and play from death and stasis. Then, almost as if to acknowledge his affinity with Sir Leoline, as a coda to his review of *Christabel* he attaches lines which he calls 'the one genuine burst of humanity' in the poem, lines he claims show what the author can do when 'no dream oppresses him, no spell binds him'. The passage he has in mind describes the ruined friendship of Roland de Vaux and the Baron. I excerpt what I suspect moves him most:

> They stood aloof, the scars remaining
> Like cliffs which had been rent asunder
> A dreary sea now flows between,
> But neither heat nor frost nor thunder
> Shall wholly do away, I wean,
> The marks of that which once had been.

My selection is not arbitrary. Not only Hazlitt, but virtually every contemporary reviewer of *Christabel*, no matter what his opinion of the poem as a whole, cites these 'manly' lines with approval. It almost seems to be a conspiracy of gentlemen – to find, in a poem which describes a mysterious contract between two women, so much to admire in these lines about manly friendship unambiguously 'rent asunder'.

13. *Lyrical Ballads 1798*, ed. W. J. B. Owen (Oxford, 1969), p. 166.

14. I discuss the poem more thoroughly in my essay 'Christabel: The Wandering Mother and the Enigma of Form', *Studies in Romanticism*, 23 (1984).

4

Feminising Keats

SUSAN J. WOLFSON

I

> an effeminacy of style, in some degree corresponding to effeminacy
> of character
>
> (Hazlitt on Keats)

Feminist literary criticism frequently theorises the 'feminine' as
the designated 'other' in a system in which the position of privi-
lege is 'masculine'. Less commonly elaborated are contestations
of gender within that masculine centre itself, especially in relation
to men such as Keats, who are often spoken of as having qualities
and attitudes 'other' than those normatively deemed masculine.
Yet a striking feature of the discourse on Keats – in both the nineteenth century and the twentieth – is the frequency with which his
gender is an issue. This is not a matter of biology, of course, but
of ideology. Like the systems that cast the feminine as 'other',
judgements about Keats appear in the language of gendered opposition and difference, in which decisions about what is not 'masculine' – in Keats's case, variously 'effeminate', juvenile', or
'puerile' – imply what is. Keats is an interesting figure in these
constructions less because of their repetition and wide circulation
(remarkable though these are) than because of the profound divisions of judgement he agitates – divisions not just in the language
of gender per se, but about the interests being served in its
application.

Why has Keats provoked such persistent – one is tempted to say obsessive – attention in these terms? This vocabulary responds in part to his literary practices, and for later readers, to comments in his letters about his character, poetic and existential. Both discourses reveal a sensibility fascinated with the permeable boundary between masculine and feminine. Keats's physical characteristics, moreover, perplexed this boundary: everyone who knew or wrote about him had to think through the question of gender when confronted with his manner, conduct, and appearance. Keats's situation in this discourse bears on more than the intrigue of his individual case, however, for the assessments are frequently produced in contexts that show him being treated as the signifier or symptom of a large-scale cultural concern. Judgements of Keats as 'unmanly' typically coincide with worries about the feminisation of men – especially men of, or under the influence of, letters; correspondingly, defences of his manliness, though couched in no less traditional terms, often seem covertly to challenge orthodox determinations of 'masculine' and 'feminine'. That Keats did not fit conventional figures made him a convenient focus for ideological debate; indeed, a manifold of literary style and sensibility, personal appearance, class origin, and the legend of his death made him a magnetic focus. Keats's peculiar position on the boundaries of discrimination, as we shall see, makes highly legible the systems of power, both social and psychological, that inform the language of gender and influence its uses.

In this essay, therefore, I will be concerned not only with Keats's practices as a poet, but also with how the language of gender operates in the literary and social culture in which he wrote and was reviewed. I will also be concerned, at the end, with where we now stand as critical inheritors of this problem. Keats's marginality typically tempts critical extremes: he either triggers efforts to stabilise and enforce standards of manly conduct in which he is the negative example, stigmatised as 'effeminate', or 'unmanly'; or he inspires attempts to broaden and make more flexible prevailing definitions, so that certain qualities, previously limited to and sometimes derided as 'feminine', may be allowed to enrich and enlarge the culture's images of 'manliness' – even to the point of androgyny. I intend for an historically based reading of this volatility to serve as a deep background for what we see at work in modern conceptions of Keats, ranging from the most traditional terms of differentiation to recent attempts by some feminist critics to redefine our understanding of 'masculine' and 'feminine'. The way Keats figures into such discussions reveals the persistence of the problems he posed to the nineteenth-century discourses of gender and the legislating functions with which these were charged.

In 1822 Hazlitt published 'On Effeminacy of Character', an essay which begins by declaring opposition to the cult of sensibility: 'Effeminacy of character arises from a prevalence of the sensibility over the will: or it consists in a want of fortitude.' As Hazlitt's blunt definition suggests, the excesses of effeminacy imply deficiency elsewhere: 'instead of voluntarily embracing pain, or labour, or danger, or death', lovers of 'exquisite indulgences' want 'every sensation ... wound up to the highest pitch of voluptuous refinement, every motion must be grace and elegance; they live in a luxurious, endless dream, or "Die of a rose in aromatic pain!"' Keats appears as Hazlitt's summary example of 'an effeminacy of style, in some degree corresponding to effeminacy of character ... one that is all florid, all fine; that cloys by its sweetness, and tires by its sameness ... Every thought must be beautiful *per se*, every expression equally fine.'[1] Though no particular text is cited, even Keats's loyal defender, Leigh Hunt, concedes the question of style: reading *Hyperion*, he regrets 'something too effeminate and human in the way Apollo receives the exaltation which his wisdom is giving him. He weeps and wonders somewhat too fondly.'[2] 'Soon wild commotions shook him, and made flush / All the immortal fairness of his limbs', Keats writes (III:124–5), his manuscript revealing an even more feminine original:

> [Roseate and pained as a ravish'd nymph –]
> Into a hue more roseate than sweet-pain
> Gives to a ravish'd Nymph [new-r] when her warm tears
> Gush luscious with no sob.[3]

Apollo's transformation is registered in sensory effects exceeding those of an exceedingly feminine nymph; Keats's only other poetic use of *luscious*, in fact, refers to the eroticism of a nymph's 'luscious lips'.[4] The verse of *Hyperion* bothers Hunt not just because of its breach of decorum (gods should not act thus) but because of its breach of gender (men should not act thus) – even though his pairing of the adjectives *human* and *effeminate* is sufficiently striking to imply a tentative subtextual critique of the inhuman purchases of manliness.

II

Cockney (noun): '"A child that sucketh long", ... a mother's darling; pet, minion; "a child tenderly brought up"; hence a squeamish or effeminate fellow.... . Sometimes applied to a squeamish, overnice, wanton, or affected woman.'
'A derisive appellation for a townsman, as the type of effeminacy in contrast to the hardier inhabitants of the country.'
'One born in the city of London, ... used to connote the characteristics in which the born Londoner is supposed to be inferior to other Englishmen.'
'One of the "Cockney School".'
(adj.): 'effeminate, squeamish'. Cockney School: 'a nickname for a set of 19th cent. writers belonging to London, of whom Leigh Hunt was taken as the representative.'
(*Oxford English Dictionary*, C: 575–6)

Keats 'was spoilt by Cockneyfying and Surburbing', Byron decides. He also thought him spoilt by sexual immaturity: he calls him 'the Mankin', and sneers at 'Johnny Keats's *piss-a-bed* poetry'; its 'drivelling idiotism' – 'the *Onanism* of Poetry'.[5] The term *cockney* implies attitudes about both, as *Blackwood's* first full attack on Keats, appearing in August 1818 as part of a series on the 'Cockney School of Poetry', makes abundantly evident. The reviewer, John Lockhart, opens the case ridiculing both female and lower-class aspirations to what he clearly felt ought to remain male aristocratic pursuits: 'The just celebrity of Robert Burns and Miss Baillie has had the melancholy effect of turning the heads of we know not how many farm-servants and unmarried ladies; our very foot-men compose tragedies, and there is scarcely a superannuated governess in the island that does not leave a roll of lyrics behind her in her band-box.'[6] Like Byron, Lockhart also summons a puerilising rhetoric to exclude Keats from adult male company, and by extension, from serious consideration as a poet. He is 'Mr John', 'good Johnny Keats', 'Johnny', the author of 'prurient and vulgar lines', and 'Mr Keats ... a boy of pretty abilities' – boy and class conflated in the summary advice to this 'young Sangrado' to return to the apothecary shop.[7] It is telling that several decades later, George Gilfillan, who admires Keats's 'elegant effeminacy' and sympathises with his unmanning by adverse circumstance, innocently introduces his subject as 'the hapless apothecary's boy' – a factual error all the more significant for its unwitting echo and testimony to the effect of *Blackwood's* mean-spirited precedent.[8]

Indeed, Lockhart's language attached itself to Keats with adhesive force. Z's letter in May 1818 to 'Leigh Hunt, King of the Cockneys' names the author of a 'famous Cockney Poem' in honour of Hunt at the 'infatuated bardling, Mister John Keats'. The lead article of the December 1819 issue joked about 'Johnny Keates' (sic), and the appellation caught on: Byron enjoyed using it; so did Arnold, when in a mood to condescend to Keats's class origins – as J. R. MacGillivray notes, whenever a nineteenth-century writer referred to 'Johnny Keats' he was signalling agreement with Lockhart.[9] Blackwood's was also rather proud of having refreshed the term cockney with all its associations of effeminacy, sexual immaturity, and social inferiority: 'The nickname we gave them, has become a regularly established word in our literature. Lord Byron, while patronising the sect, called them by no other', it boasted in the 'Preface' to the 1826 volume, which also derided Keats's poems as having 'outhunted Hunt in a species of emasculated pruriency that ... looks as if it were the product of some imaginative Eunuch's muse within the melancholy inspiration of the Haram'.[10] By 1826, of course, Byron had put Don Juan in a harem, with decidedly different inspirations; although Lord Byron was sometimes called 'unmanly' in Victorian letters, this usually meant 'ungentlemanly', lamenting his immorality or indecency, not implying effeminacy. And he, like Shelley (who was more often called 'effeminate'), benefited not only from social rank but also from a reputation for womanising.[11]

III

In poetry his was the woman's part
(Mrs Oliphant on Keats)

The feminising of Keats in nineteenth-century letters was legible not just in terms of a default from codes of manliness, but also in the ready perception of qualities in his poetry deemed to have particular appeal to women. The publishers of his first volume advertised 'Poems. By John Keatts' (sic) in The British Lady's Magazine, a journal whose masthead read, 'Greatness of mind, and nobleness, thou seat in HER build loveliest'.[12] And the epigraph for an article in an 1821 Pocket Magazine virtually handed Keats over to the feminine sphere with the prediction that 'Albion's maidens ... Will cherish thy sweet songs!', the text itself detailing the chief themes:

'general tenderness ... delicate taste and refined inclinations ... uncontroulable and unlimited sympathy with all kinds of suffering', a 'heart ... peculiarly formed for the endearments of love and the gentle solaces of friendship'. If, as Mrs Sanderford's conduct manual put it, 'Gentleness is, indeed, the talisman of woman', *Pocket* was happy to apply this badge to Keats as well, making him an honorary woman.[13] Even Gilfillan cooperated in writing Keats into the feminine sphere with a casual note about the curiously 'elegant effeminacy' of mind displayed in *The Eve of St. Agnes*: 'Its every line wears *couleur de rose*', he remarks warmly; 'No poet ever described dress with more gust and beauty'. The *Guardian*, less appreciatively, condescended to Keats's poems as no more than mere entertainments for women.[14] For better or worse, Keats continued throughout the century to be marketed to female audiences, welcomed by such publications as *The Young Lady's Book of Elegant Poetry*, *The Ladies' Companion*, and *The Girl's Second Help to Reading*, a compendium of 'such passages as referred specifically to the high duties which woman is called up to perform in life' – for example, the stanzas from *Eve of St. Agnes* quoted by Gilfillan as an instance of the 'poetry of dress'. In May 1870, *Victoria Magazine*, noting with pleasure that literary values were being 'effeminised' by women readers, published an article by a woman titled 'Keats – The Daintiest of Poets', headed by the motto, 'Glory and loveliness have passed away'.[15]

The single most influential text, both on the reception of Keats by female readers and on judgements of his unmanliness, is the legend of his death disseminated by Shelley's *Adonais*. Moved by the stories of abuse by the reviews, Shelley thought himself Keats's vindicator, and for some he was. Charles Brown prefaced his biographical sketch with lines 370–83 of *Adonais*, which image Keats's absorption into a feminine afterlife – 'He is made one with Nature: there is heard / His voice in all her music' (Rollins [ed.], *Keats Circle*, II: 52–3). For others, however, Shelley's extreme sentiment had different effects. The imagery of the 'Preface', which eulogised Keats's genius as 'not less delicate and fragile than it was beautiful ... blighted in the bud' – and of the elegy itself – which lamented the rough handling of this 'youngest, dearest ... nursling' of the muse, 'who grew, / Like a pale flower by some sad maiden cherished, / And fed with true-love tears ... whose petals, nipped before they blew, / Died on the promise' – took root in hostile as well as friendly soil, indicating a sensibility lacking sufficient 'masculine' vigour and resiliency to bear the slings and arrows of literary fortune.[16] When Byron, for one, learned from Shelley that 'Young Keats ... died lately at Rome from the consequences of breaking a blood-vessel, in paroxysms of despair at the contemptuous attack on his book in the *Quarterly*', he was incredulous: 'is it *actually* true? I did not think criticism had been so killing ... in this world of bustle and broil, and especially in the career of writing, a man should calculate upon his powers of *resistance* before he goes into the arena.' Byron was one of the first, in fact, to transplant Shelley's 'broken lily' into the garden of the faintly farcical with the famously flippant couplet in *Don Juan* (1823): 'kill'd off by one critique ... Poor fellow! His was an untoward fate; / 'T is strange the mind, that very fiery particle, / Should let itself be snuff'd out by an article.'[17]

Byron's epitaph, 'snuff'd out by an article', flourished: even when the subject was not Keats, as in *Blackwood's* review of Alexander Smith in 1854, it could be quoted with knowing effect. Over twenty years later, a critic for *Cornhill Magazine* wrote that *Adonais* could be 'justified' only 'On the theory that poetry and manliness are incompatible, that a poet is and ought to be a fragile being, ready to ["]Die of a rose in aromatic pain["]' – quoting the same line from Pope's *Essay on Man* that Hazlitt had used to characterise effeminacy.

The *New Monthly* did not help things in Keats's own day when it compared the *Quarterly's* attacks on Lady Morgan – an Irish woman of letters and defender of the French Revolution, and subject, in the *Monthly's* words, to 'one of the coarsest insults ever offered in print by man to woman' – to the same journal's 'laborious attempt to torture and ruin Mr Keats': the effect was to make Keats seem the victim of ungallant male behaviour towards women deserving kinder, gentler treatment. By the middle of the century, this chapter of the Keats legend became canonical in *Chambers's Cyclopedia*, which began its entry on Keats with a long account of how savage handling by the reviews led to his final suffering.[18]

These widely circulated reports not only dominate nineteenth-century images of Keats, but also helped draw them into the orbit of a larger cultural preoccupation: the effort to secure distinctions between the genders and stabilise codes of conduct. If Mrs Sanderford diagnosed 'the female mind' as 'constitutionally less stable than that of man', and Thomas Gisborne's manual cautioned that 'the acute sensibility peculiar to women ... is liable to sudden excesses' and 'sometimes degenerates into weakness and pusillanimity', Keats, 'pierced by the shaft' of malicious reviews, was readily translated into this feminine liability.[19] Thus Gilfillan speculates, sympathetically, that Keats's 'great defect' was 'want ... of a man-like constitution', and Carlyle, with a caustic echo of Byron, remarked that Dr Johnson 'was no man to be killed by a review', while 'the whole of Keats's poetry consists in a weak-eyed maudlin sensibility'.[20] *Blackwood's* made the point in 1820 with a mock apology for its prior manner: 'we are most heartily sorry . had we suspected that young author being so delicately nerved, we should have administered our reproof in a much more lenient shape and style.' Hazlitt takes up this theme in his essay 'On Living to One's-Self', in which he speaks of Keats as one for whom such abuse 'proved too much ... and stuck like a barbed arrow in his heart. Poor Keats! What was sport to the town, was death to him. Young, sensitive, delicate, he was like "A bud bit by an envious worm, / Ere he could spread his sweet leaves to the air, / Or dedicate his beauty to the sun" – and unable to endure the miscreant cry and idiot laugh, withdrew to sigh his last breath in foreign climes.' He is quoting Romeo's father on his lovesick son (I:i:157) – and if Romeo gets taunted in the play for being unmanned by love, the effeminacy of Keats's character receives fresh credit for Victorians reading his love letters. Swinburne, for one, sneers that 'a manful kind of man or even a manly sort of boy, in his love-making or in his suffering, will not howl and snivel after such a lamentable fashion'.[21]

Even sympathy for Keats, as Swinburne implies, may itself be read as unmanly. When a friend remarked to Carlyle that Milnes's *Life* had 'interested' him, Carlyle 'retorted, "That shows you to be a soft-horn!"'[22] This easy sarcasm in no small part reflects the way Keats had become the property of female readers. The myth of the poet who 'burst a blood vessel on reading a savage attack on his "Endymion" ... and died in Rome as a consequence' was routinely rehearsed in women's journals, such as *The Ladies' Companion* (from which I quote), while the image of the lovely genius too refined for long life gained prestige with his female biographers: Frances Mary Owen closes her study with a stanza of *Adonais*: 'He is a portion of the loveliness / Which once he made more lovely ... bursting in its beauty and its might / From trees and beasts and men into the Heaven's light.' And Dorothy Hewlett titles her 1937 biography *Adonais: a Life of John Keats*. As MacGillivray remarks, the story of Keats's frailty and unhappy end was made to order for 'the popular Victorian and feminine ideal of the unhappy and beautiful youth of genius'.[23] All those expressions of 'poor Keats!' evoked responses conventionally deemed 'feminine', activating impulses to pity, nurture, and protect. *Victoria Magazine* concludes its essay by exclaiming 'What shall we say of the malicious, the utterly brutal criticism, the hand of the cloddish boy tearing the myriad-hued fragile butterfly to fragments! No words can express the loathing every honest educated Englishman must feel for the ruffian tasks which inaugurated a long career of prosperity for the two Quarterlies.' Keats, the fragile butterfly, is implicitly cast as the wronged female, whose honour begs for all Englishmen's defence; in Mrs Oliphant's account, he is unmanned as a defenceless child, a 'poor young poet ... savagely used by the censors of literature'.

These motions are sympathetic, to be sure, but their effect was to credit the image of Keats as needing such intercession – one fulfilled by his most famous female biographer, Amy Lowell, who pauses to exclaim on one occasion, 'Poor little shaver, so pitiably unable to cope with his first great sorrow', and on another, to vilify the reviewers as 'first-class cads'.[24] George Ford nearly understates the case when he reports that 'For some women readers, the story of Keats's supposed extreme weakness had a sort of attraction'. We find no better proof than Mrs Oliphant's essay on Keats for her *Literary History*:

> He turned from the confusions of his own age, which he had neither strength nor inclination to fathom ... He was not robust enough for political strife, or to struggle as his contemporaries were doing with noisy questions about the Regent's morals or manners, or the corruptions of the state. It was so much easier and more delightful to escape into the silvery brightness... . poetry had become his chief object in life. Those whom life endows more abundantly with other interests may play with their inspiration, feeling towards that divine gift as, according to Byron, men do toward a scarcely stronger passion –
>
> > 'Man's love is of man's life a thing apart,
> > 'Tis woman's whole existence.'
>
> This was the case of Keats in respect to the heavenly gift... . In poetry his was the woman's part –

With no apologies for (and perhaps no consciousness of) untoward implication, Oliphant reverently aligns Keats with the sensibilities of a Byronic heroine.[25]

IV

> I am certain I have not a right feeling toward Women... . an obsti-
> nate Prejudice can seldom be produced but from a gordian complica-
> tion of feelings, which must take time to unravell[ed] and care to
> keep unravelled – I could say a good deal about this
>
> (Keats to Bailey, 18 July 1818)

Keats's repeated figuring in nineteenth century discussions as feminine or effeminate is not an arbitrary or wilful misreading. It
reflects and reinscribes, with varying degrees of ideological pressure,
the ambivalence in his own writing about the difference between
'masculine' and 'feminine'. In his effort to create a poetic identity
and win acceptance as a poet, he profoundly internalises and struggles with social and psychological attitudes about gender: at times
he is sensitive to tendencies in himself susceptible to interpretation
as feminine; at other times, and with more irritation, he imagines
the masculine self being feminised or rendered effeminate by
women exercising power and authority; and at still other times, he
projects feminine figures as forces against manly self-possession and
its social validator, professional maturity.

This dilemma is most clearly revealed in Keats's intense fascination with the feminine as the focus of male desire. It is significant
that his famous simile for ideal poetic power is one that conflates
sexual and visionary fulfilment, even as it suppresses the feminine in
the name of male consciousness: 'The Imagination may be compared to Adam's dream – he awoke and found it truth'.[26] To a
degree unmatched by other male Romantic poets, Keats tends to
represent ecstatic or visionary experience as an erotic encounter
with a female or feminised figure; correspondingly, his deepest
anxieties take shape in confrontations with power in a female form,
or in separations from, losses of, or betrayals by a woman. In the
early poems, various wish-fulfilling adventures of adolescent male
imagination converge on sensuous nymphs and goddesses, and the
larger plot of *Endymion* equates quest romance with erotic adventure. In the crucial post-*Endymion* sonnet on *King Lear*, 'Romance'
itself is a woman, and although her charms are antithetical to the
literary tradition Keats hopes to join, it is telling that romantic love
infuses the three poems for which the 1820 volume is named,
Lamia, *Isabella*, and *The Eve of St. Agnes*.

Yet if the feminine represents fulfilment, it is often fugitive,
elusive, or untrustworthy, and many of Keats's letters write his life

as an allegory of sexual uncertainty. His sense of powerlessness in the politics of desire impels him at times to counter with defensive contempt and condescension: the 'generality of women', he writes, 'appear to me as children to whom I would rather give a Sugar Plum than my time' (*Keats's Letters*, I, 104). Admiration is limited chiefly, sometimes exclusively, to physical attributes: when Fanny Brawne 'uttered a half complaint once' that Keats seems to love only her 'Beauty' (*Keats's Letters*, II, 275), he protests, 'I cannot conceive any beginning of such love as I have for you but Beauty... . so let me speak of you [sic] Beauty' (*Keats's Letters*, II, 127). The obverse of this aesthetic is contempt for men overpowered by the otherness of female beauty. Having transcribed a 'fine' misogynist diatribe from *Anatomy of Melancholy* detailing all 'such errors or imperfections of boddy [sic] or mind' the admiring 'Lover' will overlook in his 'Mistress', Keats remarks, 'I would give my favou[r]ite leg to have written this as a speech in a Play: with what effect could [the right actor] pop-gun it at the pit!' (*Keats's Letters*, II, 91–2). This is a provocative trade: a favourite leg for the effective verbal weapon against the felt power of female physical allure.

It is revealing that the very texts that show men subjecting women to the control of the male gaze frequently involve figures of male vulnerability. When, for instance, we hear the poet of 'Ode on Melancholy' urge men to treat women's anger as a rich spectacle – 'if thy mistress some rich anger shows, / Emprison her soft hand, and let her rave, / And feed deep, deep upon her peerless eyes' – we may think that the poem is prescribing an aesthetic ideology that denies woman's subjectivity with wilful restraint. But the real danger, it turns out, is the aesthete's self-cancelling devotion to a sensibility gendered as feminine: by the poem's close, it is 'She', 'Veiled Melancholy', who is serene and self-contained, and the male suitor who is appropriated and desubstantialised: 'His soul shall taste the sadness of her might, / And be among her cloudy trophies hung'. These figures of erotic entrapment and masculine self-dissolution are repeated in Keats's protests to Fanny Brawne: 'Ask yourself my love whether you are not very cruel to have so entrammelled me, so destroyed my freedom' (*Keats's Letters*, II, 123).

'La Belle Dame sans Merci' is a suggestive staging of these erotic politics, succinctly encoding Keats's characteristic ambivalences in the contradictory signals of the title and playing these out in the ballad itself. There is, on the one hand, a climactic revelation of female treachery: the Knight's report that in the dream that followed lovemaking, 'pale kings, and princes too, / Pale warriors' announce in concert, 'La belle dame sans merci / Hath thee in thrall!' – their 'starv'd lips' seeming in retrospect to prefigure his present depletion, their 'horrid warning' confirmed by his present state. Yet the total account defeats univocal judgement. Keats allows certain details of the Knight's narrative to suggest that if the lady had a hidden design on him, he, too, was a wielder of designs: no sooner had he met her than he courted her with flowery bindings of his own ('I made a garland for her head, / And bracelets too, and fragrant zone'), claimed possession of her ('I set her on my pacing steed'), and, figuratively repeating these motions, translated her words into terms to satisfy his own desire: 'And sure in language strange she said – / I love thee true'. These intentional actions cast 'La belle dame sans merci', in effect, less as the culpable betrayer of men's desire than as a figure defined by men's branding as 'feminine' whatever urges their withdrawal from the duties coded in the poem's other important name: 'knight at arms'.[27] It is significant that the chorus who identifies the lady as 'La Belle Dame sans Merci' – kings, princes, warriors, knight – are representative figures of a patriarchal order defined by quest, battle, conquest, and government, and secured by rejection of the indulgences the Knight associates with her, namely a zone of erotic luxury, sensuality, and near infantile pleasure.

The gendering of such conflict may be read in earlier poems as well, where the feminine, typically nymph or goddess, inhabits a world of isolation from, or on an arc of development prior to, adult demands: that 'strength of manhood' that 'must pass' such recesses of joy for 'a nobler life' of 'agonies' and 'strife', as 'Sleep and Poetry' puts it (ll. 163, 122–4), or as Keats's famous conceit of life as a Mansion of Many Apartments maps, and genders, this passage, the 'grand march' that begins only as the 'Chamber of Maiden Thought' dissolves (*Keats's Letters*, I, 281–2). Even Endymion's conflation of erotic with visionary success in Cynthia, the 'completed form of all completeness' (1:606), tests certain critical perspectives: the temptation to retreat from the social demands of adult life gets projected, here and elsewhere, as entrapment by the supernatural and the feminine, while the need to punish (or at least judge) this impulse is suggested by the way Keats typically threatens the male lover with betrayal to a fatally forlorn state.[28] We see similar trouble in *Lamia*, where erotic fascination competes, in disastrous consequence, with the claims of 'proper' manly life.

The tension between desire and self-sufficiency that drives all these plots, and seeks expression as sexual allegory, also appears, not surprisingly, in Keats's language for his vocation. If his 'chief poet[s]' and presiders are men (Homer, Shakespeare, Milton, Wordsworth), it is significant that 'Poesy' itself is frequently figured as a female 'other', and one not always susceptible to petition or appropriation. Sometimes she appears as the hostile arbiter of the poet's desire, as in Moneta's challenges to the dreamer of *The Fall of Hyperion*; sometimes the politics of courtship are reversed so that the poet can vent his hostility, degrading the feminine figure that focuses his desire, or portraying her as a flirt whose attentions prove as inconstant as they are potent. These figurings are largely conventional, of course, but Keats shows himself attracted to them, and experiencing their implications, in a uniquely intense and eroticised way. We see the consequences of this investment in the language with which he surrounds Fanny Brawne, speaking of her both as a 'dearest love' and a negative muse, a force against self-possession, and an object of deepest suspicion. His projection of his felt powerlessness as her power is often cast, revealingly, in terms that pose her as a threat to the psychic integrity needed to write: 'it seems to me that a few more moments thought of you would uncrystallise and dissolve me – I must not give way to it – but turn to my writing again – if I fail I shall die hard – O my love, your lips are growing sweet again to my fancy – I must forget them' (*Keats's Letters*, II, 142).[29]

Keats's ambivalent negotiations with the feminine as 'other' are intensified by his uncertain evaluations of those aspects of his own sensibility that he or others represent as feminine. The issue animates his statements about his 'poetical Character'. His famous claim to write with 'no self ... no identity' (*Keats's Letters*, I, 387) implicates gender, for not only does this ideal cooperate with the advice of those arbiters of conduct such as Mrs Sanderford, who urge women to 'avoid egotism',[30] but Keats himself is inclined to distinguish 'camelion' flexibility of imagination from the character of 'Men of Power', who 'have a proper self' (*Keats's Letters*, I, 184). Indeed, the 'camelion' poet may transcend male identity, having 'as much delight in conceiving an Iago as an Imogen', in cogitating on Saturn as on Ops (*Keats's Letters*, I, 387). Even in non-poetical delights, Keats admits his divergence from standard figures of manliness: he enjoys 'a sort of temper indolent and supremely careless', a state he calls 'effeminacy' (*Keats's Letters*, II, 78). And he speculates to a friend about the value of being passive, more 'the flower than the Bee', asking, 'who shall say between Man and Woman which is the most delighted?' Using standard codes of gender, Keats cogitates on the value of being the Woman: 'let us open our leaves like a flower and be passive and receptive – budding patiently under the eye of Apollo and taking hints from eve[r]y noble insect that favours us with a visit' (*Keats's Letters*, I, 232).

Keats often finds it necessary to circumscribe this playful androgyny. If he worries that the object-oriented sympathy of 'camelion' imagination may leave him, as a subjective power, 'an[ni]hilated ... among Men' (*Keats's Letters*, I, 387), we can see a desire to keep a place 'among Men' even in the flower-and-bee scenario sketched above. He turns to a second analogy that redeems passivity from the suggestion of emasculation and power-lessness: 'it is more noble to sit like Jove tha[n] to fly like Mercury – let us not therefore go hurrying about and collecting honey-bee like, buzzing here and there impatiently' (*Keats's Letters*, I, 232). It is the busy boy Mercury who seems less manly than the passive, serenely self-possessed Jove. This recovery of the masculine may also be read in the letter about 'temper indolent': this state of 'effeminacy', Keats makes certain to report, had a manly origin – he is nursing a black eye from a fight with a butcher. But even these alignments are unstable. Keats closes the meditation on Jove, confessing, 'all this is a mere sophistication, however it may neighbour to any truths, to excuse my own indolence – so I will not deceive myself that Man should be equal with jove – but think himself very well off as a sort of scullion-Mercury or even a humble Bee' – implying that he identifies more with boyish busy-ness than with manly patience, before he abandons the issue alto-gether: 'It is [no] matter whether I am right or wrong either one way or another' (*Keats's Letters*, I, 233).

These musings about the ambiguous boundaries between mascu-line and feminine are confined to friends and family. More pressing is Keats's vulnerable sense of masculinity in relation to the social world at large. He is acutely aware that his physical stature does not fill the normative figure of adult manly prowess. In the gaze of the other, especially 'Womankind', he is 'Mister John Keats five feet hight' (*Keats's Letters*, I, 342), 'quite the little Poet' (*Keats's Letters*, II, 61), a 'versifying Pet-lamb' (*Keats's Letters*, II, 116), a 'pet-lamb in a sentimental farce' ('Ode on Indolence'), or 'taken for nothing' at all (*Keats's Letters*, I, 291) – each a notable exception to Woolf's famous remark that women typically serve 'as looking-glasses possessing the magic and delicious power of reflecting the figure of man at twice its natural size'.[31] Keats's inverse fate presses in his psyche against hopes of success both as poet and lover, roles he frequently equates with or makes contingent on one another. 'Had I a man's fair form, then might my sighs [a rueful pun on "size"?] ... find thy gentle heart; so well / Would passion arm me for the enterprize: / But ah! I am no knight', he laments in a sonnet for his inaugural volume of 1817. He repeats these terms in another of its poems, 'Calidore': Sir Gondibert, 'a man of elegance, and stature tall', tells his tales of 'knightly deeds' – 'how the strong of arm / Kept off dismay, and terror, and alarm / From lovely woman' – with 'such manly ardour' that courtship seems simultaneous: 'each damsel's hand' is ready for a kiss between syllables. Keats himself will sometimes affect such worldliness. To express frustrations about writing, he imagines a sexual drama that converts failure to woo the coy muse, poetry, into the cocky confidence of a suitor well versed in courtship ritual: 'I know not why Poetry and I have been so distant lately I must make some advances soon or she will cut me entirely' (*Keats's Letters*, II, 74).

The anxiety is transparent through the wit, however, and as these figures of courtship and knightly prowess imply, Keats is sensitive to the function of class prejudice in his unmanning: 'You see what it is to be under six foot and not a lord', he grumbles; 'My name with the literary fashionables is vulgar – I am a weaver boy to them' (*Keats's Letters*, II, 61; II, 186). He counters by having certain of his poetic speakers affect the pose of the masculine aristocrat – one who, with fashionable weariness, regards the pursuit of fame as beneath him: 'Fame', he writes knowingly, is a 'wayward girl' who is 'coy / To those who woo her with too slavish knees'; even if won, she proves to be the goddess of 'a fierce miscreed', 'a Gipsey ... A Jilt' who 'fever[s]' the man who would possess her (*Keats's Letters*, II, 104–5). 'I equally dislike the favour of the public with the love of a woman', Keats claims; 'they are both a cloying treacle to the wings of independence' (*Keats's Letters*, II, 144).

These poses of masculine condescension to a femininely figured literary and erotic marketplace are fuelled by Keats's hostility to women as readers and ratifiers of his petitions for acceptance.[32] He bristles at the thought of himself and his writing subject to real as well as figurative feminine favour: he 'detest[s]' the prospect of 'Women ... tak[ing] a snack or Luncheon of Literary scraps'

(*Keats's Letters*, I, 163) and, adamant about resisting their power over his own texts, he boldly claims that the erotic wit of *The Eve of St. Agnes* is not meant for them. When Richard Woodhouse, the legal and literary adviser to his publisher, worried that this poem might be 'unfit for ladies' because no assurances are given about Porphyro's marriage to Madeline (he thinks Keats is affecting the manner of the under-six-foot Lord Byron, 'The "Don Juan" style of mingling up sentiment & sneering'), Keats retorted that 'he does not want ladies to read his poetry: that he writes for men' (Rollins (ed.), *Keats Circle*, II, 163). Significantly, when Keats thinks about selling out – that is, writing for journals while he awaits honourable literary success – he imagines that to offer his talents thus ('any thing for sale') is to become a female commodity of the most reduced kind: 'Yea I will traffic', he says in rueful and contemptuous solidarity with the streetwalker.[33] ...

V

If our century reveals the endurance of nineteenth-century oppositions, it also continues the work of overcoming such binarism. Taking on the poetry that embarrasses even the advocates of Keats's manliness, Christopher Ricks describes a Keats who explores a sense of manhood capable of full indulgence in the sensual. For him, a phrase such as 'slippery blisses', notoriously cited for immaturity or indecency, is not the 'simple infantilism or sensation' it may seem, but a 'patently audacious piece of writing' whose 'unmisgiving largeness of mind' holds a liberating psychic value for the male reader. In Endymion's 'swoon[ing] / Drunken from Pleasure's nipple' (II: 868–9), for example, Ricks reads a 'metaphor of adult love' that 'enables us, with Keats's guiding, to feel a full pleasure comparable to the infant's ... full innocence of gratification'. Trilling honours a similar guide when, with a deliberate twist on Carlyle's manly ethos, he titles his essay on Keats 'Poet as Hero' and proceeds to express admiration both for Keats's bold identification of 'diligent indolence' 'as the female principle' and his willingness to 'experience its manifestation in himself without fear or resistance'. Earlier than Trilling, Woolf had given this capacity a prestigious aesthetic value: naming Keats to her (all-male) canon of 'androgynous' writers, she wonders 'whether there are two sexes in the mind corresponding to the two sexes in the body', and 'spiritually cooperating. If one is a man, still the woman part of the brain must have effect'.[34]

For some feminists, Woolf's theory of androgyny offers a welcome deconstruction of the 'binary oppositions of masculinity and femininity'; for others, it seems an aesthetic evasion of the unalterable political and experiential reality of gender.[35] Not coincidentally, Keats's situation in modern feminist discussion, especially when it holds to binary oppositions, is equally critical. If he represented to and evoked in some of his Victorian effeminisers capacities of response that they publicly needed to disparage as feminine, he has had the equally striking fate of representing to some recent interpreters sensibilities they want to identify descriptively as 'feminine' or, more polemically, admire as 'feminist'. He is still, in other words, being treated as an exception to, or anomaly within, a monolithically conceived 'masculine' discourse. Margaret Homans, for instance, in speculating that Keats's humble origins and poverty participate in 'certain aspects of women's experience as outsiders relative to the major literary tradition ... regardless of gender', exempts him from classification with poets of the dominant 'masculine tradition', who are said to construct 'the strong self from his strong language'.[36] And before her, Adrienne Rich commented on the issue of Keats's sensibility in a way that includes him in the woman's tradition. In the course of a discussion about women's 'so-called "weak ego boundaries"', she accepts help from Keats to articulate her point: responding to her suggestion that a woman's self-effacing tendency to 'lose all sense of her own ego' might 'be a negative way of describing the fact that women have tremendous powers of intuitive identification and sympathy with other people', her interviewer remarks, 'John Keats had weak ego boundaries'. Rich replies, 'Negative capability. Exactly' – without noting that in Keats's formulation, this quality is exemplified in Shakespeare and identified as the property of 'a Man of Achievement' (*Keats's Letters*, I, 193); perhaps she paused over the implication before adding a comment that seems to want to get around Keats's capable Man by transcending gender altogether: 'Any artist has to have it to some extent'. Erica Jong had invoked the same formula for her definition of 'feminism': 'feminism *means* empathy. And empathy ... is akin to the quality Keats called 'negative capability' – that unique gift for projecting oneself into other states of consciousness'.[37] Albeit with a different emphasis, these readers perpetuate Victorian discriminations, for they have, in effect, regendered Keats by naming as 'feminist' those capacities which they find anomalous to their ideology of the 'male' character and the 'masculine' tradition, rather than studied him as an opportunity to investigate the multiple and often conflicting interests that animate men's writing within patriarchal culture. Homans has since extended her interpretation of Keats to account both for his hostility to women readers and his conspicuous efforts to participate in and take advantage of certain aspects of masculinist ideology, and she is now in the process of returning Keats to the male party.[38] Her reassessment is an interesting process in itself, however, because it suggests how Keats's own sensitivity to gender articulates itself in ways sufficiently ambivalent – in sensibilities and poetic habits traditionally construed as feminine; in attitudes and modes of behaviour recognisably sexist and reactive – to make him available for conscription into polemics active ever since the romantic era.

Each effort to gender Keats's sensibility repeats the problem of reconciling general values with a complex and elusive instance. Indeed debates about Keats by those concerned to evaluate themselves and their culture against qualities perceived in him reveal the fundamental instability of interpretive paradigms for this issue. For readings of Keats in the language of gender – by Keats himself, by his contemporaries, and by his critics – typically set into play conflicts and contradictions, the significance of which abides more in their persistent irresolution than in any possibility of a unified interpretation. If Keats continues to animate discussions of gender in literary and social experience, he continues, just as surely, to confuse the terms. Even as he provokes us to describe and differentiate among what is 'masculine', 'feminine', 'effeminate', or 'feminist', he confronts us with the need to complicate and redefine the judgements that underlie these categories – not only in literary history, but in our attempts to take the critical measure of that history.

From *Critical Essays on John Keats*, ed. Hermione de Almeida (Boston, 1990), pp. 317–30, 347–56).

NOTES

[Susan Wolfson's important discussion of the ways in which contemporary critics of John Keats, along with their nineteenth- and twentieth-century successors, have concentrated on the feminine aspects of his life and writing

impressively combines detailed research with feminist insight. She regards
Keats not simply as early 'feminist' or, alternatively, as an opponent of
feminism (both positions which some feminist critics have held), but rather
approaches the poet as an opportunity to investigate the multiple and often
conflicting interests that animate men's writing within patriarchal culture.
Her article focuses on the contestation of gender within the masculine self:
in this context Keats becomes not just an individual case for investigation
but a sign of a large-scale cultural anxiety about the feminisation of the
male in the Romantic period. Keats, whose literary position was very marginal in his own age, tempted a certain degree of extreme critical judgement. By Wolfson's account, Keats is writing at a time of a determined
critical attempt to enforce standards of manly conduct, and he is thus
regarded either as effeminate or the inspiration for attempts to make more
flexible the prevailing definitions of masculinity. For most of his critics,
from William Hazlitt onwards, Keats demonstrates the feminine qualities
of weakness, liability to sudden excess, and passivity. Section IV of
Wolfson's article deals with the problematic depictions of the masculine
and feminine in Keats's own poetry and letters, and his ambivalence about
the differences between the two gendered positions. Wolfson's detailed discussion of Victorian representations of Keats or his poems, including visual
ones (in which Keats is usually pictured as delicate, indeed almost feminine
in features), has regrettably been left out due to reasons of space. Ed.]

1. William Hazlitt, 'On the Effeminacy of Character', Essay 9, *Table-
   Talk; or, Original Essays*, 2 vols (London, 1822), II, 204, 202–3, 215.

2. James Henry Leigh Hunt, *The Indicator*, 2 (9 August 1820), 352.

3. Jack Stillinger (ed.), *The Poems of John Keats* (Cambridge, MA,
   1978), p. 356. All quotations, cited by line number, follow this
   edition.

4. John Keats, *Endymion. A Poetic Romance*, II, 942. I am indebted to
   Miriam Allott's note, *The Poems of John Keats* (New York, 1970),
   p. 440. This complaint about Apollo persists late into the century; W. J.
   Courthorpe, for example, comments that with such an 'effeminate notion
   of Apollo, [Keats] could never have invented any kind of action which
   would have explained his subsequent triumph over Hyperion' (*The
   Liberal Movement in English Literature* (London, 1885), pp. 18–22.

5. *Byron's Letters and Journals*, ed. Leslie A. Marchand, 12 vols
   (Cambridge, MA, 1973–82), VII, 200; VII, 102; VII, 202; II, 217. For
   a very sharp study of the justice of Byron's assessment of Keats in
   ways that Byron himself was not prepared to appreciate, see Marjorie
   Levinson, *Keats's Life of Allegory: The Origins of Poetic Style*
   (London, 1988), pp. 18–22.

6. 'On the Cockney School of Poetry, No 4', *Blackwood's Edinburgh
   Magazine*, 3 (August 1818), p. 519.

7. Ibid., variously, pp. 519–24. *Blackwood's* subsequent caricature of 'Mr John Keats standing on the sea-shore at Dunbar, without a neckcloth, according to custom of Cockaigne' (vol. VI [December 1819], 239) is fuelled in part by Keats's presumption in affecting an aristocratic fashion, described by a contemporary in fact as 'à la Byron' (*The Keats Circle*, ed. Hyder E. Rollins, 2 vols [Cambridge, MA, 1948], II, 211).

8. George Gilfillan, 'John Keats', in *First and Second Galleries of Literary Portraits* (Edinburgh, 1854), p. 258.

9. *Blackwood's*, 3 (May 1818), 197 and 6 (December 1819), 239; *Lord Byron, Letters and Journals*, VII, 200 and 229; J. R. MacGillivray, *Keats: A Bibliography and Reference Guide with an Essay on Keats's Reputation* (Toronto, 1949), p. xii.

10. *Blackwood's*, 19 (19 January 1826), xvi and xxvi.

11. 'Lord Byron is a pampered and aristocratic writer, but he is not effeminate', Hazlitt explains ('Of Effeminacy', 215); Thomas Carlyle in fact found him 'almost the only man' among English poets 'faithfully and manfully struggling, to the end' in the cause of 'spiritual manhood' ('Goethe', *Foreign Review*, 3, reprinted in *Critical and Miscellaneous Essays* [London, 1899]; reprint, New York, 1969), 5 vols, I, 243). The discourses on Shelley are much more divided. When G. H. Lewes said that he was 'par excellence, the "poet of women"' he was referring not to effeminacy but to the ideals of feminism (with which he sympathised): 'woman' as 'a *partner* of your life' (*Westminster Review*, 35 [April 1841], 169). But Charles Kingsley derided Shelley's nature as 'utterly womanish'; it is he, rather than the wrongly cited Byron ('who amid all his fearful sins, was a man'), on whom one ought to blame the present age's spasmodic, vague, extravagant, effeminate, school of poetry' (*Fraser's Magazine*, 48 [November 1853], 572, 573, 574.

12. *British Lady's Magazine*, 25 (1 May 1817), 262.

13. 'Remarks on Keats' (J. W. Dalby), *Pocket Magazine of Classic and Polite Literature*, 7 (4 April 1812), 333 and 335. Mrs John Sanderford, *Woman, In Her Social and Domestic Character*, 7th edn (London, 1842), p. 16

14. Gilfillan, 'John Keats', 260. For *Guardian* Review, see Lewis M. Schwartz, *Keats Reviewed by His Contemporaries: A Collection of Notices for the Years 1816–87* (Metuchen, NJ, 1973), pp. 228–32.

15. *The Young Lady's Book of Elegant Poetry* (Philadelphia, 1835); 'To Autumn', pp. 314–15; *Ladies' Companion* (August 1837), 186–7, includes 'Hither, Hither love', 'Fame, like a wayward girl', 'On a Dream', and 'Tis the witching hour'; *The Girl's Second Help to Reading* (1854; see G. M. Matthews (ed.), *Keats. The Critical Heritage* [New York, 1971], p. 10); 'The Daintiest of Poets – Keats', *Victoria Magazine*, 15 (May 1870), 55–67; Mrs Fields (Annie Adams) prints a MS page of 'I

stood tip-toe' concluding with the poet's exhortation to 'Ye ardent marigolds!' (*A Shelf of Old Books* [New York, 1894], p. 43).

16. I follow *Shelley's Poetry and Prose*, ed. Donald H. Reiman and Sharon B. Powers (New York, 1977); I quote from p. 390, and stanza 6 of the poem.

17. Shelley, *Letters 1818 to 1822*, ed. Roger Ingpen, in *The Complete Works of Percy Bysshe Shelley*, ed. Roger Ingpen and Walter E. Peck, 10 vols (New York, 1926), X, 225; *Byron, Letters and Journals*, VIII, 103, and *Don Juan*, Canto XI, 60, *Lord Byron: The Complete Poetical Works*, ed. Jerome J. McGann, 5 vols (Oxford, 1980–6, vol. V).

18. *Blackwood's*, 75 (March 1854), 346; *Cornhill*, 34 (1876), 558; *New Monthly*, 14 (September 1820), 306; 'John Keats', *Chambers's Cyclopaedia of English Literature*, ed. Robt Chambers, 2 vols (Boston, 1866), II, 402–3.

19. Thomas Gisbourne, *An Inquiry into the Duties of the Female Sex* (1796; 7th edn, London, 1806), pp. 34–5; Sanderford, *Woman*, p. 35.

20. Gilfillan, 'John Keats', p. 261–2; Thomas Carlyle, 'Burns', *Edinburgh Review*, 48 (1828); reprinted in *Critical and Miscellaneous Essays*, I, 277.

21. *Blackwood's*, 7 (September 1820), 686; Hazlitt, 'On Living to One's-Self', *Table-Talk*, I, 229–30; A. C. Swinburne, 'Keats', *The Complete Works of Algernon Charles Swinburne*, ed. Edmund Gosse and Thomas James Wise, 20 vols (London, 1925–7), XIV, 297.

22. William Allingham, *William Allingham: A Diary, 1824–1889*, ed. H. Allingham and D. Radford (1907; reprinted Harmondsworth, 1985), p. 205.

23. *Ladies' Companion* (August 1837), p. 186; Frances Mary Owen, *John Keats*, p. 183; Dorthy M. Hewlett, *Adonais: A Life of John Keats* (London, 1937); J. R. MacGillivray, *Keats*, p. xiii.

24. 'The Daintiest of Poets', 67; Margaret Oliphant, 'John Keats', *The Literary History of England in the End of the Eighteenth and Beginning of the Nineteenth Century*, 3 vols (London, 1925), I, 14 and II, 80.

25. Ford, *Keats and the Victorians*, p. 68; Oliphant, 'John Keats', pp. 137–8.

26. *The Letters of John Keats*. ed. Hyder E. Rollins, 2 vols (Cambridge, MA., 1958), I, 185[cited hereafter in this volume as *Keats's Letters* with volume and page – Ed.

27. Noticing that the Knight at the end of the poem joins an all-male chorus, Karen Swann asks: 'Could this community, and not the ideal or even the fatal woman, be the true object of his quest?' For her negotiation of this question, see 'Harassing the Muse', in *Romanticism and Feminism*, ed. Anne K. Mellor (Bloomington, IN, 1988), pp. 81–92, esp. 90–2.

28. See Stuart M. Sperry, *Keats the Poet* (Princeton, NJ, 1973), pp. 101–9; and Christopher Ricks, *Keats and Embarrassment* (London, 1974), pp. 12–14. Helen B. Ellis ('Food, Sex, Death, and the Feminine Principle in Keats's Poetry', *English Studies in Canada*, 6 [1980], 56–74) also gives a compelling discussion to the psychological implications. See esp. 56–7.

29. I study the literary consequence of Fanny's resistance to Keats's desire in 'Composition and "Unrest": The Dynamics of Form in Keats's Last Lyrics', *Keats–Shelley Journal*, 34 (1985), 58–82.

30. Sanderford, *Woman*, p. 9.

31. Virginia Woolf, *A Room of One's Own* (1929; reprint, New York, 1957), p. 35.

32. Theoretical contexts for examining Keats in relation to women readers and an increasingly feminised literary marketplace are developed by Sonia Hofkosh ('The Writer's Ravishment: Women and the Romantic Author – The Example of Byron', in *Romanticism and Feminism*, pp. 93–114) and Margaret Homans ('Keats and the Women Readers', English Institute paper, 1986).

33. *Keats's Letters*, II, 178.

34. Ricks, *Keats and Embarrassment*, pp. 104–5, 89. Lionel Trilling, 'The Poet as Hero: Keats in His Letter', reprinted in *The Opposing Self* (New York, 1955); Woolf, *A Room of One's Own*, pp. 107, 102. Even Coventry Patmore is willing to argue that 'the spirit of the great poet has always a feminine element' ('Keats', reprinted in *Principle in Art, Religio Poetae, and Other Essays* [1889, reprint, London, 1913] p. 62).

35. I quote Toril Moi (*Sexual/Textual Politics: Feminist Literary Theory* [London, 1985], p. 13) who is disputing Elaine Showalter's critique of Woolf's theory of androgyny as an aesthetic ideal based on a problematic 'class-oriented...ideal – the separation of politics and art'; as such, androgyny offered Woolf a myth of escape to 'the sphere of the exile and the eunuch' that allowed her to 'evade confrontation' with the political consequences of her femaleness (*A Literature of Their Own: British Women Novelists from Brontë to Lessing* [Princeton, NJ, 1977], pp. 288, 285, 264).

36. Margaret Homans, *Women Writers and Poetic Identity* (Princeton, NJ, 1980), pp. 240n, 25, and 33.

37. Adrienne Rich, 'Three Conversations', in *Adrienne Rich's Poetry*, ed. Barbara Charlesworth Gelpi and Albert Gelpi (New York, 1975), p. 115; Erica Jong, 'Visionary Anger', Ms 11 (July 1973), p. 31.

38. Margaret Homans, 'Keats and Women Readers', English Institute paper 1986.

5

Keats's Lisping Sedition

NICHOLAS ROE

Keats's friend Richard Woodhouse wrote in his copy of *Endymion*, 'K. said, with much simplicity, "It will easily be seen what I think of the present Ministers by the beginning of the 3d Book"'.[1] One can see readily enough from the opening of *Endymion* Book III that Keats was unimpressed by the government. The *British Critic*, however, was unalarmed by this example of Keats's political verse, observing that the poet had neglected to mention half of the establishment he was attacking: 'The third book begins in character, with a jacobinical apostrophe to "crowns, turbans, and tiptop nothings"; we wonder how mitres escaped from their usual place.'[2] John Lockhart, writing on the passage in *Blackwood's Magazine*, commented:

> We had almost forgot to mention, that Keats belongs to the Cockney School of Politics, as well as the Cockney School of Poetry... . Hear how their bantling has already learned to lisp sedition.[3]

Lockhart associated Keats's politics with Leigh Hunt, poet, editor of the liberal *Examiner* newspaper, and – as Lockhart described him – 'potent and august King of the Cockneys'. The terms of Lockhart's criticism have received less attention than they deserve. Keats is a 'bantling' – a bastard child – taught in Hunt's Cockney School to versify in a 'lisp', associated at this period with a childish or 'effeminate' sensibility. The opening lines of *Endymion* III are indeed characterised by a sort of childish exuberance. But the verse is clogged with awkward parentheses: 'or – O, torturing fact!/Who'; forced rhymes, 'fact!/unpack'd', 'gone – /Babylon'; obscure words such as 'dight'; and elliptical phrases like 'There are who lord it', 'a sight/Able to face an owl's', 'unladen breasts,/Save of blown self-applause'.[4] As political invective, the lines are almost wholly obscure. In the *Quarterly Review*, September 1818, John Wilson Croker contended that Keats had written 'at random', so that the poem wandered from one subject to another merely as rhymes suggested fresh thoughts and images, but to Lockhart the poem's marred and imperfect verse, its 'lisping' voice, was the expression of a subversive design. Was this merely a gibe to ridicule the 'young Cockney rhymester', or should one take Lockhart's observation seriously as an insight that reveals the ideological grounds on which Keats's early poems were condemned as a melodious plot against the establishment?

Keats's first collection, *Poems* (1817), was divided into five sections: first, a dedicatory poem, followed by Poems, Epistles, Sonnets, and, lastly, Keats's meditation on his calling as a writer, 'Sleep and Poetry'. Many of the poems were 'occasional' verses ('To Some Ladies', 'On receiving a curious Shell', 'On leaving some Friends'), or imitations of Spenser ('Specimen of an Induction', 'Calidore'), or familiar and fraternal verse epistles to friends and to his brother George. Some of them were explicit in announcing Keats's liberal politics, most obviously in the sonnets to Leigh Hunt and to the Polish patriot Kosciusko. The epistle 'To George Felton Matthew' celebrated heroes of 'the cause of freedom' – the patriots King Alfred, William Tell, William Wallace, and Robert Burns. 'To my Brother George' welcomed the poet's duty '"To startle princes from their easy slumbers"'. 'To Hope' (written in February 1815, probably after Hunt's release from jail on 2 February) declared:

> Let me not see the patriot's high bequest,
>   Great Liberty! how great in plain attire!
> With the base purple of a court oppress'd,
>   Bowing her head, and ready to expire ...[5]

'To Hope' is written in a conventional eighteenth-century libertarian idiom. But, along with the other poems already mentioned, it reinforces the political interests directly announced by Keats's first book. In some of these early poems Keats interweaves explicit liberal sentiments with passages of luxurious description in which a decorative, Spenserian bower is identified as a place of imaginative (and erotic) retirement:

> a bowery nook
> Will be elysium – an eternal book
> Whence I may copy many a lovely saying
> About the leaves, and flowers – about the playing
> Of nymphs in woods, and fountains; and the shade
> Keeping a silence round a sleeping maid;
> And many a verse from so strange influence
> That we must ever wonder how, and whence
> It came
>
>   ('Sleep and Poetry', ll. 63–71)

These arbours of fancied sequestration can be read as an expression of Keats's wish to lose the responsibilities of life to the 'strange influence' of poetry, but the luxurious bower defines a space of imaginative 'elysium' that is also intelligible as an expression of the liberal ideals directly announced elsewhere in the poems. When critics noticed Keats's 'natural freedom of versification', or disclosed Keats's principle 'that plan and arrangement are prejudicial to natural poetry', they were responding to the stylistic signature of the 'natural freedom' that defined his political opposition to 'the present Ministers'.[6]

Keats's 'bowery nooks' are resorts of imaginative life which also mediate the ideological context of his creativity. In 'Sleep and Poetry', for instance, withdrawal into 'the bosom of a leafy world' gives place to thoughts of the fully humanised poetry which Keats hoped to write in the future:

> And can I ever bid these joys farewell?
> Yes, I must pass them for a nobler life,
> Where I may find the agonies, the strife
> Of human hearts ...
>
>   (ll. 122–5)

Here, and elsewhere in Keats's early poems, the bower thus serves as a temporary refuge in the poet's quest towards a humane, historicised imagination. A similar progression appears in 'Ode to a Nightingale', in which the 'embalmed darkness' of reverie discloses a bower of floral beauty where the poet may 'guess each sweet' – much as he had enumerated 'luxuries' in his earlier poems. But in 'Ode to a Nightingale' this child-like poring over 'sweets' (which Yeats thought was a characteristic of Keats's imagination) is gradually informed by a fuller awareness of mortality, the passage of time, and the tread of 'hungry generations' of humankind. This movement of Keats's vision, from the sweets of 'embalmed darkness' to a chastened awareness of history, resembles some of his early verse in which comparable imaginative patterns are accompanied by a more evident preoccupation with politics.

The title page of *Poems* (1817) was in fact carefully arranged to announce the relationship between liberal politics and the poet's imaginative life. Opening the book, Keats's first readers saw an epigraph from Spenser's complaint *Muiopotmos: or the Fate of the Butterfly* –

> 'What more felicity can fall to creature,
> Than to enjoy delight with liberty'

–and, just beneath this verse, a laurelled head of William Shakespeare. Keats's epigraph couples 'delight' with 'liberty', although in Spenser's poem 'felicity' had immediately given place to 'mishap' and an elegiac meditation on the vulnerability of joy:

> But what on earth can long abide in state?
> Or who can him assure of happie day;
> Sith morning faire may bringe fowle evening late,
> And least mishap the most blisse alter may?
> (ll. 217–20)[7]

Earthly mutability also informed the first poem in Keats's volume, the dedicatory sonnet to Leigh Hunt (or 'Libertas' as Keats named Hunt at this time). The sonnet echoes the 'Immortality Ode', recalling (and affirming) Wordsworth's loss of visionary power as the occasion for Keats's compliment to Hunt:

> To Leigh Hunt, Esq.
> Glory and loveliness have passed away;
>   For if we wander out in early morn,
>   No wreathed incense do we see upborne
> Into the east, to meet the smiling day:
> No crowd of nymphs soft voic'd and young, and gay,
>   In woven baskets bringing ears of corn,
>   Roses, and pinks, and violets, to adorn
> The shrine of Flora in her early May.
> But there are left delights as high as these,
>   And I shall ever bless my destiny,
> That in a time, when under pleasant trees
>   Pan is no longer sought, I feel a free
> A leafy luxury, seeing I could please
>   With these poor offerings, a man like thee.

The impact that this dedicatory poem would have made on Keats's contemporary readers and reviewers should not be underestimated. By placing it on the first page of his first collection, Keats had deliberately identified himself with an outspoken figure of public opposition to government and crown. As journalist and editor of the *Examiner* Hunt was repeatedly and unsuccessfully charged with seditious libel until 1813, when he was jailed for two years for a libel on the Prince Regent. Charles Cowden Clarke remembered how as a schoolboy at Enfield Keats had read the *Examiner* and Bishop Burnet's liberal and reformist *History of His Own Times*, and said that this reading had 'laid the foundation of [Keats's] love of civil and religious liberty'.[8] Keats celebrated Hunt's release from jail in his sonnet of February 1815 (also included in *Poems* 1817), although he did not meet Hunt in person until October 1816 when their friendship developed swiftly. The dedicatory sonnet in *Poems* was therefore a personal tribute, which also assumed Hunt's reputation in contemporary public life in its final compliment to 'a man like thee'.

Keats's admiration for Hunt as politician and poet has too frequently been regarded as a derivative product of their friendship. Some of Keats's earliest reviewers framed him as Hunt's junior 'bardling', and later critics (when they noticed Keats's politics at all) have perpetuated the idea that his political opinions were no more than a reflection of Hunt's. In 1971 Geoffrey Matthews announced Keats's subordination to Hunt's politics as if this were incontrovertible: 'The real target of the *Quarterly*'s and *Blackwood*'s attacks was not Keats at all, but Hunt'.[9] Although Hunt was indeed important as poet and politician to Keats, Keats's political imagination had its own integrity. Charles Cowden Clarke recalled that the *Examiner* had encouraged Keats's liberal opposition years before the poet's relationship with Hunt developed, and the immediacy of the *Examiner* reports would have been reinforced by the powerful arguments for liberty and freedom of conscience in Burnet's *History*. It was primarily the seditious force of Keats's poetic style that roused the critics' hostility; indeed, according to Cowden Clarke 'word had been passed that [Keats] was a Radical; and in those days of "Bible-Crown-and Constitution" supremacy, he might have had better chance of success had he been an Anti-Jacobin'. In this perspective the poet's friendship with Hunt was seen as a secondary matter.

John Barnard's recent Penguin selection of Keats begins with his republican poem 'Lines Written on 29 May The Anniversary of the Restoration of Charles II':

> Infatuate Britons, will you still proclaim
> His memory, your direst, foulest shame?
>   Nor patriots revere?
>
> Ah! when I hear each traitorous lying bell,
> 'Tis gallant Sidney's, Russell's, Vane's sad knell,
>   That pains my wounded ear.

The poem (first published by Amy Lowell in 1925) was probably written in 1814–15, well before Keats's first meeting with Hunt. It echoes Burnet's disgust at the 'darkness and disgrace' of Charles II's reign, and indicates Keats's awareness of the English republican tradition which had inspired an earlier generation of radicals during the 1790s.[10] However, John Barnard rightly discriminates between Keats's political imagination and the more palpable ideological motives of Shelley's writing. He reaffirms the traditional idea of Keats as the poet of 'realms of gold' where 'Art and Beauty' exist apart from history, and in so doing echoes the terms in which Keats's friends had replied to the political attacks of the *Quarterly* and *Blackwood's*. John Hamilton Reynolds, for example, asserted Keats's rural 'independence':

> We have the highest hopes of this young Poet. We are obscure men, it is true ... We live far from the world of letters, – out of the pale of fashionable criticism, – aloof from the atmosphere of a Court; but we are surrounded by a beautiful country, and love Poetry, which we read out of doors, as well as in. We think we see glimpses of a high mind in this young man ...[11]

The poet's 'high mind', by implication, is disengaged from the traffic of letters, criticism, and politics. Reynolds's purpose was to defend Keats by insulating him in 'beautiful country', yet from a suspicious point of view the poet's distance from 'fashionable criticism' and 'the atmosphere of a Court' might be interpreted as the measure of a threatening unorthodoxy. Certainly, John Lockhart took this view and contrived to frustrate Keats and the other 'Cockneys' by banishing them to a cultural limbo on the fringe of metropolitan civilisation, yet not quite removed to the country. This strategy of enforcing Keats's isolation from 'the world' initiated the long-standing critical consensus which agreed that historical analysis was 'irrelevant' to an understanding of Keats's poetry.[12]

The London, 'mob' had always been seen as a vulgar, turbulent mass, and it was probably this historical association with social upheaval that Lockhart wished to invoke with the 'Cockney' label. But his criticism displaced the Cockney territory from the inner city to the northerly village of Hampstead, and confined it there by coining the disagreeable adjective 'suburban'. OED dates the pejorative sense of 'suburban' to 1817, its first recorded use being in Byron's *Beppo* – completed October 1817, published February the following year: 'vulgar, dowdyish, and suburban' (stanza 66). It could also be argued that it was Lockhart's essays on 'The Cockney School of Poetry' – which also date from October 1817 – that served to fix the modern, pejorative senses of 'suburban' as part of his hostile characterisation of Hunt and Keats.

In his first essay Lockhart writes about Hunt's poetry of nature and place:

> He is the ideal of a Cockney Poet. He raves perpetually about 'green fields', 'jaunty streams', and 'o'er-arching leafiness', exactly as a Cheapside shop-keeper does about the beauties of his box on the Camberwell road. Mr Hunt is altogether unacquainted with the face of nature in her magnificent scenes; he has never seen any mountain higher than Highgate-hill, nor reclined by any stream more pastoral than the Serpentine River. But he is determined to be a poet eminently rural, and he rings the changes – till one is sick of him, on the beauties of the different 'high views' which he has taken of God and nature, in the course of some Sunday dinner parties, at which he has assisted in the neighbourhood of London.
>
> (*Blackwood's*, October 1817)

Cockney poetry, for Lockhart, expressed a Cheapside sublime in catch-phrases and jingles. Nature's 'magnificent scenes' had been reduced to familiar, local prospects; Romantic ecstasy had dwindled to table talk. A comparable duality appeared in Byron's 'Second Letter on Bowles's Strictures', which discriminated 'two sorts of Naturals; – the Lakers, who whine about Nature because they live in Cumberland; and their *under-sect* (which some one has maliciously called the "Cockney School"), who are enthusiastical for the country because they live in London'. Byron agreed with Lockhart in that he too associated Cockney imagination with the bogus sublimities of Hunt's poetic landscape: 'the wilds of

Middlesex', 'the Alps of Highgate', and 'the Nile of the New River'.[13] And although Byron was principally concerned in his 'Second Letter' to vindicate Pope as a nature poet, his essay also shows that the Cockney controversy generated a public revaluation of Wordsworth as an ornament of the literary and political establishment. The consequences of this alteration for later criticism of Wordsworth and Keats are notable. Generally speaking, modern scholars and critics lose interest in Wordsworth from this period in the poet's career. On the other hand, hostile criticism of Keats at this time has obscured the ideological force of his early poems, which contemporary readers understood as a revival of the English jacobin movement of the 1790s.

Lockhart's attacks on the Cockney School continued in 1819, with a mock-obituary of Hunt which established the terms of suburban vision for the nineteenth and twentieth centuries:

> It is much to be regretted, that the deceased bard's rural life was so limited and local. He had no other notion of that sublime expression, 'sub Dio', than merely 'out of doors'. One always thinks of Leigh Hunt, on his rural excursions to and from Hampstead, in a great-coat or spencer, clogs over his shoes, and with an umbrella in his hand. He is always talking of lanes, and styles, and hedgerows, and clumps of trees, and cows with large udders. He is the most suburban of poets. He died, as might have been prophesied, within a few hours saunter of the spot where he was born, and without having been once beyond the well-fenced meadows of his microcosm. Suppose for a moment, Leigh Hunt at sea – or on the summit of Mont Blanc! It is impossible. No. Hampstead was the only place for him ... Only hear how he revels in the morning before breakfast, when out on an adventurous constitutional stroll.
>
> Then northward what a range, – with heath and pond,
> Nature's own ground; woods that let mansions through,
> And cottaged vales with pillowy fields beyond,
> And clump of darkening pines, and prospects blue,
> And that clear path through all, where daily meet
> Cool cheeks, and brilliant eyes, and morn-elastic feet.
>
> Mr Hunt is the only poet who has considered the external world simply as the 'country,' in contradiction to the town – fields in place of squares, lanes *vice* streets, and trees as lieutenants of houses.
>
> (*Blackwood's*, October 1819)

For Lockhart, Leigh Hunt's poetry urbanised nature, creating a suburban prospect that was domesticated and familiar, known and frequented by all. Hunt's sonnets 'To Hampstead' were coy, sure enough, and were fair game for Lockhart. His criticism succeeded in making suburban life and literature synonymous with cultural vulgarity, and later generations have followed Lockhart in regarding the *'Suburban School'* of English writing (so Byron termed it) as beyond the pale of serious critical attention.[14] The 'Cockney School' essays simultaneously prejudiced understanding of Keats's political radicalism from an early date, by establishing a powerful idea of Keats as an immature poet and thinker.

John Hamilton Reynolds had recommended Keats's poetry by emphasising his youth, and other critics made similar points, so that William Rossetti, writing in 1887, could claim that Keats had been 'doomed to be the poet of youthfulness'.[15] Leigh Hunt had introduced Keats in the *Examiner*, 1 December 1816, under the heading 'Young Poets': 'youngest of them all, and just of age ... is JOHN KEATS'. Reviews of the early volumes refer to Keats as 'the young writer', 'a young poet giving himself up to his own impressions', 'an immature promise of possible excellence', 'sentiment sometimes bordering upon childishness'. For Wordsworth, too, 'young Keats' was 'a youth of [great] promise'.[16] Nevertheless, in April 1818, when *Endymion* was published, Keats was twenty-two and a half years old: hardly young any longer, and certainly not 'bordering on childhood'. Wordsworth had been not quite twenty-three when he published *An Evening Walk* and *Descriptive Sketches* in 1793. Byron was just twenty-four when *Childe Harold* was published in 1812, and the reviews certainly did not dwell upon his young manhood. So while many of Keats's first reviewers welcomed his poetry, their preoccupation with youth pointed to something that other less sympathetic critics found politically suspect: the callow sentiments of a poet 'just of age', the unformed imagination of a man 'bordering on childishness', the 'lisped' verses of a 'bardling'.

Keats himself tried to deflect hostile criticism of *Endymion* by alerting readers to his own 'great inexperience, [and] immaturity'. 'The imagination of a boy is healthy,' Keats wrote in his Preface to the poem,

> and the mature imagination of a man is healthy; but there is a space of life between, in which the soul is in a ferment, the character undecided, the way of life uncertain, the ambition thick-sighted: thence proceeds mawkishness ...

'Mawkishness' is derived from 'mawk', a maggot, and in this context may also be related to the auxiliary sense of 'maggot', meaning 'a whimsical fancy'. However, Keats associated mawkishness particularly with a transitional space of life at which the imagination is 'sickly' (not whimsical) in that it lacks character and purpose. In December 1817 Keats had identified a comparable uncertainty of self as one characteristic of imaginative genius, a quality he defined as 'negative capability'.[17] Reviews of *Poems* and *Endymion* described the poetry as 'indistinct', 'indiscriminate', and 'confused' – but they also acknowledged the disturbing force of Keats's imagination. For example, the *Edinburgh Magazine* drew attention to Keats's 'licentious brilliancy of epithet', describing his style as 'vivacious, smart, witty, changeful, sparkling, and learned – full of bright points and flashy expressions that strike and even seem to please by a sudden boldness of novelty'. Keats's poetry here is 'changeful', 'novel', a challenge to received literary values and specifically to the neo-classical ideal of stylistic and intellectual 'decorum'. Croker, in the *Quarterly*, elucidated the politics of Keats's changeful style by characterising his poetry as an anarchy of neologisms and run-on couplets, to be understood only in so far as Keats was 'a copyist of Mr Hunt'.[18] Byron, like Croker, also felt obscurely threatened by Keats's mawkish novelty. But for him Keats's imagination was less involved with 'soul ... character ... [and] way of life' and rather more absorbed by the sexual awakening of adolescence. The 'Mankin', Byron called Keats, 'that little dirty blackguard', 'this miserable Self-polluter', '[his] writing is a sort of mental masturbation', 'the *Onanism* of Poetry'. Byron's social-sexual slander of Keats betrayed his own insecurities, his need to deny Keats's imaginative presence and reaffirm his own socio-poetic virility as a member of the aristocracy.[19] The Tory journals demonstrated a comparable preoccupation with Keats's 'Mankin' sexuality, but more distinctly in the context of 'effeminate' sensibility and political subversion.

The politics of 'childish' poetry link hostile reviews of Keats with the critical reception of the earlier generation – Coleridge, Southey, and Wordsworth – in the revolutionary 1790s. Criticism of Keats's poems from 1817 was, as Jerome McGann has said, 'in many respects a repetition of the attack upon Wordsworth's programme in the Lyrical Ballads'.[20] Favourable reviews of Keats's 1817 volume were attracted by Keats's devotion to poetic simplicity. J. H. Reynolds praised the 'genuine simplicity' of the poems:

'artless' yet 'familiar with nature', with a 'natural freedom of versification'. Leigh Hunt found in the poems a 'most natural and least expressible simplicity'; the *European Magazine* and the *Eclectic Review* pointed respectively to poetry 'innocent as childishness' and 'sentiment ... bordering upon childishness'.[21]

Early reviews of *Lyrical Ballads* (1798) had been remarkably similar. The *Analytical Review* praised 'the studied simplicity which pervades many of the poems'; for the *British Critic* the poems aimed at 'simplicity and nature'; the *Monthly Review* found in the volume 'natural delineations of human passions, human characters, and human incidents' and in one poem, 'We are Seven', 'innocent and pretty infantine prattle'.[22] All these reviews responded to Wordsworth's desire to reproduce the 'essential passions of the heart' in an appropriately democratic idiom. But to a suspicious anti-Jacobinical reader poetry (and poetic theory) of this character might appear dangerously radical and levelling. The reactionary *Anti-Jacobin* magazine (20 November 1797) substantiated this political context by elaborating 'the elements of a *Jacobin* Art of Poetry' to illustrate 'the poetical, as well as the political, doctrine of the NEW SCHOOL'. The 'Ode to Jacobinism' (26 March 1798) represented the French Revolution as a 'darling child' whose 'infant mind' had been infected by Voltaire's writings. The satirical poem 'New Morality' (9 July 1798) identified a proto-Keatsian 'mawkish strain' as the residue of '*French* Philanthopy ... filtered through the dregs of Paine'. And the same poem offered another genealogy, this time of Rousseau's foster-child, 'Sweet Sensibility':

> Sweet child of sickly Fancy! – her of yore
> From her loved France Rousseau to exile bore;
> And, while midst lakes and mountains wild he ran,
> Full of himself, and shunn'd the haunts of man,
> Taught her o'er each lone vale and Alpine steep
> To lisp the story of his wrongs, and weep;
> Taught her to cherish still in either eye,
> Of tender tears a plentiful supply,
> And pour them in the brooks that babbled by; –
> – Taught by nice scales to mete her feelings strong,
> False by degrees, and exquisitely wrong; –
> – For the crushed beetle *first*, – the widow'd dove,
> And all the warbled sorrows of the grove; –
> *Next* for poor suff'ring *guilt*; – and *last* of all,
> For Parents, Friends, a King and Country's fall.[23]

For the *Anti-Jacobin* sensibility was the medium of a subversive design, in which Rousseau and Paine had collaborated to enlist sympathetic and tender feeling as motives for democratic revolution: a revolutionary mawkishness. Indeed, James Gillray's cartoon 'New Morality' (which illustrated the poem) showed the English friends of liberty (including Coleridge, Southey, Thelwall, and – as 'toad and frog' – the Charleses Lamb and Lloyd) paying homage to an icon of 'Sensibility'. Sensibility was equated with subversion by the *Anti-Jacobin* because its franchise extended beyond social and political boundaries to hitherto marginal and vulnerable sections of society – especially women and children. 'Prodigals of grief', such individuals possessed the capacity to feel ('falsely', 'wrongly', according to the *Anti-Jacobin*) for all humankind, generating a democratic vision in which established social structures had no validity.

Besides giving a revolutionary intensity to Keats's mawkishness the democratic sensibility of the 1790s foreshadowed the unselfish principle of Keats's negative capability, which identified universal sympathy as the prerogative of poetic genius. When Keats pondered negative capability in his letter of late December 1817, he concluded: 'This pursued through Volumes would perhaps take us no further than this, that with a great poet the sense of Beauty overcomes every other consideration, or rather obliterates all consideration.' Here, Keats's idea of beauty authenticated creative genius – especially Shakespeare's – but its power to 'overcome' and 'obliterate' presented a distinctly militant aesthetic appropriate to an age of revolutionary struggle. Writing sixty years previously, Edmund Burke had said that beauty 'carries with it an idea of weakness and imperfection' and argued that women accordingly took pains to counterfeit 'weakness, and even sickness' in their behaviour.[24] For Keats, though, sickliness and imperfection were overcome and assimilated by the imagination as a paradoxical source of human strength which, unlike the French Revolution, could offer a lasting renewal for the world: 'a joy for ever'. And the diction of Keats's poetry, glossed by reviewers as an 'effeminate' and childish lisp, articulated the subversive challenge of beauty to the discourse of the political and cultural establishment.

So, twenty years after the publication of 'New Morality', hostile critics of Keats identified him as the latest offspring of 'sickly Fancy': Leigh Hunt's foster-child, or 'bantling' illegitimate son, taught to 'lisp' sedition not 'mid lakes and mountains wild' but in a suburban villa at Hampstead. By insisting on Keats's 'youth' and 'effeminacy', these critics sought to dissipate a subversive potential in his poems that they recognised and acknowledged. And the extent to which later generations have been unwilling to treat Keats seriously as a political writer is one measure of the reviewers' success in enforcing earlier, Burkean standards according to which Keats's distinctive poetic voice could be identified with stereotypes of passivity and weakness, and thus accommodated to prevailing structures of society.

For Lockhart childishness was an essential characteristic of the 'Cockney School' of 'politics, versification, and morality', and of Keats in particular as 'a bardling', 'a young Cockney rhymester'. In Lockhart's essays the following profile of Cockneyism emerges: 'exquisitely bad taste', 'vulgar modes of thinking', 'low birth and low habits', 'ignorant', 'under-bred', 'suburban', 'paltry', 'morally depraved', 'indecent and immoral', 'licentious', 'obscene and traitorous'. The occasion for this sexual slander was Hunt's poem *The Story of Rimini* (1816). Lockhart's purpose was to smear Hunt's political character by depicting him as 'the man who had dared to write in the solitude of a cell ... a lewd tale of incest, adultery, and murder' (*Blackwood's*, July 1818). This strategy of sexual-political defamation was perhaps unremarkable enough: Byron used the same language in his comments on Keats.[25] Yet in Lockhart's essay on Keats, the social-sexual abuse aimed at Hunt gives place to the different, more radical sense of 'Cockneyism' associated with childishness. In Lockhart's fourth 'Cockney School' essay the political charge of 'Cockneyism' had less to do with Keats's social circumstances as a Londoner like Hunt than with Lockhart's recognition of the subversive function of Keatsian 'childishness'. The poet is described as a 'young man', 'Mr John', 'so young a person', 'the wavering apprentice', one of 'the rising brood of Cockneys', 'Johnny Keats', 'our youthful poet', a 'flimsy stripling', 'Johnny', 'a boy of pretty abilities', 'a young Cockney rhymester' (*Blackwood's*, August 1818). But what precisely did Lockhart intend, beyond simple abuse, by disparaging Keats as a young *Cockney* rhymester? In the OED, the four primary senses of 'Cockney' are glossed as follows:

> *Cockney*: egg; lit. 'cocks' egg;'
> 1. An egg ... hen's egg ... one of the small or misshapen eggs occasionally laid by fowls ... 2. 'A child that sucketh long', 'a nestlecock', 'a mother's darling' ... 'a child tenderly brought up' hence, a

squeamish or effeminate fellow, 'a milksop'. 3. A derisive appellation for a townsman, as the type of effeminacy in contrast to the hardier inhabitants of the country. 4. One born in the city of London ...

For Lockhart Keats is a Cockney not merely because he is supposedly a young man, and an admirer of Leigh Hunt. The charge is more specific: Cockney Keats is an unweaned boy-child, unwilling to 'bid farewell' to the joys of early sensual experience at his mother's breast. His vulnerable 'tenderness' enervates the discourse of masculine authority, which Lockhart now associates with those writers who had formerly appeared in the Jacobin rabble of 'New Morality'. In his first essay on the Cockney School (*Blackwood's*, October 1817), Lockhart admires the one-time republican William Wordsworth as a figure of austere 'patriarchal simplicity'. Charles Lamb, Gillray's subversive toad or frog, is happily re-embodied by Lockhart in his last Cockney School essay as 'that simple-minded man of genius' (*Blackwood's*, October 1819). Keats, meanwhile, has become potentially more dangerous than this natural father Leigh Hunt, as the 'new brood' of a treacherous sensibility that had formerly been associated with the French Revolution.

As the political unrest of the post-Waterloo years grew more distant, or moved through different channels, the unsettling potential of Keats and Hunt (which had seemed alarming in an age of revolutions) gradually dispersed. During the nineteenth century both writers were accommodated by sustaining the stereotypes of childishness and effeminacy established by Lockhart and others after 1817. In this manner, Hunt and Keats were publicly depoliticised, and disengaged from the ideological context which had so powerfully informed their creativity.

Lockhart's caricature in *Blackwood's* transformed Hunt into a figure of fun. Thirty-five years later Hunt was no longer a force in political affairs, although still very much alive. In 1853 he reappeared as the childish, disarming Harold Skimpole in *Bleak House*:

> 'I don't mean literally a child,' pursued Mr Jarndyce; 'not a child in years. He is grown up – he is at least as old as I am – but in simplicity, and freshness, and enthusiasm, and a fine guileless inaptitude for all worldly affairs, he is a perfect child.'
>
> (ch. 6)

Hunt (once jailed for a libel on the Prince Regent) was doomed by Dickens to eternal childishness, and Keats's reputation developed in a similar manner during the nineteenth century. Once his mawkish sensibility no longer seemed likely to promote subversion, Keats survived as the unworldly poet of 'delicate and fragile' genius celebrated by Shelley in *Adonais*. According to William Howitt in 1847: 'On this world and its concerns he could take no hold, and they could take none on him'; for David Macbeth Moir, in 1851: 'all ... was the result of imaginative wealth and youthful inexperience'; the *Encyclopaedia Britannica* of 1857 (Alexander Smith) thought that 'he still wrote in a style of babyish effeminacy ... [and] of a ... nauseous sweetness'. These judgements were echoed by weightier critics: David Masson wrote of 'an intellectual invalid, ... a poor youth too conscious of "the endeavour of the present breath", watching incessantly his own morbid symptoms' (1860); Algernon Swinburne of 'a vapid and effeminate rhymester in the sickly stage of whelphood [who] lived long enough only to give promise of being a man' (1886). Gerard Manley Hopkins thought Keats 'one of the beginners of the Romantic movement, with all the extravagance and ignorance of his youth ... His contemporaries, as Wordsworth, Byron, Shelley, and even Leigh Hunt, right or wrong, still concerned themselves with great causes, as liberty and religion; but he lived in mythology and fairyland the life of a dreamer' (1887–8). Matthew Arnold commented that Keats was 'let and hindered with a short term and imperfect experience, – "young" as he says of himself' (1880, 1886).[26]

The feminising of Keats during the nineteenth century, apparent in some of these criticisms, has recently been analysed in detail by Susan Wolfson.[27] She shows how during his period Keats was 'deemed to have particular appeal to women'; his poetry was marketed in particular 'to female audiences'. This was one way of assimilating Keats's threat to prevailing codes of manliness, a continuation of Lockhart's politically-motivated criticism in *Blackwood's*. This prolonged feminising of Keats helps one to make sense of the otherwise laughable masculine over-compensation in David Masson's Sweeney-Keats: 'a slack, slouching youth, with a thick torso, a deep grave voice, and no fixed principles [who] kept aloof from opinion, doctrine, controversy, as by a natural instinct.'[28]

In all of these nineteenth-century responses to Keats, the revolutionary potential of his 'style of babyish effeminacy' has been forgotten. Indeed, Keats survived as the Romantic poet widely believed to have had no interest in politics and the events of contemporary history until quite recently. Recovering the historical and ideological contexts in which Lockhart could detect Keats's poems' lisping sedition reveals that his poetry was more thoroughly (and from some perspectives, dangerously) politicised than has been allowed hitherto. Furthermore, Keats's theories of genius, negative capability, and ideal beauty (so often regarded as aesthetic 'escapism') can be seen as developments of a democratic sensibility formerly identified with Jacobin revolution. In retrospect, Lockhart's campaign to destroy Keats because his poetry had a disturbing potency for his first readers was only too successful. Byron was closer to the mark than he knew, when he wrote in *Don Juan* that Keats had been 'snuffed out by an article'.

From *Essays in Criticism*, 42 (1992), 36–55.

NOTES

[Nicholas Roe's essay is an historicist account of the ways in which Keats's politics have been obscured by the class- and gender-based criticisms of his contemporaries who sought to categorise his poetry as both suburban and mawkish, and who identified Keats himself as lower class and effeminate. Roe is particularly concerned with the critical reception of Keats's substantial poetic romance *Endymion* (1818) and his first collection of *Poems* (1817). In reclaiming the ostensibly non-political Keats for the left, Roe demonstrates how the stylistic liberties the poet took in writing his verse implied both a belief in freedom and an opposition to the 'present Ministers'. It was this seditious force of his writing that roused the critics' hostility. As in his earlier work *Wordsworth and Coleridge: The Radical Years* (1988), Roe argues that the Romantic Imagination was originally constituted out of dissenting political commitment. This essay is reprinted complete; there are, however, several minor revisions and corrections that have been added at the request of the author. Ed.]

1. See, *The Poems of John Keats*, ed. Miriam Allott (London and New York, 1970), p. 206fn.

2. *The British Critic* (June 1818) in *Keats. The Critical Heritage*, ed. G. M. Matthews (London, 1971), p. 94.

3. 'Cockney School of Poetry', No. IV, *Blackwood's Magazine* (August 1818), p. 524. Further references to the 'Cockney School' essays appear in the text.

4. John Keats, *Endymion. A Poetic Romance* (London, 1818), references hereafter to this edition.

5. John Keats, *Poems* (London, 1817), p. 42. Subsequent quotations from poems in this volume are to this edition. See also Vincent

Newey's analysis of Keats's 'declared political interests' in '"Alternate uproar and sad peace": Keats, Politics, and the Idea of Revolution', *MHRA Yearbook of English Studies*, ed. J. R. Watson, 19 (1989), pp. 267–8.

6. *The Champion* (9 March 1817) and the *European Magazine* (May 1817), in *Keats. The Critical Heritage*, pp. 49, 52. For the politics of Keats's style, see also William Keach, 'Cockney Couplets: Keats and the Politics of Style', *Studies in Romanticism, 25* (1986), 182–96.

7. *Spenser. Poetical Works*, ed. J. C. Smith and E. de Selincourt (Oxford, 1912).

8. Charles Cowden Clarke, 'Recollections of John Keats', *The Gentleman's Magazine*, new series, XII (January–June 1874), p. 180.

9. *Keats. The Critical Heritage*, p. 15.

10. *John Keats. A New Selection*, ed. John Barnard (Harmondsworth, 1988), p. 1, and *Bishop Burnet's History of His Own Time*, 2 vols (London 1724–34), I, 826.

11. *Alfred, West of England Journal and General Advertiser* (October 1985), p. 26. *Keats. The Critical Heritage*, p. 26.

12. See Jerome McGann, 'Keats and Historical Method' in *The Beauty of Inflections. Literary Investigations in Historical Method and Theory* (Oxford, 1985), p. 26.

13. 'Observations upon "Observations". A Second Letter to John Murray Esq. on the Rev. W. L. Bowles Strictures on the Life and Writings of Pope', in *The Works of Lord Byron*, 17 vols (London 1832–3), VI, 410, 412.

14. Byron to John Murray, 4 August 1821, *Byron's Letters and Journals*, ed. Leslie A. Marchand, 12 vols (Cambridge, MA, 1973–82), VIII, 166.

15. See William M. Rossetti, *Life of John Keats* (London, 1887), p. 209.

16. For Hunt on Keats see *Keats. The Critical Heritage*, p. 42. Other early reviews noticing Keats's youth are quoted from *The Examiner* (1 June 1817) and *The Eclectic Review* (September 1817), *Keats. The Critical Heritage*, pp. 55, 67. For Wordsworth on Keats see *The Letters of William and Dorothy Wordsworth*, ed. E. de Selincourt, 2nd edn, *The Middle Years, Part II 1812–1820*, rev. M. Moorman and A. G. Hill (Oxford, 1970), pp. 360, 578.

17. See Keats's letter to George and Tom Keats, 21 27 (?) December 1817, in *Letters of John Keats*, ed. Robert Gittings (Oxford, 1970), p. 43. Subsequent references to Keats's letters are to this edition.

18. *Edinburgh Magazine, and Literary Miscellany* (October 1817), *Keats. The Critical Heritage*, pp. 71–4, *Quarterly Review* (September 1818), *Keats. The Critical Heritage*, pp. 110–14.

19. For Byron on Keats, see *Byron's Letters and Journals*, VII, 202, 217, 225, 229, and Marjorie Levinson, *Keats's Life of Allegory. The Origins of a Style* (Oxford, 1988), pp. 15–19.

20. McGann, *The Beauty of Inflections*, p. 30.

21. *The Champion* (9 March 1817), *The Examiner* (1 June 1817); *European Magazine* (May 1817); *Eclectic Review* (September 1817), *Keats. The Critical Heritage*, pp. 16, 59, 53, 67.

22. The reviews are reproduced in *Lyrical Ballads*, ed. R. L. Brett and A. R. Jones (London and New York, 1963), pp. 319–23.

23. *The Poetry of the Anti-Jacobin* (6th edn, 1828). For the politics of childish poetry in the 1790s, see David Fairer, 'Baby Language and Revolution: the Early Poetry of Charles Lloyd and Charles Lamb', *The Charles Lamb Bulletin* (April 1991), 33–52.

24. Edmund Burke, *A Philosophical Enquiry into the Origin of Our Ideas of the Sublime and the Beautiful* (London, 1757), p. 91.

25. The taint of sexual corruption and incest had also lurked in a spy's report about those 'French people' William and Dorothy Wordsworth at Alfoxden in 1797: 'the master of the House has no wife with him, but only a woman who passes for his Sister', Dr Daniel Lysons to the Duke of Portland, 11 August 1797, in Nicholas Roe, *Wordsworth and Coleridge. The Radical Years* (Oxford, 1988), p. 248.

26. See *Keats. The Critical Heritage*, pp. 311, 351, 356, 371. See also A. C. Swinburne, *Miscellanies* (London, 1886), pp. 211, 213; G. M. Hopkins to Coventry Patmore, 20, 24 October 1887 and 6 May 1888 in *G. M. Hopkins, Selected Prose*, ed. G. Roberts (Oxford, 1980), pp. 154, 159; Matthew Arnold, 'John Keats', first published in 1880, reprinted in *Essays in Criticism, Second Series* (London, 1888) quoted from *The Complete Prose Works of Matthew Arnold*, ed. R. H. Super (11 vols, Ann Arbor, 1960–77), IX, 214.

27. See Susan J. Wolfson, 'Feminising Keats', in *Critical Essays on John Keats*, ed. Hermione de Almeida (Boston, 1990), pp. 317–56. [Reprinted in this volume – see previous essay. Ed.]

28. *Keats. The Critical Heritage*, pp. 373–4.

6

Keats in the Museum: Between Aesthetics and History – 'Ode on a Grecian Urn'

A. W. PHINNEY

Among the many readers of 'Ode on a Grecian Urn', Cleanth Brooks was the first to consider in any detail the poem's portrayal of the urn as a historian. Yet, as the subtitle of his essay – 'History without Footnotes' – suggests, Brooks ultimately emphasises the urn's universality, rather than its historical particularity. As a 'Sylvan historian' the urn tells only tales, rather than 'formal history', and it 'certainly supplies no names and dates'. Indeed, in an especially paradoxical formulation, Brooks asserts that the urn's 'history is beyond time, outside time'. But this apparent lack of historical content is not a defect in his eyes, for the 'autonomous world' of the urn 'comes to have a richer and more important history than that of actual cities'.[1]

Brooks's own attitude concerning the relation between history and criticism is evident here. Just as the urn is said to ignore 'names, dates, and special circumstances' (p. 164), so Brooks reads the poem without reference to its historical context. As he argues in a later chapter of *The Well Wrought Urn*, 'to treat the poems discussed primarily as poems is a proper emphasis, and very much worth doing. For we have gone to school to the anthropologists and the cultural historians assiduously, and we have learned their lesson almost too well' (p. 215). If there is to be a discipline that is a specifically *literary* criticism, rather than merely a branch of some other discipline such as history or sociology or anthropology, then one must be able to define an aesthetic structure that remains essentially the same over time, a 'formal pattern' that 'seems to carry over from poem to poem' and that allows us 'to approach a poem by Donne in the same general terms through which we approach a poem by Keats' (p. 218). Like the urn, poetry must embody certain qualities that transcend history.[2]

From another perspective, then, we might say that both 'Ode on a Grecian Urn' and Brooks's reading of it participate in the same ideological illusion. For such faith in the transhistorical nature of art can be shown to be itself historically conditioned. By the Romantic period, art has become an ornamental commodity whose value must be justified in a utilitarian society. The poet and the critic affirm the timeless iconicity of art precisely because art has lost its immediate relevance to the history of its time. 'The relative dissociation of the work of art from the praxis of life in bourgeois society thus becomes transformed into the (erroneous) idea that the work of art is totally independent of society.'[3] Christopher Caudwell's *Illusion and Reality* offers a good example of how this analysis has been applied to Keats:

> Keats is the first great poet to feel the strain of the poet's position in this stage of the bourgeois illusion, as producer for the free market.... The poet now escapes upon the 'rapid wings of poesy' to a world of romance, beauty and sensuous life separate from the poor, harsh, real world of everyday life, which it sweetens and by its own loveliness silently condemns.... [This world] is the golden-gated upper world of Hyperion, the word-painted lands of the nightingale, of the Grecian urn, of Baiae's isle. This other world is defiantly counterposed to the real world.
>
> 'Beauty is truth, truth beauty' – that is all
> Ye know on earth, and all ye need to know.
>
> The poet now begins to show the marks of commodity production....
> The poem has become already an end in itself.[4]

By reframing the poem in this way we would not falsify Brooks's reading, but we would be showing that the poem's apparent affirmations about the relations between history and art, and the reiteration of these views in the New Criticism, are only instances of Romantic ideology. As Jerome McGann has argued. 'The idea that poetry, or even consciousness, can set one free of the ruins of history and culture is the grand illusion of every Romantic poet', an illusion that has continued to dominate subsequent criticism of the Romantics.[5]

Of course many scholars have defended Keats against this kind of critique by arguing that the poet himself recognised the impossibility, and, indeed, the undesirability, of escaping from the world of process, and that 'Grecian Urn' implies as much.[6] But I think we have yet to explore the extent to which the ode anticipates the very confrontation that has emerged in the history of its reading.[7] Keats's poem is not just concerned with the tensions between art and life; it also dramatises the conflicting claims of aesthetic criticism and historical critique in the understanding of a work of art. As I will be trying to show, the ode suggests that neither mode of understanding is sufficient by itself, and that both necessarily intermingle in any interpretive act. While neither the work of art nor its interpreter can escape history, one's interpretation of the work must, for this very reason, partake of the nature of an aesthetic fiction.

Before turning directly to the ode, however, I would like to examine some of the historical context that haunts about *its* shape. For as we shall see, the poem's dramatisation of the conflict between aesthetics and history is not solely a product of Keats's imaginative genius but also a reflection of the contradictions inherent both in the age's approach to ancient art and in Keats's own contemporary position as an artist.

The 'Ode on a Grecian Urn' was a child of the vogue for Greek art ushered in by Winckelmann in the latter half of the eighteenth century. Popularised in England by Fuseli's translation of *Reflections on the Painting and Sculpture of the Greeks* (1765), Winckelmann's idealised vision of Greek culture quickly became a commonplace of contemporary art criticism. While we cannot be sure that Keats actually read Winckelmann, it seems probable that he would have heard of the great German art critic from Haydon, since Haydon had been a student of Fuseli and owned a copy of the *Reflections*.[8] Whether directly or indirectly, Keats certainly seems to have been inspired by Winckelmann's apotheosis of antiquity, so much so that he in turn imparted the same enthusiasm to others. Joseph Severn, for instance, fondly recalled Keats's discourses about 'the Greek spirit, – the Religion of the Beautiful, the Religion of

Joy, as he used to call it': 'Keats ... made me in love with the real living Spirit of the past. He was the first to point out to me how essentially modern that Spirit is: "It's an immortal youth", he would say, "just as there is no *Now* or *Then* for the Holy Ghost".'[9]

Keats's personification of 'the real living Spirit of the past' as 'an immortal youth' and the timeless, idyllic scene of stanzas 2 and 3 of 'Grecian Urn' both recall Winckelmann's own enraptured description of the Apollo Belvedere: 'Of all the works that escaped the havock of time, the statue of *Apollo* in *Belvedere*, is the sublimest idea of art.... [A]n eternal spring, like that of *Elysium*, blends the grandeur of man with the charms of youth.... [H]ere sick decay, and human flaws swell not, blood palpitates not here.... [P]eace dwells in blest tranquillity, and the smiles that beam in his eye seem to invite the love-sick muses.'[10] Like the speaker of 'Grecian Urn', Winckelmann finds in Greek art a world of unchanging beauty, free from the defects of poor humanity. But in order to maintain this vision, he must exclude the world of historical process as something that is outside the work. Contemplating the Apollo Belvedere, Winckelmann sees the images not of a particular place in time but of eternity. There is 'no *Now* or *Then*', as Keats says. Time is only what the work escapes.

This kind of dehistoricising of the artwork exemplifies what Hans-Georg Gadamer calls 'aesthetic differentiation' – 'disregarding everything in which a work is rooted (its original context of life, and the religious or secular function which gave it its significance)' so that 'it becomes visible as the "pure work of art"'.[11] For Gadamer, this aesthetic attitude is what produced such cultural phenomena as 'the "universal library" in the sphere of literature, the museum, the theatre, the concert hall, etc.,' which all juxtapose the accumulated artifacts of the past in a kind of artificial 'simultaneity' (*Truth and Method*, p. 78). One might prefer to reverse cause and effect in Gadamer's account, arguing instead that such institutions as the museum produced 'aesthetic differentiation'. As André Malraux suggests, 'Museums have imposed on the spectator a wholly new attitude towards the work of art. For they have tended to estrange the works they bring together from their original functions and to transform even portraits into "pictures".'[12] I mention this institutional context because it too would have played a role in Keats's perception of antiquity. Unlike Winckelmann, who had the opportunity to visit the archaeological sites of Pompeii and Herculaneum, Keats knew antique art only through books, such as the *Musée Napoléon*, and, most especially, through frequent visits to the British Museum.[13] Indeed, we might say that it was the museum that made possible Keats's treatment of the urn as an artistic symbol. By freeing the work from its original context, the museum transformed it into an objet d'art, to be contemplated in and of itself. Thus emptied of its original historical content, it could become the vehicle of the poet's own speculations about art.

Yet neither Keats nor his age uniformly viewed antique art from an historical perspective.[14] While Keats's urn has been cut off from the past, stanzas 1 and 4 of the ode nevertheless bear witness to an attempt to recover that past. Aesthetic consciousness was never fully disengaged from the consciousness of history. Indeed, the very claims made by Winckelmann for the superiority of Greek art involved historical arguments (see Gadamer, p. 176). In order to justify his assertions, Winckelmann offered an account of the world that produced that art, attributing the refinement of Greek taste not only to climate but also to cultural factors such as mythology, political systems, sports, and even clothing. Thus Winckelmann acknowledged the extent to which art is a social production, rooted in a localised historical matrix, and in doing so he implicitly raised the question of whether ancient artistic practice could be imitated by the moderns. This ideal taste, he notes, 'was not only original among the Greeks, but seemed also quite peculiar to their country: it seldom went abroad without loss'.[15] Paradoxically, Winckelmann's attempt to define an eternally valid aesthetic ideal was contradicted by the very historical claims that undergird his argument.

The renewed interest in Greek art that was Winckelmann's legacy to European collectors and artists, and which spurred on efforts to retrieve classical artworks and place them in museums, was thus already fissured by this conflict between historicism and aestheticism. ... A specific example of this tension between historicism and aestheticism in contemporary discussions of classical art – an example with which Keats would have been intimately familiar – can be found in the debate over the value and authenticity of the Elgin marbles. Championed by Haydon, Lord Elgin's collection was disparaged by the respected and influential antiquarian Richard Payne Knight. Payne Knight questioned the originality and significance of the marbles primarily on historical grounds. 'You have lost your labour', he initially told Lord Elgin; 'your marbles are overrated; they are not Greek, they are Roman of the time of Hadrian.'[16] Although Payne Knight later conceded that the marbles were indeed classical Greek works, he still maintained that they were 'merely architectural sculptures' not intended for close scrutiny, and that they had probably been executed only by 'workmen scarcely ranked among artists', rather than by Phidias himself.[17]

While these strictures may have been partially motivated by petty jealousy, they were also founded on Payne Knight's belief that the unbridled enthusiasm of his contemporaries for antique art too often failed to take into account the original situation in which that art was produced. In his *Analytical Inquiry into the Principles of Taste*, for instance, he ridiculed the imitations of Greek temples that had recently become such ubiquitous ornaments in English country gardens:

> In the rich lawns and shrubberies of England ..., they lose all that power to please which they so eminently possess on the barren hills of Agrigentum and Segesta, or the naked plains of Pœstum and Athens.... the scenery, in which they sprang; and in which the mind, therefore, contemplates them connected and associated with number-less interesting circumstances, both local and historical – both physical and moral, upon which it delights to dwell. In our parks and gardens, on the contrary, they stand wholly unconnected with all that surrounds them – mere unmeaning excrescences. ...[18]

Though a collector of antiquities himself, Payne Knight believed that the attempt to re-create the art of the past in the world of the present was bound to fail. While one might succeed in reproducing the art object itself, one could never bring back the cultural situation that had given purpose and meaning to the original work.

For Haydon, by contrast, imitation was the only true method of ascertaining the authenticity and greatness of the Elgin marbles. Mere historical conjecture carried little weight in a case of aesthetic judgement. ... Although Haydon was a historical painter, he thought of his art first and foremost as the imitation of nature. Rather than disputing Knight's claims on historical grounds, therefore, Haydon displaced the field of debate to the realm of artistic practice. For him, the value of the marbles was evident from their anatomical realism, which he had discovered through the process of copying the marbles themselves: 'Let him who doubts [this truth], study them, as I have done, for eight years daily, and he will doubt it no longer.'[19]

As we can see, then, the debate between Payne Knight and Haydon raised a number of issues already implicit in Winckelmann's appreciation of Greek art. How can one best understand and judge the art of the past, through an internal aesthetic analysis, or through historical contextualisation? Can one effectively imitate antique art in the modern world, or is such art inextricably bound up with its historical origin?

Keats's sonnet 'On Seeing the Elgin Marbles', written shortly after his visit to the British Museum with Haydon in March 1817, shows the young poet wrestling with these questions, trying to mediate between a historical and an aesthetic approach. Initially, the sonnet confronts the creative issue. While Keats adopts Winckelmann's view of Greek art as ideal, that ideal is also posited as unattainable, crushing the poet with the recognition of his own inadequacy. Nevertheless the sonnet makes claims for a certain pathetic sublimity in this tension between the poet's personal and historical limitations and the grandeur of the mythological world suggested by the marbles. As a modern poet, Keats cannot relive the past, but as an interpreter he can at least imagine the past and derive pleasure from the awareness of his difference from it:

> Yet 'tis a gentle luxury to weep
> That I have not the cloudy winds to keep
> Fresh for the opening of the morning's eye.[20]
> (ll. 6–8)

Indeed, Keats suggests that the power of the marbles derives not simply from their timeless beauty but from the conjunction of that beauty with history:

> Such dim-conceived glories of the brain
> Bring round the heart an undescribable feud;
> So do these wonders a most dizzy pain,
> That mingles Grecian grandeur with the rude
> Wasting of old time – with a billowy main –
> A sun – a shadow of a magnitude.
> (ll. 9–14)

If on one hand the marbles represent the eternal idea of 'Grecian grandeur' – and here the sonnet uses the English word employed by Fuseli to translate Winckelmann's 'Größe' – on the other hand Keats seems to be equally affected by the fact that the marbles belong to a world that is chronologically and geographically distant, that they bear the marks not only of their culture but of the intervening centuries. Here Keats seems to be trying to synthesise the alternative positions of Haydon and Payne Knight. To see the marbles, for Keats, is not just to see their beauty but to become aware of their history – both of the world that created them ('A sun') and of their history since (their transport by Elgin on the 'billowy main') – and finally of the fact of history itself, the 'Wasting of old time' that reduces greatness to 'a shadow of a magnitude'. 'On Seeing the Elgin Marbles' thus terminates in a series of increasingly elliptical phrases that imitate the fragmented marbles themselves in their power of suggestion. ... Part of their fascination for Keats may have come from the possibility that, in addition to conjuring up thoughts of 'Grecian grandeur' and 'the rude wasting of old time', the marbles called to mind the situation of his own art. As Gadamer has suggested, there is a similarity between the isolation of the artwork as an aesthetic object in the museum and the alienation of the artist in modern society. While 'the work loses its place and the world to which it belongs insofar as it belongs to aesthetic consciousness', this estrangement 'is paralleled by the artist also losing his place in the world' (Gadamer, p. 78).

We can trace this parallel quite precisely in the case of Keats, since he explicitly countered his failure to find a large contemporary public by placing his hopes in poetic immortality. Just as antique art could supposedly be rescued from the ruins of history by putting it in the museum and considering it in purely aesthetic terms, so Keats sought to rescue himself from his own contemporaries by projecting himself into the canon of great writers, the literary equivalent of the museum. Referring to the attacks on *Endymion*, for instance, he responds with astonishing self-assurance: 'This is a mere matter of the moment – I think I shall be among the English Poets after my death.'[21] Instead of writing merely for the moment, Keats sees himself as writing for all time.

But given the acuteness of his own historical consciousness, the notion of writing for the future could not have been uniformly reassuring to Keats.[22] As can be seen from his comments in the famous letter to Reynolds comparing Milton and Wordsworth, Keats clearly believed that poetry is not strictly a product of individual genius. All poetry, he recognised, is also conditioned by its historical moment. ...

A confrontation with the art of the past, then, would have been important to Keats because it also represented a confrontation with the destiny that he had willed for himself. ...

In her penetrating study of Keats's odes, Helen Vendler divides 'Ode on a Grecian Urn' into three movements, which she characterises as mimetic, archetypal, and aesthetic moments in the speaker's contemplation of the urn. While I agree with this tripartite division of the poem, I would prefer to label these movements as historicist, aesthetic, and hermeneutic.[23] The structure of the ode is that of a dialectical argument, in which the conflicting claims of history and aesthetics are dramatised and finally sublated into a third attitude – the hermeneutic – that includes them both as necessary but partial moments in the understanding of the artwork. But while the hermeneutic moment in this sense can be seen as the conclusion of a dialectical movement, this does not imply, as we shall see, that the meaning of the urn or the poem can be reduced to an essential formula.[24]

I think we can characterise the speaker's encounter with the urn in the first stanza as an attempt to understand the urn in historical terms, to see it as the expression of a foreign culture. The speaker approaches the urn as an antiquarian, like Payne Knight. From the outset, the urn is located in the general medium of time, its foster-parent, and is apostrophised as an historian. Understanding the urn historically is not an easy task, however, because of the temporal distance that separates the poem's speaker from the world of the urn's making. ... Interpretation is further complicated by the fact that the urn does not offer a direct account of history; it represents not its own time but the ideal time of pastoral. The locales of Tempe and Arcady were indeed real places in ancient Greece, but much more importantly they were the settings of romance. Thus the speaker realises that what he is inquiring into is a matter of 'legend', not fact, and that the urn is a 'Sylvan historian'. To call this historian 'Sylvan', however, is not necessarily to relinquish the historical question so quickly as Brooks implies when he says that the urn's histories 'may be characterised as "tales" – not formal history at all' (*Well Wrought Urn*, p. 155). For the ability to tell such tales and believe in them was for Keats part of an ideological moment. Already in 'Sleep and Poetry', he had characterised the 'lovely tale of human life' in the realm 'Of Flora, and old Pan' as a stage to be outgrown in favour of more realistic narratives of 'the agonies, the strife / Of human hearts' (ll. 110, 102, 124–5). One of Keats's persistent themes is the belatedness of the modern poet, who, like Psyche, is born 'too late for antique vows, / Too, too late for the fond believing lyre, / When holy were the haunted forest boughs' ('Ode to Psyche', ll. 36–8).[25] To say that the urn can 'thus express / A flowery tale more sweetly than our rhyme', then, is not only to make a statement about the relative advantages of the visual as opposed to the verbal arts but to fix a historical difference between the world that could make the urn and Keats's own, since Keats could not in conscience tell a 'flowery tale' sweetly, that is, without the ironies and dashes of realism that he adds to 'Isabella' and 'The Eve of St. Agnes'. The poem's first stanza thus situates the urn in the world of the past, and performs a kind of sympathetic ideological critique, similar to the critique of Milton in the letter to Reynolds cited above.

In spite of this historical distance, however, the urn can still exercise an erotic charm. The breathless questions that conclude the first stanza – 'What men or gods are these? What maidens loth? / What mad pursuit? What struggle to escape? /What pipes and timbrels? What wild ecstasy?' – suggest a mounting sexual tension that matches the ecstasy represented on the urn. Thus the apparently antiquarian curiosity of the speaker is transformed into a passionate and self-involved examination. ...

How is it that an artifact from a historically remote era can still affect us? The question that faces Keats here is essentially that later posed by Marx: 'The difficulty lies not in understanding that the Greek arts and epic are bound up with certain forms of social development. The difficulty is that they still afford us artistic pleasure and that in a certain respect they count as a norm and as an unattainable model.'[26] Stanzas 2 and 3 of the ode suggest two answers to this problem. One answer can be found in the subject matter itself. While cultures change, Keats seems to be saying, there remain certain passions, such as love and desire, that are so basic to the human condition that their portrayal will always maintain an immediate hold upon our imagination. But these two stanzas also seem to enact a second, more sophisticated explanation for the continuing appeal of the aesthetic work. 'Heard melodies are sweet, but those unheard / Are sweeter' focuses our attention on the play between the expressed and and unexpressed in the work of art, a form of play that necessarily involves the audience. As E. H. Gombrich reminds us, all art must involve a form of symbolisation of the represented, since the work of art cannot simply be what it represents. This process of symbolisation endows the work with a certain openness, which in turn requires various forms of concretisation by the audience. 'Any picture, by its very nature', Gombrich notes, 'remains an appeal to the visual imagination; it must be supplemented in order to be understood.'[27] Keats's own example of this process extends beyond the realm of the merely visual, calling into play the auditory imagination, but the point is similar. The melodies of the piper on the urn are sweeter than those actually heard because they address not the 'sensual ear' but the 'spirit'; that is, they exist only in a potential form that allows the imagination a certain freedom in the process of actualising them.

In this sense, it becomes the task of the audience to perform the work of art. The urn, as [W. J.] Bate observes, 'remains ready to come alive ... as music on the printed page becomes alive when the inked notes are scanned and interpreted by some later imagination'.[28] Significantly, whereas the first stanza records a series of questions, suggesting that the urn presents an independent world to be interrogated by the speaker, the imperatives of the second stanza – 'play on', 'Pipe to the spirit', 'do not grieve' – now imply that it is the speaker who gives life to the scene before him, putting it in play through his directions.[29] Indeed, we might even venture to say that all of the statements in stanzas 2 and 3 seem to carry this imperative overtone, telling the figures on the urn what they can and will do. Thus the speaker can endow the urn's representations with a life of their own, speculating on the joys and frustrations of the fair youth, and attributing emotions even to the trees that shelter the lovers. Keats's point here, I take it, is that our interest in art often involves the pathetic fallacy, projecting our own feelings onto inanimate objects. As the speaker thus enacts in his imagination the drama portrayed on the urn, it seems to be lifted out of the past into the present; it seems to be happening 'now'. This feeling of contemporaneous performance dissolves the historical distance that separates the speaker from the urn and allows him to identify with it. Furthermore, this 'now' seems to be infinitely repeatable, as is suggested by the echoing repetitions in these two stanzas of 'nor ever', 'never', and 'for ever', 'lover' and 'love', and 'happy'. Out of such repetition the speaker conjures an image of eternal bliss, a perpetually postponed climax that cannot cloy. Thus the urn makes it possible for the speaker to fantasise about a world without flux, not only because it is in the nature of visual art to deny temporality but because the performability of the aesthetic object allows him to repeat the same scenario over and over again. And in so far as the urn allows these fantasies, catering to recurrent human desire, it appears itself to have transcended time and annihilated history.

But Keats also implies that this kind of identification with the urn's representations and the resulting belief in the possibility of transcending history may depend upon a certain bad faith. In the end the speaker's echoing incantations begin to ring hollow; as every schoolchild knows, the same word repeated too many times begins to lose all meaning. Infinite repetition may only lead to numbness. Interleaved among the 'love', there is the undertone of 'leave', 'leaves', 'leaves', implying that departures are inevitable.[30] As Brooks points out (*Well Wrought Urn*, p. 159), to say that the love depicted on the urn is 'far above' 'All breathing human passion' is not only to indicate its ideal incorporeality but also to suggest that it is altogether outside the realm of what is recognisably human. And, by the same token, to say that the urn transcends history because it is art, and art represents the eternal essences of human being, is precisely to abstract art from any real human context.

As if to insist on these points, Keats turns in stanza 4 to a scene that cannot be conceived as universal – a sacrificial procession. Not only does this procession hint at a darker side of life concealed by the picture of young love given in stanzas 2 and 3, it also returns the urn to an alien, 'mysterious' world of ritual, reminding us again that the culture represented by the urn is foreign to us, and that the urn is a historical artifact. Whereas in the previous two stanzas the speaker's apostrophes insist on the urn's capacity to escape time, here the questions reassert a temporal modality, insisting on ends and beginnings – 'To what green altar?' and from 'What little town?'

But is the temporality now that of fiction or that of history? On one hand, these questions seek to extend the story that is implied by the scene of sacrificial procession. On the other hand, they are also archaeological questions, the kind that might be asked by someone trying to locate the historical and geographical origin of the urn. Here the poem seems to blur the line between fiction and history, insisting on the extent to which both rely on the elaboration of a narrative schema. The extension of that narrative inevitably requires the speaker to move beyond the boundaries of representation, imagining a town and an altar that are not actually pictured on the urn. Whether we consider the urn as historical artifact or as fictional representation, then, it needs someone to tell its story. By itself it is not self-complete and self-explanatory; it is the fragment of a world that can only be reconstructed through the work of an interpreter. As many commentators have noted, the urn might be classed among what Keats called 'Things semireal ... which require a greeting of the Spirit to make them wholly exist' (*Keats's Letters*, I, 243). While on one hand the kind of ahistorical self-projection into the urn's representations undertaken by the speaker in stanzas 2 and 3 can be seen as an act of bad faith, on the other hand it would be an illusion to believe that historical inquiry can somehow proceed without the aid of interpretive imagination.[31] As Keats observed in one of his letters, '[N]o Man can live but in one society at a time – his enjoyment in the different states of human society must depend upon the Powers of his Mind – that is you can imagine a roman triumph, or an olympic game as well as I can' (*Keats's Letters*, II, 18). History is a real and binding force in human affairs, but historical understanding must also always be a form of storytelling, since, from our own standpoint in history, we can only know the past through a kind of imaginative projection.

The haunting power of the speaker's questions in stanza 4 results from this attempt to recover the distant past as a fictive presence. The world of the urn is imagined as if its drama were unfolding in an ahistorical 'now' – 'this pious morn'. Yet at the same time the stanza insists upon the gulf of silence that separates the speaker from that world, just as the speaker's return to the questioning attitude of the first stanza seems to acknowledge that this world can never be known except as a matter of conjecture. The town at the origin of the procession is created by the speaker's imagination, only to be abandoned as forever desolate, lost in history. Thus the fourth stanza evokes the dual sense of presence and absence, proximity and distance, that troubles all interpretation.

Stanza 5 begins by recapitulating these issues in a kind of coda. The urn is an 'Attic shape' – historically determined, yet still an aesthetic form, a wrought, marble artifact that nevertheless invites the speaker to re-experience its scenes as immediate and organically alive. As a 'silent form', the urn requires that its audience speak for it. And yet to interpret the urn honestly is also to confront the spectre of eternity, which reminds us that the enterprise of speaking for the urn is necessarily presumptuous, in that it assumes that one has overcome history and achieved a transcendental standpoint of non-contingent knowledge. Hence the urn is figured as a riddle without a solution, teasing 'us out of thought', compelling and repelling the interpreter's attempts at understanding.

The urn is, finally, a 'Cold Pastoral', for while it supposedly represents a timeless world, it also reminds us of our own temporality. Keats's epithet recalls the expression 'cold beauty' in his sonnet 'On Visiting the Tomb of Burns', which is applied to a landscape that, though beautiful in itself, cannot be enjoyed apart from the consciousness of natural ephemerality and human mortality. In that sonnet, Keats opposes this troubled consciousness to the Greek world, which could relish the 'real of beauty'. Burns's misfortune, according to Keats, was to be born into a northern world and a 'barbarous age' in which pleasure and beauty are divorced from life by 'the kirk' and the 'doctrine of thrift' (*Keats's Letters*, I, 319–20). Thus while 'Cold' has usually been interpreted as a reference to the urn's own marble hardness, its inhuman quality as artifact, it may also be taken as an expression of the speaker's historical distance from the urn. The urn's pastoral, warm and inviting as it may appear, must remain a kind of 'cold beauty' for him, since he cannot, in the world and time in which he lives, relish 'the real of beauty'.

Whereas the speaker previously sought to locate the urn in history, he has now become aware of his own historicity. Like the little town at the other end of the processional route, 'this generation' shall also be wasted by time, and the urn shall 'remain, in midst of other woe / Than ours'. The speaker's encounter with the urn can only be understood as a single episode in its history. Like the figures in the sacrificial procession, the urn is involved in a perpetual journey that never goes anywhere, apparently moving forward in time without ever coming to a point where its significance can be summed up.

The urn's concluding message, however – 'Beauty is truth, truth beauty' – would seem to offer just such a summation, apparently asserting the universal and implicitly timeless meaning of the work of art. Yet if one takes seriously the tension between history and aesthetics that seems to pervade the rest of the poem, it is difficult to read this phrase simply as the unequivocal affirmation of the timeless truth of the aesthetic object. We could of course take such a simplistic declaration as an indication of either the limitations of the urn itself or the speaker's desperate will to meaning. There is however another possible interpretation, one less at odds with the rest of the poem, namely, that the line states a hermeneutic principle – that all truth in interpretation depends upon a process of imaginative projection by the interpreter. As Gadamer writes, 'A person who is trying to understand a text is always performing an act of projecting. He projects before himself a meaning for the text as a whole as soon as some initial meaning emerges in the text. Again, the latter emerges only because he is reading the text with particular expectations in regard to a certain meaning. The working out of this fore-project, which is constantly revised in terms of what emerges as he penetrates into the meaning, is understanding what is there' (*Truth and Method*, p. 236). It is just this process of projection and revision that the ode dramatises. As the speaker gradually moves through his alternative approaches to the urn, he comes to a better understanding of how it speaks and what it has to say.

Indeed, I would argue that in the famous passage from the letters that is so often cited as a gloss to the urn's sentence – 'What the imagination seizes as Beauty must be truth – whether it existed before or not' (*Keats's Letters*, I, 184) – Keats espouses a view of the relations between part and whole, meaning and projection, that is in some ways comparable to Gadamer's description of the hermeneutic circle.[32] Keats's concern in this passage, I think, is not with timeless Neoplatonic essences but with the *act* of imagination *seizing* truth. Imagination, Keats goes on to suggest, is a heuristic tool, supplementing logic, in any cognitive process. ...

The qualification that follows – 'that is all / Ye know on earth, and all ye need to know' – might be taken then as a recognition of the role that imagination must inevitably play in human knowledge, because of the very limitations of our mortal state. In this sense, it both echoes and answers the conclusion to Byron's own meditation on a Grecian urn in Canto 2 of *Childe Harold*: 'Well didst thou speak, Athena's wisest son! / "All that we know is, nothing can be known"' (ll. 55–6). Like Byron, Keats recognises humanity's essential ignorance, but he also suggests that imagination allows us to surmise about the past. When *Childe Harold's* narrator, contemplating a human skull, asks 'Can all Saint, Sage, or Sophist ever writ, / People this lonely tower, this tenement refit?' (ll. 53–4), the speaker of 'Grecian Urn' answers, 'No, and yes'.

Read in these terms, 'Beauty is truth, truth beauty' deserves its place as the urn's message to future generations – not because the urn itself has transcended history but because it is this process of interpretive projection and revision that each generation will enact in its effort to understand the urn. This reading would still be subject to potential ironisation by the quotation marks in the *Lamia* volume, however, since it is in the nature of such a view of truth to destabilise itself, recognising all statements of truth, including its own statement, as provisional. Indeed, we might say that this very provisionality is encoded into the poem's conclusion, since we are not really sure who is speaking, the urn or the poem's speaker. Though the speaker attributes the message to the urn, it must be the speaker's own sentence, one would think, since the urn itself is silent.

In this case, the textual controversy over the punctuation of the poem's last two lines becomes all the more interesting, since it gives material substance to the question of who is speaking, the interpreter or the material interpreted, in any interpretive act. Despite our desire for a definitive text, it seems to me that we need to be open to the possibility that the variations in punctuation may reflect Keats's own indecision as to who should have the poem's final word.[33] Should the speaker be shown as merely transmitting to future readers the wisdom of an earlier age, or should that wisdom be displayed as the speaker's own, discovered through the encounter with the urn? The fact that the later version of the poem printed in the *Lamia* volume encloses 'Beauty is truth, truth beauty' in quotation marks, apparently leaving the ode's last thirteen words to the speaker, suggests that in the end Keats may have chosen to try to make clearer the speaker's role as an interpreter and mediator of the urn's message. However we decide this controversy, it seems to me that its most interesting aspect is that as interpreters of the poem we find ourselves in exactly the same position as the poem's speaker. Just as the speaker attributes to the urn a message that he must himself produce, so we try to ascertain the 'truth' about the poem, without fully realising perhaps the extent to which that 'truth' will be a function of our own notions of 'beauty'. In this century, for instance, we have gone through a continual process of reinterpreting the ode's conclusion and its relationship to the rest of the poem because we have developed the notion that 'true' art avoids simplistic didacticism.

In effect, Keats's poem turns upon itself and on us, so that the question of how to understand the urn progressively becomes a reflection on the process of interpretation itself, thereby entangling both the poem's speaker and ourselves as its readers. Like the urn, the poem functions in two ways, both as a fictive representation that can be given a certain historical context and as an aesthetic structure that still invites our participation. Thus while we can locate the poem's dilemmas in terms of certain historical issues, as I have tried to do in the first half of this essay, this does not close the poem, turning it into a set of historically determined and determinate assertions. The poem continues to intrigue and fascinate us. If the 'Ode on a Grecian Urn' has become an enduring object of interpretation, this is because the ode, like the urn, like eternity, 'tease[s] us out of thought'. The persistence of art lies in its enigmas, in the way in which it holds open certain questions for further interpretation.[34] The effort to 'think' this poem, to assign it to a particular ideology and close off its questions, is called into question by the poem itself, not only in its dramatisation of the urns' continuing appeal to the aesthetic imagination but in terms of its rhetoric and fiction as well.

Rhetorically, the ode's repeated questions, overinsistent repetitions, riddling puns and oxymorons, and ambiguous syntax tease us with multiple possibilities, inducing in us the same kinds of doubts that plague the poem's speaker. ... The poem's questions, for instance, rather than determining contexts for the urn's representations, merely suggest possible conjectures without deciding between them: deities or mortals, or both; Tempe or Arcady; a little town by a river or the seashore or in the mountains. Or how do we understand a line like 'More happy love! more happy, happy love!'? Is Keats being ironic at his speaker's expense, or is this a failure of poetic invention? How do we read the word 'still', as adverb or adjective, as 'not yet' or 'motionless', eternally prolonged, or merely dead? Is 'All breathing human passion far above' intended as praise or blame? And what of the urn's final oracular pronouncement, which has been the source of constant dispute? While I have attempted to interpret this phrase, it remains equally true that the urn's hermetic sentence, like the rest of its rhetoric, seems deliberately calculated to resist interpretation.

In terms of its fiction, the poem's story about interpreting the urn is one that mirrors our own activity, so that to look at the poem is also to look at ourselves looking at the poem. We cannot disentangle ourselves from Keats's fiction, since it already incorporates our own interpretive activity within it, anticipating our responses to the poem. Through its own self-consciousness about being interpreted, the ode forces us to be self-conscious about our positions as interpreters. It reminds us that just as the speaker's understanding of the urn depends upon his perspective, so our understanding of the poem will depend upon the way in which we choose to view it.

In 'Ode on a Grecian Urn', Keats weighs the hermeneutic claims of both aestheticism and historicism, pointing out their weaknesses while retaining their truths. Aestheticism abstracts too easily from the real human world of history, while historicism must acknowledge both the aesthetic potentiality of art and the extent to which historical interpretation itself depends upon a form of aesthetic activity. In dramatising these modes of reading, the poem also exposes the deficiencies in certain ways of reading the Romantics. To see in Keats's poem the affirmation of the transhistorical truth of the aesthetic object, or alternatively to say that one can historicise this affirmation as an unconscious form of ideology, seems to me to underestimate Keats's own awareness of the paradoxes of writing for the future. The ode attempts to suggest a third alternative, a mode of reading that does not take the story out of history, and vice versa, acknowledging the role of the interpreter as participant in the interpretive act. But in taking up this stance, the poem must also renounce any claim to be able to determine its own interpretation definitively, just as I must renounce any claim that this essay might close the history of its reading. In committing his work to the future, Keats realised, he was also committing it to the medium of history, to the perpetual reading and reinterpretation that maintains our dialogue with the past.

From the *Journal of English and Germanic Philology* (April 1991), 208–29.

NOTES

[A. W. Phinney's discussion of Keats's 'Ode on a Grecian Urn' mediates between the purely formalist readings of a New Critic like Cleanth Brooks (who produced a justly celebrated analysis of the verbal and structural effects of the poem in his book *The Well Wrought Urn* [New York, 1947]) and historicist critics, like Jerome McGann, who argue that the poem reflects the ideology of its time. As a way of evading the exclusivity of these two positions, Phinney turns to the work of Hans-Georg Gadamer who, in his *Truth and Method* (1975), postulated the idea that a literary work does not appear in the world as a neatly packaged object of meaning. Meaning for Gadamer and his followers depends on the historical situation of the reader or interpreter. Gadamer claimed that all interpretations of past literature arise from a dialogue between the past and the present. At one level we seek to discover the questions which the work of art asks about its own time and yet, at another, the kinds of question we ask about a poem such as Keats's ode depend on those issues which are current for us. Thus our present perspective always involves a relationship with the past, but at the same time the past can only be interpreted through the filter of the present. Gadamer argued for the method of 'Hermeneutics', which views understanding as a 'fusion' of past and present in which the truth of interpretation depends on a process of imaginative projection by the interpreter. For Phinney, Keats's ode anticipates the very conflicts which have resulted from the history of its interpretation, dramatising the conflicting aims of aesthetic criticism and historical critique. A number of brief cuts have been made to Phinney's article. Ed.]

1. Cleanth Brooks, *The Well Wrought Urn* (New York, 1947; reprint, 1975), pp. 156, 163, 162. Among Brooks's predecessors, H. W. Garrod (*Keats* [Oxford, 1926] and Kenneth Burke ('Symbolic Action in a Poem by Keats', *Accent*, 4 [1943], 30–42) were most sensitive to the implied limitations of the figures on the urn, but neither dealt specifically with the theme of history in the poem.

2. See the discussion of this tension in Brooks's reading by Stuart Sperry, *Keats the Poet* (Princeton, NJ, 1973), pp. 275–6.

3. Peter Burger, *Theory of the Avant-Garde*, trans. Michael Shaw (Minneapolis, 1984), p. 46.

4. Christopher Caudwell, *Illusion and Reality: A Study of the Sources of Poetry* (1937; reprint, New York, 1973), pp. 107–8.

5. Jerome J. McGann, *The Romantic Ideology: A Critical Investigation* (Chicago, 1983), p. 91. See also McGann's critique of the tradition of formalist readings of Keats in 'Keats and the Historical Method in Literary Criticism' in *The Beauty of Inflections. Literary Investigations in Historical Method and Theory* (Oxford, 1985). The relations between Keats's poetry and the aesthetic ideas and their historical and political context have become a prevalent topic in recent criticism. See, for example, Thomas Reed, 'Keats and the Gregarious Advance of Intellect in *Hyperion*' (*ELH*, 55 [1988], 195–232); Marjorie Levinson, *Keats's Life of Allegory: The Origins of a Style* (Oxford, 1988); and *Studies in Romanticism*, 25 (1986) which includes essays by Susan J. Wolfson, Morris Dickstein, William Keach, David Bromwich, Paul Fry, and Alan Bewell [The New Criticism to which Phinney refers was an American school of criticism of which Brooks was a pioneer. It argued that a poem should be analysed in terms of its formal structure and verbal patterns, in isolation from its biographical and historical context. For McGann and the New Historicism in Romantic studies, see the Introduction. Ed.]

6. For example, David Perkins, *The Quest for Permanence: The Symbolism of Wordsworth, Shelley, and Keats* (Cambridge, MA, 1959); Walter Jackson Bate, *John Keats* (Cambridge, MA., 1963); and Douglas Bush, *John Keats: His Life and Writings* (New York, 1966) all emphasise the poet's 'imperfect contentment with the eternal but unfelt happiness of the figures on the urn' (Bush, p. 141).

7. See, however, the essays by Philip Fisher ('A Museum with One Work Inside: Keats and the Finality of Art', *Keats–Shelley Journal*, 33 [1984], 85–102) and by Douglas B. Wilson ('Reading the Urn: Death in Keats's Arcadia', *Studies in English Literature, 1500–1900*, 25 [1985], 823–44), both of which anticipate some of my own concerns here, emphasising the poem's historical self-consciousness and the parallel situations of the poem's speaker and its reader.

8. Ian Jack, *Keats and the Mirror of Art* (Oxford, 1967), p. 38. [Benjamin R. Haydon was an artist and friend of Keats. Ed.]

9. William Sharp, *The Life and Letters of Joseph Severn* (London, 1982), p. 29.

10. Johann Joachim Winckelmann, 'Description of the Apollo Belvedere', *Universal Museum* (1768), p. 56. I would like to thank Mr Frank K. Lorenz, Curator of Special Collections at Hamilton College, for providing me with this text.

11. Hans-Georg Gadamer, *Truth and Method* (2nd edn, 1965), trans. Garrett Barden and John Cumming (New York, 1975), p. 76.

12. André Malraux, *The Voices of Silence* (1951), trans. Stuart Gilbert (New York, 1953), p. 14.

13. See Jack, *Keats and the Mirror of Art* for an extensive account of Keats's knowledge of art and of possible models for the Grecian urn.

14. See R. G. Collingwood, *The Idea of History* (Oxford, 1946), for a general account of the development of historical consciousness during this period. Both René Wellek (*The Rise of English Literary History* [Chapel Hill, NC, 1941] and Walter Jackson Bate, *The Burden of the Past and the English Poet* [1970; reprint New York, 1972]) detail the growth of a historical view of literature in the eighteenth century.

15. Johann Joachim Winckelmann, *Reflections on the Painting and Sculpture of the Greeks: With Instructions for the Connoisseur, and an Essay on Grace in Works of Art* (1755), trans. Henry Fuseli (London, 1765), p. 2.

16. *Autobiography of Benjamin Robert Haydon* (Oxford, 1927), p. 276.

17. Quoted in William St Clair, *Lord Elgin and the Marbles* (London, 1967), pp. 177–8.

18. Richard Payne Knight, *An Analytical Inquiry into the Principles of Taste*, 4th edn (London, 1808), pp. 169–70, 181–2.

19. Benjamin R. Haydon, 'On the Judgment of Connossieurs Being Preferred to that of Professional Men, – Elgin Marbles, &c', *Examiner*, 429 (17 March 1816), pp. 162–3.

20. All quotations from Keats's poems are from John Keats, *Complete Poems*, ed. Jack Stillinger (Cambridge, MA, 1982).

21. John Keats, *The Letters of John Keats, 1814–1821*, ed. Hyder Rollins (Cambridge, MA, 1958), I, 394.

22. See Ronald Sharp, *Keats, Skepticism, and the Religion of Beauty* (Athens, GA, 1979), pp. 114–58, and J. Philip Eggers, 'Memory in Mankind: Keats's Historical Imagination', *PMLA*, 86 (1971), 990–8.

23. Helen Vendler, *The Odes of John Keats* (Cambridge, MA, 1983), pp. 118–21. My own analysis remains strongly indebted to Vendler's work. See also the excellent discussion of 'Grecian Urn' in Paul Fry, *The Poet's Calling in the English Ode* (New Haven, CT, 1980), which notes the hermeneutic dimensions of the poem.

24. As Fry observes, Keats 'submits all bias to the sublations of dialectic' (p. 220). Fry goes on to emphasise that 'many aspects of the odes are *not* confined within the shaping of dialect' (p. 221). See also the open-ended discussions of the structures of Keats's odes in Perkins, *The Quest for Permanence* and in Jack Stillinger, 'Imagination and Reality in the Odes' (*The Hoodwinking of Madeline, and Other Essays on Keats's Poems* [Urbana, IL, 1971], pp. 99–119).

25. On Keats's sense of modernity and belatedness, see Bate, *John Keats*, pp. 321–38; and Harold Bloom, 'Keats and the Embarrassments of Poetic Tradition', *The Ringers in the Tower: Studies in the Romantic Tradition* (Chicago, 1971), pp. 130–42, and *Poetry and Repression: Revisionism from Blake to Stevens* (New Haven, CT, 1976), pp. 112–42.

26. Karl Marx, *Grundrisse: Foundations of the Critique of Political Economy*, trans. Martin Nicolaus (New York, 1973), p. 111.

27. E. H. Gombrich, *Art and Illusion: A Study in the Psychology of Pictorial Representation* (Princeton, NJ, 1969), pp. 242–3.

28. Bate, *John Keats*, p. 518. Vendler, discussing the fourth stanza, writes that 'the audience, prompted by the visible artifact, engages by its interrogation in the act of cooperative mutual creation with the artist' (*Odes*, p. 122). See also Sperry, *Keats the Poet*, who repeatedly emphasises the speaker's role in bringing the scenes on the urn to life.

29. See Wasserman's fine analysis of the poem's 'grammatical moods', Earl Wasserman, *The Finer Tone: Keats's Major Poems* (Baltimore, MD, 1953), pp. 30–1.

30. I owe this recognition to Fisher ('A Museum with One Work Inside') who points out the importance of the pun in 'leave' and 'leaves' (p. 92).

31. As Fry notes, 'the urn as historian is shown to fail because it offers the past without interpretation' (*The Poet's Calling*, p. 251).

32. I should note, however, that Gadamer takes considerable pains to distinguish his position from Romantic hermeneutics, which he conceives as being oriented primarily toward 'the reproduction of an original production' (*Truth and Method*, p. 263). While this characterisation is unduly narrow, in my opinion, there certainly remain significant differences between Gadamer and Keats.

33. See Jack Stillinger, 'Who Says What to Whom at the End of "Ode on a Grecian Urn"?' in *The Hoodwinking of Madeline and Other Essays on Keats's Poems*, pp. 167–73, for an account of the various versions and alternative interpretations of these lines. I agree that two of the various versions are effectively refuted by the objections Stillinger raises. As he observes, it makes no sense to see the last thirteen words as being addressed to the urn, since 'ye' is ordinarily plural and the urn has been addressed as 'thou'. Nor does it seem reasonable to think that the speaker is addressing the figures on the urn, since they are not 'on earth'.

34. See Sperry, 'What the ode expresses is the difficulty and yet the necessity of remaining content with the way art speaks to us, with the kind of "half-knowledge" it offers' (*Keats the Poet*, p. 278).

7

'To Autumn'

ANDREW BENNETT

The criticism of 'To Autumn' has articulated a clear discrepancy between the apparent denial of historical and political analysis in the poem and the events of the second decade of the nineteenth century, including economic and political crisis, the suspension of Habeas Corpus, the Spa Fields riot, Luddism, sporadic but widespread food riots in rural areas, and, most specifically, the Peterloo Massacre of August 1819, just one month before the composition of Keats's poem. The apparent silence of 'To Autumn' on the subject of politics tends to be read as evidence of a Keatsian desire to abstract poetic language from history, a desire to write perfected language into which the disruptions of history do not intrude. 'To Autumn' has been read as a poem of perfection, a poem in which language is perfected in form and in the exclusion of history. A. C. Swinburne classed it with 'Ode on a Grecian Urn' as the 'nearest to absolute perfection' of Keats's odes;[1] more recently, Walter Jackson Bate has called 'To Autumn' 'one of the most nearly perfect poems in English', Aileen Ward has remarked that it is Keats's 'most perfect and untroubled poem', and Douglas Bush has stated that the poem is 'flawless in structure, texture, tone, and rhythm'.[2] This 'perfection of language, a perfection apparently undaunted by contemporary political events, has led politically minded critics to describe 'To Autumn' as an escape from history. Attempting to account for the discrepancy between the perfected language of the poem and the contemporary disruptions of politics, Jerome McGann, for example, has analysed 'To Autumn' as 'an attempt to "escape" the period which provides the poem with its context'.[3]

Similarly, in a recent essay which has perceptive things to say about politics in Keats's poetry, Vincent Newey has argued that 'To Autumn' celebrates a capacity quite opposite to that of political engagement.[4] In this chapter, I attempt to situate 'To Autumn' within its political context of agrarian economics in the early nineteenth century in order to suggest ways in which the perfected critical response to 'To Autumn' is both figured by the text, and, crucially, disrupted by the subtextual pressures of politics on the poem. Figures of reading become, literally, economic figures and the silencing of politics and history in 'To Autumn' is repeated in the silence of critical response to the implicit political 'subtext' of the poem.

'To Autumn', then, is embedded within both the context of a Keatsian anxiety over the economics of writing which I have outlined in my discussion of the letters written between May and September [in ch. 2 of Bennett's book. Ed.], and a more general anxiety of economics in England in 1819. The Keatsian rhetoric of harvesting in 'To Autumn' may be read both as a figure of political discourse and as a self-description of poetry and poetic making. On a number of occasions in his poems and letters, Keats inscribed the economics of harvesting within the terms of the economics of poetic writing: in a letter of July 1819, for example, in reference to the publication of his poetry, Keats says 'the very corn which is now so beautiful, as if it had only <taken> took to ripening yesterday, is for the market: So, why shod I be delicate' (Keats's Letters, II, 129). The rhetoric of gleaning also provides an amphibology of harvesting and writing in a number of poems, most clearly expressed in the desire to glean the poet's 'teeming brain' in 'When I have fears that I may cease to be'.[5] 'To Autumn', as a poem of harvesting, represents Keats's most fully worked nexus of such homologies: among other things the poem is an articulation of the politics and economics both of agriculture and of writing.

In this chapter, I shall depart somewhat from the dual focus of this book – narrative and audience, what I term 'figures of reading' – in order to suggest ways in which Keats's most 'perfected' of poems engages with the discourses of politics and economics. Implicit in such a reading is the recognition that increasingly during 1819 the question of writing for a living, and thus of finding a public, becomes more and more urgent. But this chapter also presents an exercise in reading 'against the grain': by reading 'To Autumn' intertextually, through intertexts which fracture the surface poise of the poem, I shall suggest that one way to read a poem which so signally represses solecism is to make of reading itself a solecism.

As I have suggested, "To Autumn' has been read as a poem of perfection, a poem which suppresses the cacophonous noises of history: it is a poem which seems to exclude the language of politics from its rhetoric, to silence the noise of history, politics, economics. Without such purchase on the text, readers stand powerless in front of the irrefragable beauty of language, they are left to luxuriate in the fecund textuality of words, and, in the face of such poetry, critics generally speak in languid autumnal tones, in extended nostalgic periods, intoning the litany of perfection, the organic, the whole. To historicise Keats's poem, however, would be to read against the grain, to listen to the fractious intertextual cacophony of history, politics, economics, noises which Autumn seems to silence. My analysis of Keats's letters in terms of the relationship between writing, work, and economics, suggests that, on one level, 'To Autumn' was generated out of the ideological tensions to which the writer in the early nineteenth century was subject. Written just before the letters announcing his abandonment of the notion of writing for money, 'To Autumn' may be read as a crucial text in Keats's developing economics of writing. The perfection of language which critics have discerned in the poem is fractured by the economics of writing.

Part of the perfection of language in 'To Autumn' involves a density of intertextuality, an inclusion of other voices into a univocal exclusivity of Keatsian voice, which both textures and textualises the poem. Although, as Helen Vendler has noted, 'To Autumn' denies specific allusion,[6] the echoes that critics have heard in the poem are legion: they include, for example, echoes from Virgil, Shakespeare, Spenser, Milton, Thomson, Wordsworth, Coleridge, Chatterton. Rather than disrupting the univocality of Keats's poem, these echoes are seen as texturing the poem's literariness and homogenising its monolithic voice – the voice of the literary. Keats's 1816 sonnet 'How many bards gild the lapses of time' provides, in itself, an intertextual commentary on the intertextuality of 'To Autumn'. The earlier poem explicitly argues for the 'pleasing chime' of the literary tradition – a music which 'occasions' 'no confusion, no disturbance rude' – as a generating impulse for writing, and compares such music to 'the unnumber'd sounds that evening store[s]' which 'Make pleasing music, not wild uproar'. The sonnet interacts fruitfully with the later ode in a number of ways, not least in the economics of the opening line's 'gild' (a word which, as I show below, will be erased in/by 'To Autumn'), and in the 'lapses of time', the discontinuities of history, which such gilding suppresses. But Keats's crisis of writing during the summer and autumn of 1819 means that such an aesthetics of literary perfection/exclusion is deeply fractured by the intrusive discourses of economics. By focusing on a different set of 'intertexts', it is possible to describe 'To Autumn' as an intervention in a series of discourses, literary and political, which both disrupt the poem's 'perfection' and situate it within the political events of autumn 1819.

There is, then, a double intertextuality of 'To Autumn': an intertextuality of the literary, and an intertextuality – still mediated to a large extent by literary texts – of the historical. The literary intertextuality of 'To Autumn' posits an ideology of literary language as separated from history precisely through its exclusion of other voices: the literary is presented as a closed and enclosed discursive space immune to the infringements of other discourses. In this model of intertextuality the text is enclosed, an enclosure bounded by the limits of a specifically literary history. The boundaries of the literary exclude the illicit incursions of transgressive (non-literary) language into the space of poetry. The poem's historical intertextuality, on the other hand, involves the antagonistic intertexts which the poem's literariness attempts to suppress – the texts of economics, history, politics. The fractures in the poem's literary logic – the famous syntactical suspension in stanza 1, the thematic laziness of the workers in stanza 2, the semantic ambivalence of the word 'conspiring', the use of the apostrophic convention in a poem which otherwise refuses the outworn formulations of the eighteenth-century ode[7] – all suggest fault-lines which mark the repression of history by textuality. By attending to a number of intertextual echoes we might discern a number of ideological fault-lines in Keats's poem in which we might trace the text's engagement with the discourses of history.

The politics of 'To Autumn' are most explicitly articulated within the terms of the contemporary politics of agriculture. The politics of agriculture had potentially revolutionary implications in the early nineteenth century due to the repeated minor uprisings of rural workers agitating against the 1815 corn law, enclosures, and generally against oppressive economic conditions. In 'To Autumn', however, these matters are displaced into a mythological figure of

Ceres. A number of critics have recently suggested that Ceres, the goddess of corn and harvests, is a pervasive absent presence in 'To Autumn', a presence which is unstated, unspecified, and disseminated throughout both the pastoral tradition and Keats's poem.[8] The agrarian politics of the early nineteenth century are mediated by the unnamed mythological discourse 'Ceres': by looking closely at this mythological substitution, we may be able to position 'To Autumn' within contemporary political discourses.

Keats's contemporary poem 'Lamia' offers an intriguing insight into the significance of Ceres in the lines 'and the store thrice told / Of Ceres' horn' (part 2, ll. 186–7). The phrase 'Ceres' horn', which is an expansion of the word 'cornucopia' (literally, 'horn of plenty') represents an example of Keats's generative solecisms. Ceres, goddess of abundant food (particularly corn) is not, in any of Keats's sources, nor in the mythological tradition, described as possessing a horn: the cornucopia, in fact, belongs to an entirely unrelated deity, Amalthea.[9] Keats's reference to 'Ceres' horn' is, then, a kind of corny illicit pun on cornucopia, which is 'thrice told' in that 'cornucopia' may be translated into 'Ceres' horn' in three different ways: plenty of corn; horn of plenty; Ceres' [corn's] horn. Unravelling this ravelled pun we find a tautology in the association of 'Ceres' horn' with cornucopia: Ceres = corn (by metonymy); horn = cornus (by translation); so the pun reads 'Corn's (Ceres') corn[us] (horn)' – and 'copia' is omitted except in the copious linguistic play involved. Ceres' horn is thrice-told as well as thrice-counted in this cornucopia of linguistic compression.

Within the context of an economic analysis of 'To Autumn', this paronomastic [dealing with punning or wordplay. Ed.] play on Ceres is significant because of the figure's relationship with property, law, and the politics of agriculture. In classical mythology, Ceres represents not only agrarian plenitude but also the transition from a pre-monetary and, indeed, communistic, economy to a fully commercial and proto-capitalist economy of monetary exchange, a transition which brought with it the institution of the law. The seventeenth-century encyclopaedist Andrew Tooke explains this in his *Pantheon* in a passage which reverberates with significance for the discourse of agricultural politics in the early nineteenth century:

This you may learn from *Ovid*, who tells us that *Ceres* was the first that made laws; provided wholesome food; and taught the art of husbandry, of ploughing and sowing. For before her time, the earth lay rough and uncultivated, covered with briars, and unprofitable plants; when there were no proprietors of land, they neglected to cultivate it; when nobody had any ground of his own, they did not care to fix landmarks: but all things were common to all men, till *Ceres* who had invented the art of husbandry, taught men how to exercise it; and then they began to contend and dispute about the limits of those fields, from the culture of which they reaped so much profit: and hence it was necessary that laws should be enacted to determine the rights and properties of those who contended. For this reason *Ceres* was named the foundress of laws.[10]

Ceres, then, represents the origins of lawful and economic exchange and of topographical boundaries, and we might gloss Keats's illicit paronomastic play on cornucopia in 'Lamia' as a subtextual, and perhaps subliminal, revolt against such order, exchanging the illicit coinage of puns for the true currency of etymology: Keats presents the reader with a 'Pun mote' (*Keats's Letters*, II, 214). If, as seems to be the case, Ceres is the pervasive unstated presence in 'To Autumn', then the perfected language of pastoral description is invaded by political questions of lawful exchange, agricultural boundaries, private property and labour relations. That critics have noted Ceres' pervasive but unnamed presence in 'To Autumn' is suggestive: Keats appropriates the mythology but explicitly excludes the nominal property of the mythological originator of private property. Indeed, this denial of Ceres's name is particularly remarkable in a poet who, as John Clare wryly commented, 'keeps up a constant a[l]lusion or illusion to the grecian mythology'—and who 'behind every rose ... looks for a Venus & under every laurel a thrumming Apollo'.[11] The exclusion of Ceres' proper name – her property – in the poem represents a transgression of the law of property.

Furthermore, the association of the origins of law with the demarcation of boundaries in the mythology of Ceres is particularly significant in a poem based on the boundary season, autumn.[12] Between the eighteenth-century analysis of the origins of property (mythologised in Ceres) and the contemporary controversy over enclosures, there is a homology in the movement from a communistic pre-agrarian past before the law of Ceres and its transmutation into 'modern' agriculture on the one hand, and the movement from common agricultural usage to the privatisation of land in enclosures on the other. Other things being equal (and the history of enclosures is, of course, far more complex than this reduction allows), enclosure reproduces the structure of the mythological origins of (agricultural) private property, the bounding of land ownership.[13] As a boundary, however, autumn is unbounded, as the poem's notorious ambivalence over the precise temporal location of the season suggests: the poem is located within both summer and autumn, and points forward to winter, it is located at the beginning as well as at the end of harvest, the bees in stanza 1 are dislocated in their sense of time, and the lambs in stanza 3 are ambivalent sheep. Similarly, these temporal transgressions of bounding-lines are repeated in the topographical violation of boundaries as the poem moves out in space from the cottage to the garden to the fields to the hills and finally upwards to the unbounded skies. This movement, in itself, suggests a denial of enclosure, a political gesture of defiance against the appropriation of public property in the contemporary enclosure movement.

It is, of course, the second stanza of 'To Autumn', with its images of rural workers, which most clearly articulates the discourse of agricultural labour relations. Although the unstated figure of the goddess Ceres activates the discourses of labour, property, lawful exchange, and legal boundaries, it is possible to hear in 'To Autumn' the noise of the politics and economics of agriculture in a hitherto unnoticed verbal echo of Pope's *Epistle to Bathurst*. It has been well documented that, in preparing to write 'Lamia' in the summer of 1819, Keats had been rereading Dryden's poetry to get the feel of a 'flint-worded' poet (*Keats's Letters*, II, 214).[14] But the fact that Keats appears to quote Pope at least three times in the letters of that summer (*Keats's Letters*, II, 133, 164, 210), including a quotation from *Eloisa to Abelard* on the day he wrote 'To Autumn', strongly suggests that he was also reading the poet who had previously been something of a Keatsian *bête noire*. Pope's *Epistle to Bathurst*, one of his 'Moral Essays' whose 'Argument' is subtitled 'Of the Use of Riches', satirically examines the knotty question of whether, as the Argument has it, 'the invention of Money has been more commodious, or pernicious to Mankind'.[15] In particular, Pope attacks the extremes of Avarice and Prodigality. A personification occurs at a key point in Pope's poem in order to satirise avaricious hoarding:

> Riches, like insects, when conceal'd they lie,
> Wait but for wings, and in their season, fly.

> Who sees pale Mammon pine amidst his store,
> Sees but a backward steward for the Poor
> (ll. 171–4[16])

Although the first two lines might provide a secondary echo of the last stanza of 'To Autumn', which moves from insects to flight, the third line offers an echo which, in rhythm and verbal cadence, is a precise model for the opening to stanza 2 of Keats's poem:

> Who sees pale Mammon pine amidst his store

in Pope is translated into the rhetorical question of

> Who hath not seen thee oft amid thy store?

in Keats. 'Seeing' this hidden intertext within the Keatsian store of Romantic luxuriance allows us to discern a rich economic and political subtext within Keats's overtly naturalistic and 'disin-terested' poem: it alerts us to the fact that the turbulent, fractious subtext of 'To Autumn' involves a problematic relationship between, on the one hand, the capital accumulation of stanza 1 – loading, bending, filling, swelling, budding – a kind of 'natural' accumulation which constitutes a displaced representation of financial accumulation, and, on the other hand, work and its nega-tion in stanza 2 – expressed in the phrases 'sitting careless', 'sound asleep', 'thy laden head', 'with patient look / Thou watchest'.

The echo of Pope's Moral Essay not only activates the subtextual economics of 'To Autumn' but also suggests an ideological explana-tion of aristocratic accumulation: 'pale Mammon' who 'pine[s] amidst his store' is a 'backward steward for the Poor'. Similarly, the representation of rural leisure is double-edged in that not only are the workers incongruously leisurely but their lassitude reflects the seasonal nature of the work and the fact that their relaxation will soon become unemployment: if the bees are seduced into believing that warm days will never cease, the workers have similarly con-fused the seasons.[17] Just as the full granaries will soon start to empty, the warm days will soon turn cold. The third stanza already – even within the frame of this pressingly plenitudinous and affluent poem – marks a declining repletion (or, indeed, an over-repletion) in its diction ('soft dying', 'wailful', 'mourn', 'lives or dies') and imagery. Indeed, we might argue that it is precisely because of the plenitude, the generosity, of autumnal days, that work is left undone, just as Keats's poem, with its slow, lush, plenitudinous generosity almost convinces its readers that the work of history may be abandoned in aesthetic contemplation. And, indeed, the act of writing 'To Autumn' was specifically recorded by Keats as a leisurely affair, engendered by a walk which constituted a break from writing – a holiday not only from the more serious business of rewriting 'Hyperion' but also from work proper.

But the silent intertextual echo of Pope's Mammon also suggests that money may be silenced, may be barred from Keats's poem in significant ways, and we might ask what is invested in this silent barring of money from 'To Autumn'. Money is explicitly suppressed by Keats in an alteration to line 25: 'barred clouds bloom' was, in the first draft of the poem, altered from 'a gold cloud gilds': the alteration – from 'gold' to 'barred', from 'gilds' to 'bloom' – bars the noisy intrusion of economics into the poem. The suppressed word 'gilds' threatens to open up a number of semantic seams in 'To Autumn': one archaic sense of 'gild' is a noise or clamour;[18] 'gild' also involves the payment of taxes and the covering of an object with a thin layer of gold, as well as the common metaphorical development of this latter sense in the idea of giving a specious brilliance to an unworthy object. These noisy economic sememes of 'gild', however, are literally barred – they are crossed out – by the final text: they are explicitly barred by the word 'barred'. The verb 'to bar' is associated with exclusion, with the law, with property, with limiting, confining, and enclosing: in order to read these sememes of 'barred' in Keats's poem, however, we must read the text as a palimpsest – literally, because 'barred ... bloom' is written over 'gold ... gilds'[19] – we must transgress the space of words in the poem, and deny the law of authorial exclusion. Similarly, 'barred' gives us a key to the poem's attempted exclusivity of intertextuality, its barring of heterogeneous noises from its perfected surface – a barring which is represented phonetically by the alteration from the harsh noise of the velar to the softer harmony of the bi-labial plosives, and which is represented throughout the poem by Keats's notoriously mellifluous harmonics. And to say, as we might want to, that 'barred clouds bloom' is simply more beautiful, more perfect, than 'a gold cloud gilds', is both to register the aesthetic force of the 'natural' plenitude which structures the poem and, at the same time, to beg the question of the poem's engagement with the economics of the aesthetic.

John Clare's poetry provides an interesting commentary on the relationship between law, wealth, and enclosure in the early nineteenth century which helps to illuminate the subtextual economics of Keats's poem. In a number of poems,[20] Clare comments nostalgically on the damage done by enclosures to the rural scene, but he also writes perceptively on the economic matrix of values that produces such ecological damage. In the early poem 'Helpstone', for example, Clare laments the destruction caused by enclosures and comments:

> Acursed wealth o'er bounding human laws
> Of every evil thou remainst the cause
> Victims of want those wretches such as me
> Too truly lay their wretchedness to thee
> Thou art the bar that keeps from being fed
> And thine our loss of labour and of bread
>   (ll. 127–32)

Although 'Helpstone', written in 1812, was not published until 1820, reading Keats's poem through the perspective of Clare's helps to elucidate the complex ideological matrix in the verbal cluster 'wealth', 'bounding', 'laws', 'victims', 'bar', 'fed', 'labour', 'bread', explicit in Clare's poem, and fracturing the surface poise in Keats's: if one of the subtextual pressures of 'To Autumn' is the refusal of the physical, economic, and legal limitations of enclosure, we might read Keats's poem as in some sense correlative with the explicit denunciation of the transgression of humanitarianism and the picturesque which Clare's poem articulates. In 'The Mores' Clare is even more explicit in his locution 'lawless laws' (l. 178), a formulation which expresses the fundamental injustice of enclosures (fundamental because the rationale for enclosure – private property and legal ownership – deconstructs itself in its gesture of legalising such appropriation; the change from public to private ownership reveals the arbitrary basis of private property: Clare's point is that the arbitrary legality of enclosures deconstructs the very concept of legality upon which laws are founded). As Robert Malcolmson has noted, the justification for private property seems to have undergone a conceptual shift during the eighteenth century (generated, in part at least, by the enclosure movement), from the notion of use-right to that of absolute property ownership: Malcolmson points out that it is in practices such as gleaning that the conflict between the two conceptions of rights is most clearly articulated.[21] Clare's 'lawless laws' points to the fact that from one perspective, at least, enclosures involved the institution of, for example, gleaning as robbery through, precisely, robbery – as E. P. Thompson has commented, 'Enclosure (when all the sophistications are allowed for) was a plain enough case of class robbery, played according to fair rules of property and law laid down by a Parliament of property-owners and lawyers'.[22]

Although the mythological figure of Ceres, representing copious luxury, property, proper boundaries, and the law, is ambiguously absent from 'To Autumn', Keats explicitly includes the reciprocal figure of the anonymous gleaner in stanza 2. The figure of the gleaner activates the vocabularies of want, the appropriation of property, the violation of proper boundaries, and the transgression of the law. The affluence suggested by the richness of literary language in the poem is undercut by the discourse of gleaning: the pressures of linguistic plenitude, the wealthy luxuriance of language, are counter-pointed by this explicit reference to the plight of the poor.

When we examine the contemporary discourse of gleaning, then, we discover a final intertextual pressure on the perfected language of 'To Autumn'. Gleaning was particularly controversial in the autumn of 1819 due to a contemporary controversy over its legality. It was an ancient custom, ideologically overdetermined by the biblical story of Ruth, producing a symbolic significance which reinforced its practical importance for the diet of agricultural workers. The gleaner was a common figure in poetry and painting up to and indeed throughout the nineteenth century as a signifier of the balancing of avarice and charity. Although gleaning was sanctioned by the Bible and traditionally permitted by landowners, at the end of the eighteenth century landowners began to claim that gleaning transgressed laws of property, and started to bring prosecutions against gleaners. The nineteenth century saw numerous attempts by landowners to restrict the practice through the use of the law, by prosecution for trespass and theft. The inclusion of the gleaner figure in stanza 2 of 'To Autumn', together with the stanza's silence over the political question of gleaning, may be understood to mark a reappropriation of the figure for poetry and simultaneously for agricultural workers.[23] By presupposing the legitimacy of the gleaner figure for poetry, Keats also assumes the legality of gleaners. At the same time, however, Keats's representation of the gleaner – as with other nineteenth-century pictorial representations of this pastoral figure[24] – involves a nostalgic objectification and elision of the suffering which gleaning involved: not only was gleaning generated by poverty, but physically it was extremely demanding.[25] The poised steadiness of Keats's gleaner only hints – with 'laden', and perhaps with the assertion of steadiness in its negated implication of unsteadiness, weariness, fatigue – at the physical exertions involved in gleaning.

I would like to suggest that gleaning is the constitutive trope in an intertextual reading of 'To Autumn': indeed, the older word 'leasing' expresses the whole gamut of concerns in my reading of Keats's poem – as a legal term 'leasing' involves the letting of property and at the same time a legally binding or constricting contract; as a synonym for gleaning it involves the (re)appropriation of others' property; etymologically the word also signifies reading. In 'To Autumn' Keats gleans anterior texts, exterior discourses: the Keatsian text is, like all texts, a tissue of gleanings. The opposition of the unnamed Ceres to the anonymous gleaner figures the poem's play of property: such an opposition may itself be read as an allegory of intertextual interpretation. In its various manifestations and transformations in the work of critics such as M. M. Bakhtin, Julia Kristeva, Roland Barthes and Michael Riffaterre, intertextuality tends to demand a dual reading: on the one hand it is understood as a strategy of dissemination, a radical dispersal of origins, and on the other hand it seems to be constituted by a precise specificity of intertextual location and filiation:[26] in 'To Autumn' this play of absence and presence is figured in the dual nominality of the unnamed Ceres and the anonymous gleaner. And the duality of Ceres and the gleaner also reminds us that the gleanings of intertextuality constitute an illicit appropriation of others' property – that, as T. S. Eliot would have it, 'mature poets steal'.[27] Keats's text no longer properly demarcates itself and is no longer properly demarcated: as the extending boundaries of the last stanza suggest, it eliminates all textual boundaries. The poem is unbounded in a movement which refuses (en)closure as it enacts the structure of illicit appropriation implicit in intertextuality.

'To Autumn' ends with noise, and with the question of noise: 'Where are the songs of spring?' 'The noises made in the third stanza by gnats, sheep, hedge-crickets, birds, are the attenuated sounds of buzzing, bleating, whistling, twittering, noises which Keats enumerates as poetically illicit – they are not the noises of spring nor are they the noises of the literary tradition – and which are specifically presented as an alternative music. These noises provide a final model for our intertextual reading of the poem. If textuality is to be defined in terms of intertextuality, then we should recognise that poems include the noise made by textual imposters in the literary tradition, imposters which impose illicit sounds on poetry. Similarly, we should recognise that, because, as Roland Barthes says 'any text is an intertext' and 'any text is a new tissue of past citations'[28] – because textuality is intertextuality – in their turn, poems constitute just such illicit noises, the tintinnabulous noises of language disempowered, made by poetic language within the discourse of history. By attending to the disruptive intertextual noises of history, politics, economics we find that the attempt to silence the noise of history in 'To Autumn', rather than an escape from the historical, is itself a strategic silencing, a silencing which echoes most profoundly the political effacement, which we might call the 'noise', of the oppressed. And the recuperative reading which is figured in intertextuality should also be understood to figure the political dynamics of 'To Autumn'. The peculiar resistance to the political which has been read into 'To Autumn' can be disfigured by the transgressions which constitute the politics of intertextuality in the poem: in order to read the politics of 'To Autumn' we must transgress the boundaries of authorial property, we must refuse to be figured within, or by, the bounds of the text.

From Andrew Bennett, *Keats, Narrative and Audience: The Posthumous Life of Writing* (Cambridge, 1994), pp. 159–71, 224–8.

NOTES

[This essay on Keats's late poem 'To Autumn' is taken from Andrew Bennett's recent book on Keats's poetry which argues that the poet's writing contains certain 'figures of reading' which have determined the ways future readers will respond to the text. There are two schools of thought on the politics of Keats's 'To Autumn': some comment on the silence of the ode on questions of the turbulent agrarian political unrest that characterised the early nineteenth century. These critics argue that Keats uses an abstract poetic discourse to write a perfected language into which the disruptions of history do not intrude. Other critics, however, who comment on the repression of historical events in the poem, then go on to show how the poem relates to these events and the contemporary commentary upon them. Bennett adopts a different stance: he suggests ways in which the critical response to 'To Autumn' is figured by the text and disrupted by the subtextual politics of the poem. Bennett's essay is informed by poststructuralist theories of literature and he makes particular use of theories of 'intertextuality'. Intertextuality is a view of the text particularly associated with the contemporary critics Roland Barthes and Julie Kristeva, who argued that we must not think in terms of the intention of the author when reading a text. Rather we must be aware that each text is really a site or intersection of the language of other texts that exist within and around the text under consideration. 'Any text', writes Barthes, 'is an intertext; other texts are present in it, at varying levels, in more or less recognisable forms: the texts of the previous and surrounding culture' (Barthes, 'Theory of the Text' in *Untying the Text: A Post-Structuralist Reader*, ed. Robert Young [London, 1981], p. 39). Using intertextuality, Bennett as a reader of Keats can find echoes and punning allusions to agrarian political discourse in the poem (see, in particular, his discussion of the puns on Ceres' horn and the cornucopia). For Bennett, the most significant 'figure of reading' which Keats's poetry engages is that of 'Solecism'. Bennet defines Solecism as ' an impropriety of language, a violation of the rules of grammar or syntax, a breach of good manners or etiquette, a social blunder, an error, incongruity or inconsistency' (*Keats, Narrative and Audience*, p. 2). He argues that 'To Autumn' so obviously represses incongruous political meanings (which themselves would constitute a 'Solecism' in the poem) that it forces the reader of the poem to read 'against the grain' (itself also a 'Solecism'). Bennett, in short, is interested in the 'fault lines' which mark the repression of history by the literary textuality of the poem. Ed.]

1. Quoted in G. S. Fraser (ed.), *John Keats: Odes, A Casebook* (London, 1971), p. 48.

2. Walter Jackson Bate, *John Keats* (Cambridge, MA, 1963), p. 58; Aileen Ward, *John Keats: The Making of a Poet* (London, 1963), p. 321; Douglas Bush, *John Keats: His Life and Writing* (New York, 1966), p. 176.

3. Jerome J. McGann, 'Keats and Historical Method' in *The Beauty of Inflections. Literary Investigations in Historical Method and Theory* (Oxford, 1985), p. 61. See Paul H. Fry, 'History, Existence, and "To Autumn"', *Studies in Romanticism*, 25 (1986), 211–19, for a response to McGann's reading which argues for an understanding of the poem as concerned with 'the ontology of the lyric moment'; while McGann argues that Keats suppresses history, Fry asserts its irrelevance, but both read the poem in terms of the exclusion of the historical.

4. Vincent Newey, '"Alternate uproar and sad peace": Keats, Politics, and the Idea of Revolution', *MHRA Yearbook of English Studies*, ed. J. R. Watson, 19 (1989), p. 288. William Keach's political reading of the bees in stanza 1 of 'To Autumn' is, perhaps, the nearest that critics have come to a 'political' reading of the poem ('Cockney Couplet: Keats and the Politics of Style', *Studies in Romanticism*, 25 [1986],

pp. 193–6). For recent more general considerations of Keats and politics, see Marjorie Levinson, *Keats's Life of Allegory: The Origins of a Style* (Oxford, 1988); Paul Hamilton, 'Keats and Critique', in Marjorie Levinson et al., *Re-Thinking Historicism: Critical Readings in Romantic History* (Oxford, 1989); and Daniel Watkins, *Keats's Poetry and the Politics of Imagination* (Princeton, NJ, 1988).

5. See also Keats, 'Sleep and Poetry', lines 290–3, and 'The Fall of Hyperion', I, 467; see also *Keats's Letters*, II, 211.

6. Helen Vendler, *The Odes of John Keats* (Cambridge, MA, 1983), p. 276.

7. See John Creaser, 'From "To Autumn" to Autumn in Keats's Ode', *Essays in Criticism*, 38 (1988), 190–214, for an analysis of the disruptive implications of the use of apostrophe in the poem.

8. See Ian Jack, *Keats and the Mirror of Art* (Oxford, 1967), p. 236. Annabel M. Patterson, '"How to load and...bend": Syntax and Interpretation in Keats's "To Autumn"' *PMLA*, 94 (1979), 449–58; McGann, *The Beauty of Inflections*, p. 54; Vendler, *The Odes of John Keats*, ch. 7; Richard Macksey, 'Keats and the Poetics of Extremity', *Modern Language Notes*, 99 (1984), 845–84 (875, 879); Creaser, 'From "To Autumn" to Autumn' pp. 211–12; Kara Alwes, 'Moneta and Ceres: The Final Relationship Between Keats and the Imagination', *Nineteenth Century Literature*, 43 (1988) 212–19.

9. In a sense it might be argued that the solecism is that of the critical tradition, in that Keats does not explicitly mention the cornucopia and it is various annotated editions of Keats's poems that gloss the line in terms of the equation of Ceres and cornucopia: see, for example, M. Robertson (ed.), *Keats: Poems Published in 1820* (Oxford, 1980), p. 209; Roger Sharrock (ed.), *Keats: Selected Poems and Letters* (Oxford, 1964), p. 212; D. G. Gillham (ed.), *John Keats: Poems of 1820* (London, 1969), p. 141; Miriam Allott (ed.), *The Poems of John Keats* (London, 1970), p. 642; John Barnard (ed.), *John Keats: The Complete Poems*, 2nd edn (Harmondsworth, 1980), p. 702 (but see Douglas Bush (ed.), *John Keats: Selected Poems and Letters* [Boston, 1959], p. 354: 'The horn of plenty is usually associated with Amalthea'). Annotators tend to give similar glosses to 'The Fall of Hyperion', I, ll. 35–7 where Proserpine and 'the fabled horn' are mentioned together. The absence of any connection between Ceres and the cornucopia in the mythology or the iconography of Ceres (she is generally described as having a crown made from ears of corn and as holding a lighted torch in one hand and poppies in the other) seems to suggest that it was Keats's own invention, and one which involves a significant redescription of the figure: Ceres taught men how to work in order to gain abundance, whereas the horn of plenty simply produces abundance without the need for work. On the importance of

Ceres for Keats, see Helen Vendler's comment that 'Keats's mind was never far from Ceres' (*The Odes of John Keats*, p. 234).

10. Andrew Tooke, *The Pantheon, Representing the Fabulous Histories of the Heathen Gods and Most Illustrious Heroes* (1698), 31st edn (London, 1803), p. 162: this is only the most convenient of the formulations provided by a number of classical dictionaries available in the early nineteenth century, all of which provide similar descriptions. Significantly Jean-Jacques Rousseau makes a very similar analysis in *A Discourse Upon the Origin and Foundation of the Inequality among Mankind* (1761): 'To the tilling of the Earth the Distribution of it necessarily succeeded, and to Property once acknowledged the first Rules of Justice: for to secure every Man his own, every Man must have something...The Ancients, says Grotius, by giving to Ceres the Epithet *Legislatrix*, and to a Festival celebrated in her Honour the name *Thesmophoria*, insinuated that the Distribution of Lands produced a new kind of Right; that is, the Right of Property different from that which results from the Law of Nature' (pp. 124–6).

11. G. M. Matthews (ed.), *Keats. The Critical Heritage* (London, 1971), pp. 155, 156.

12. See Arnold Davenport, 'A Note on "To Autumn"' in Kenneth Muir (ed.), *John Keats: A Reassessment* (Liverpool, 1958), p. 96 on autumn as a boundary season.

13. Tooke's mythological explanation of the origins of private property, agriculture, and law, should be read in the context of other eighteenth-century explanations of the origins of property, such as that of Rousseau, quoted above, note 10. For accounts of the enclosure movement in the late eighteenth and early nineteenth centuries, see W. A. Armstrong, 'Rural Population and Growth, Systems of Employment and Incomes', ch. 7 in G. E. Mingay (ed.), *The Agrarian History of England and Wales: Volume VI, 1750–1850* (Cambridge, 1989), pp. 721–8; Raymond Williams, *The Country and the City* (London, 1973), pp. 96–107; Michael Turner, *Enclosures in Britain, 1750–1860* (London, 1984); Pamela Horn, *Life and Labour in Rural England, 1760–1850* (London, 1987), pp. 46–51, *The Rural World, 1780–1850: Social Change in the English Countryside* (London, 1980), pp. 51–7.

14. See, for example, Bate, *John Keats*, pp. 546–7, on Keats's use of Dryden in 'Lamia'.

15. *The Twickenham Edition of the Poems of Alexander Pope*, ed. John Butt, 7 vols (London, 1961), III, pt. 2, 107.

16. On the importance and significance of lines 155–78, see, for example, Earl R. Wasserman, Pope's *Epistle to Bathurst: A Critical Reading with an Edition of the Manuscripts* (Baltimore, MD, 1960), p. 40; and

John Barrell and Harriet Guest, 'On the Use of Contradiction: Economics and Morality in the Eighteenth-Century Long Poem', in *The New Eighteenth Century: Theory, Politics, English Literature*, ed. Felicity Nussbaum and Laura Brown (New York, 1987), p. 124.

17. See, Patterson, '"How to load and ... bend": Syntax and Interpretation in Keats's "To Autumn"', pp. 454–6.

18. The most recent example of this usage given by the *OED* is from a 1599 poem by the poet Alexander Hume: 'Throw all the land great is the gild/Of rustik folks that crie'.

19. See, *The Odes of John Keats and Their Earliest Known Manuscripts in Facsimile*, ed. Robert Gittings (London, 1970), pp. 58–9, which shows that in the first Keats drew a line through 'gold' and 'gilds', and then wrote 'barred' and 'blooms' just above.

20. For examples of Clare on enclosures, see 'Helpston Green'. 'The Lamentations of Round-Oak Waters', 'The Lament of Swordy Well' (esp. lines 183–91), 'The Fens' (lines 69–116), 'Remembrances' (lines 41–50): quotations from *The Oxford Authors: John Clare*, ed. Eric Robinson and David Powell (Oxford, 1984). On Clare and enclosures, see John Barrell, *The Idea of Landscape and the Sense of Place, 1730–1840: An Approach to the Poetry of John Clare* (Cambridge, 1972), pp. 110–20, 189–215; and Bob Heyes, 'John Clare and Enclosures', *John Clare Society Journal*, 6 (1987), 10–19.

21. Robert W. Malcolmson, *Life and Labour in England, 1700–1780* (London, 1981), pp. 34, 144, 166, note 30; see also Heyes, 'Enclosures', p. 16.

22. E. P. Thompson, *The Making of the English Working Class* (London, 1964), p. 218. Compare Williams's comment on enclosures as a 'form of legalised seizure enacted by representatives of the beneficiary class' (*The Country and the City*, p. 98). Both comments are somewhat controversial, but have the advantage of echoing contemporary (radical) opposition to enclosures – expressed, for example, by Clare. For a more 'balanced' recent analysis of the evidence, see, for example, W. A. Armstrong, 'Rural Population Growth', pp. 721–8.

23. See Andrew Bennet, 'The Politics of Gleaning in Keats's "Ode to a Nightingale" and "To Autumn"', *Keats–Shelley Journal*, 39 (1990), 34–8, in which I attempt to show, through reference to a very specific articulation of the discourse of gleaning in the early nineteenth century, the engagement of 'To Autumn' in the debate. For biblical references to gleaning and charity, see Ruth ii, 9–17; Leviticus xix, 9–10, xxiii, 22; Deuteronomy xxiv, 19–21. On the history of gleaning in the nineteenth century see W. A. Armstrong, 'Food, Shelter and Self-Help, The Poor Law, and the Position of the Labourer in Rural Society', ch. 8 in Mingay, *Agrarian History*, pp. 734–5; and David

Hoseason Morgan, *Harvesters and Harvesting, 1840–1900: A Study of the Rural Proletariat* (London, 1982), pp. 151–61.

24. See, for example, John Constable's 'The Gleaners: Brighton' (1823), Samuel Palmer's 'The Gleaning Field' (*c.*1833), Jean-François Millet's 'Des glaneuses' (1857), and Jules Breton's 'Le rappel des glaneuses (Artois)' (1859).

25. See Ivy Pinchbeck, *Women Workers and the Industrial Revolution, 1750–1850* (London, 1930), p. 103.

26. M. M. Bakhtin, 'Discourse in the Novel', in *The Dialogic Imagination: Four Essays*, trans. Caryl Emerson and Michael Holquist (Austin, TX, 1981), pp. 259–422; Julia Kristeva, *The Kristeva Reader*, ed. Toril Moi (London, 1986), p. 111; Michael Riffaterre, *Semiotics of Poetry* (Bloomington, IN, 1978); Roland Barthes, 'Theory of the Text' in *Untying the Text: A Post-Structuralist Reader*, ed. Robert Young (London, 1981), pp. 31–47. See Jonathan Culler, 'Presupposition and Intertextuality', in *The Pursuit of Signs: Semiotics, Literature, Deconstruction* (London, 1981), pp. 169–87, on the ambivalent status of intertextual referents.

27. *Selected Prose of T. S. Eliot*, ed. Frank Kermode (London, 1975), p. 153.

28. Barthes, 'Theory of the Text', p. 39.

8

Shelley's *Mont Blanc*: What the Mountain Said

FRANCES FERGUSON

Critics seem to have agreed on one thing about *Mont Blanc* – that it is a poem about the relationship between the human mind and the external world. After that, the debates begin – over whether the mind or the world has primacy, over whether 'The veil of life and death' of line 54 has been 'upfurled' or 'unfurled' in line 53, over whether 'but for such faith' in line 79 means 'only through such faith' or 'except through such faith', and so on.[1] It is not surprising that debates should have arisen, because the poem moves through a variety of different ways of imagining the mountain and the power of which it is symbolic (or synecdochic); and although the poet may do the mountain in different voices, the variety of conceptions and the rapidity with which they succeed one another are possible largely because the mountain is like the tarbaby in Uncle Remus and says nothing.

The question that arises, of course, is, How is the mountain's silence any different from the silence of the objects of any other poem? Grecian urns are likewise silent; and nightingales may sing, but they do not talk. In the case of *Mont Blanc*, the interest lies, curiously enough, in the palpable improbability of looking for anything but silence from the mountain, which is repeatedly seen as the ultimate example of materiality, of the 'thingness' of things, so that its symbolic significance is quite explicitly treated as something added to that materiality.

At moments Shelley seems to be almost defiantly trying to think of the mountain (and the entire landscape connected with it) as a

172

brute physical existence. Such an effort would have to be at least somewhat defiant, both because of the inevitable difficulty of trying to imagine anything completely without history and context (and thus associations) and because of the multiplicity of associations that had accrued to the idea of this mountain. Whereas it is crucial to the mountain's force as an example of pure materiality that it can never know that it is the highest mountain in Europe, it – and the vale of Chamonix generally – had, as Richard Holmes nicely observes, developed a reputation among the 'travelling English' of the time 'as a natural temple of the Lord and a proof of the Deity by design'.[2] The famous story of Shelley's travelling through the region, entering his name in the hotel registers in Chamonix and Montavert, and listing his occupations as 'Democrat, Philanthropist and Atheist' serves to indicate the level of his indignation at the way in which religion attributes spiritual qualities to a brute material object when it assimilates such an object to a proof of the deity by design.[3] It serves as well to suggest how difficult it is to think of the mountain as a merely physical object. For in his efforts to counter the myth of natural religion that is attached to Mont Blanc, Shelley does not destroy the mountain's symbolic value but merely inverts it.

To say that Shelley attempts to conceive Mont Blanc in terms of sheer physical force may sound like a movement toward recognising a gap between signifier and signified and toward trying to accept the mountain not just as pure physicality but also of necessity as pure non-referentiality. The mountain would function, in such an account, as a linguistic signifier that would reveal the ironic distance between its material presence and any possible signified. Yet I would argue that the poem insists, most importantly, on the inability of one's resting in such irony as it exhibits its own repeated failures to let Mont Blanc be merely a blank, merely a mass of stone: *Mont Blanc* leads to attempts to think of the mountain as physical and without metaphysical attributes, and fails; it attempts to imagine a gap between the mountain and the significances that people attach to it, and fails. But if one way of talking about the poem is to suggest that Shelley is here restricted because of the inadequacy of language, or the way in which language blocks one from saying certain things or certain kinds of things, the other side of that image of blockage – of the inability to break through – is a contrary movement made manifest by the way in which the relationships that are sketched out in the poem are not merely adequate

but so abundant and well-fitting as almost to inspire claustropho-
bia. In this respect, the poem is more nearly akin to Wordsworth's
lines about how exquisitely the human mind and the world are
fitted to one another than even those lines that Harold Bloom and
others have seen echoed in the opening section of *Mont Blanc* – the
lines from 'Tintern Abbey' in which Wordsworth speaks of having
'felt / A presence that disturbs [him] with the joy / Of elevated
thoughts .../ A Motion and a spirit, that ... / ... rolls through all
things' (ll. 93–102).[4]

Thus although the motive behind the poem appears to be conceiving of Mont Blanc not just as the white mountain but also as a
massive version of blankness – or 'solitude / Or blank desertion'
(*The Prelude*, I, 394–5), the poem has already in its first few lines
become a poem about the impossibility of seeing the mountain as
alien. As Earl Wasserman observes, the 'everlasting universe of
things' is like the Arve flowing through the Ravine that is like the
'universal mind', and the Ravine of 'universal mind' and the
Channel in which the brook of the individual mind flows merge
with one another.[5] In the midst of all the convergence and congru-
ence of the schema, however, Wasserman very convincingly notes a
sensory overload in the image of the brook: 'The simile, which has
no significant function except to transform the mode of vision, by
its very tautology opens the door to an abundance of supposedly
external objects that exceed the requirements of the comparison, as
though the tendency to conceive of images as external were too
great for the poet to resist.'[6]

Wasserman's central point here is that the poet conceives of
metaphors in which he then finds 'a remarkably consistent objective
correlative for his metaphor for a total universe that is indifferently
things or thoughts and that is located in the One Mind'.[7] It is not,
of course, particularly surprising that Shelley should see the scene,
when he finally looks at it, in the terms in which he thought about
it before he looked at it; what is, however, remarkable is not just
that the interpretation and the perception are aligned with one
another but that the various portions of the imagery are as well.
The river, of necessity, fits the ravine perfectly – and in a way that
makes it impossible to say which has priority and determines the
other. Whereas a glass of water may be said to be prior to the water
in it, in that its shape is one that any water in it must conform to,
the course and shape of a riverbed may be said to be determined by
the waters that flow through it just as much as the riverbed may be

said to determine the course of the river. Yet it is not merely the river and the riverbed that are interdependent and mutually creative, for the height of the mountain and the depth of the ravine have an analogous relation to one another: there is a ravine – and a ravine this deep – because there is a mountain – and a mountain this high – and vice versa.

An additional complication appears, however, in the image of the brook that Wasserman describes as exceeding 'the requirements of the comparison'.[8]

> The source of human thought its tribute brings
> Of waters, – with a sound but half its own,
> Such as a feeble brook will oft assume
> In the wild woods, among the mountains lone,
> Where waterfalls around it leap for ever,
> Where woods and winds contend, and a vast river
> Over its rocks ceaselessly bursts and raves.
>
> (ll. 5–11)

The 'feeble brook' is not described simply as a tributary to the 'vast river'; instead, the river is said to 'burst and rave' over its – the brook's – rocks, thus introducing the question of whether a brook is still a brook when a river runs in its channel. Although the question itself seems like a bad riddle, it forcibly demonstrates Shelley's procedure throughout the poem of insisting on the changeableness of the identity of any individual entity. For the brook, in becoming a part of the river, both loses its identity as a brook and transcends itself, gaining access to a forcefulness it never had as a 'feeble brook'.

We have here, in the cluster of images that are continually put into relation with one another, an elaborate schema of reciprocity. The universe of things exists to be perceived by the universal mind, so that the mind does not create things in its acts of perception but rather keeps the things of the world from going to waste. The river that courses along the channel of the brook enables the individual mind to participate in thought and sensation without ever having to originate them for itself. As we do not make up the world of things as we go along, so we do not discover all of human thought on our own. The relationship between the river and the brook may be seen not only as analogous to that between all of human knowledge and an individual knowing subject but also as similar to all human language in relation to an individual speaker.

It is, however, when the terms that are put into relationship with one another get proper names that the poem begins to flirt with relational punning. Bloom has stressed the importance of Shelley's addressing the ravine and the mountain as 'Thou' and has seen it as emblematic of the poem's conjecturing 'the possibility of a Thou as a kind of universal mind in nature'.[9] Although there are no proper names in the first section of the poem, the second section offers not just the pronoun 'Thou' but also the names 'Ravine of Arve' and 'Arve'. The appearance of the names registers the shift from Shelley's imagining a schematic relationship for the ravine and the river to his seeing this particular ravine and this particular river. But the address to the ravine is repeated enough for it to become, as Wasserman might have said, 'excessive'. For when Shelley turns to look at and speak to the ravine, he calls it 'thou, Ravine of Arve – dark, deep Ravine', and in the nomenclature 'Ravine of Arve' is another way of suggesting the interdependence of the ravine and the river. There is also, however, a linguistic *tour de force* – or cheap trick – at work here: the river that has been imagined in the first section to 'burst and rave' ceaselessly is identified as the Arve, so that the 'Arve raves'. And it of course turns out that the 'Arve raves in the Ravine'. (If you drop the article 'the' from the previous clause, you have four words that are all contained in the letters of the word 'ravine', and it might, with a bit of work, be made into another song for *My Fair Lady*.)

This species of relational punning underscores the symbiosis of things and mind, of river and ravine, that Shelley has earlier been sketching. Further, it raises some interesting questions about the status of language in the poem. Although the punning is a kind of technological trick with language, it is hard to see how this language can really be described as duplicitous, for all it does is reiterate the earlier message: thought takes the world of things to be inextricable from the mind: the actual perception of the scene confirms this message, in taking the river to be inextricable from the ravine, and at this point in the poem the language itself rather glaringly insists that the Arve exists because it is in the Ravine of Arve. The importance of the language trick lies not, however, in the fact that this language is human and might thus reveal the primacy of the human and the priority of the human mind. Rather, the anagram suggests the inevitability of any human's seeing things in terms of relationship.

The significance of this love language, moreover, goes beyond the familiarity built into a poet's addresses to the personifications that he creates. For the questions about epistemology that Wasserman has very convincingly seen to dominate the poem appear very different if epistemology is correlated with ontology on the one hand or, alternatively, with love. In the one account – that which continually seeks to align epistemology with ontology so that one's knowing always struggles to coincide with the real existence of what one knows – the adequacy of one's ability to know is always suspect. In the other account – that which aligns epistemology with love – emotional profligacy that continually postulates and assumes the existence of an interlocutor supplants any notion of matching one's knowledge with things as they really are.

In the remarkable fragment 'On Love', Shelley approvingly remarks that 'Sterne says that if he were in a desert, he would love some cypress'.[10] In *Mont Blanc* Shelley falls in love with a ravine, a river, and a mountain not because of the nature of those objects but because of his own, his human, mind, which cannot imagine itself as a genuinely independent, isolated existence. Love is, he says,

> that powerful attraction towards all that we conceive, or fear, or hope beyond ourselves, when we find within our own thoughts the chasm of an insufficient void and seek to awaken in all things that are a community with what we experience within ourselves. If we reason, we would be understood: if we imagine, we would that the airy children of our brain were born anew within another's: if we feel, we would that another's nerves should vibrate to our own, that lips of motionless ice should not reply to lips quivering and burning with the heart's best blood. This is Love. This is the bond and the sanction which connects not only man with man but with everything which exists.[11]

When Shelley views the natural landscape, he immediately begins to speak familiarly to it, not just because poets traditionally personify natural objects and address them with terms of endearment, but because he cannot imagine himself without imagining an anti-type that will enable him to be assured of his own existence. For 'the invisible and unattainable point to which Love tends', he says, is 'the discovery of its anti-type; the meeting with an understanding capable of clearly estimating our own'.[12]

Edmund Burke had identified as sublime not only the experience of contemplating enormous heights and depths but also, and most particularly, the experience of being isolated from other humans.[13]

From one perspective, Shelley seems to provide a textbook example of how to experience the sublimity of Mont Blanc as he registers his consciousness of the mountain's force while appearing to speak from a condition of isolation (where no human aid can intervene between him and the mountain's power). It is from this perspective unremarkable that Shelley's account of the mountain continually recurs to the subject of its wildness, of its being a wilderness remote from all that civilisation involves. By a peculiar twist, however, Shelley converts the isolation of the mountain from a threat into an opportunity – as if he were not so much alone with the mountain as 'alone at last' with it. For the act of imagination or intellection by which he moves from the description of the portion of the mountain that remains hidden to him is an act of sympathy; although he speaks merely of the portion of the mountain that really exists, he in effect woos the mountain with an 'imagination which … enters into and seizes upon the subtle and delicate peculiarities' that the mountain (if it were human) would have 'delighted to cherish and unfold in secret'.[14]

Thus Shelley's addressing the ravine and the mountain as 'Thou' is only one aspect of the poet's effort to convert epistemological language into love language. For although *Mont Blanc* is a sublime poem upon a sublime subject, it projects an air of sociability. As soon as the poet depicts the 'Dark, deep ravine', he provides it with companionship in the persons of 'Thy giant brood of pines', those 'Children of elder time' (ll. 20–1). Even when he imagines Mont Blanc as a fierce and ravening force, he cannot imagine it as a real desert; it is 'A desart peopled by the storms' and a place where the poet immediately starts constituting a domestic circle as he asks, 'Is this the scene / Where the old Earthquake-daemon taught her young / Ruin? Were these their toys?' (ll. 71–3).

Yet Shelley's famous letter to Thomas Love Peacock describing his first viewing of Mont Blanc makes the poem's love-longing for the mountain seem particularly one-sided, not just unrequited but positively scorned:

> I will not pursue Buffon's sublime but gloomy theory, that this earth which we inhabit will at some future period be changed into a mass of frost. Do you who assert the supremacy of Ahriman imagine him throned among these desolating snows, among these palaces of death and frost, sculptured in this their terrible magnificence by the unsparing hand of necessity, and that he casts around him as the first essays of his final usurpation avalanches, torrents, rocks and thunders – and

above all, these deadly glaciers at once the proofs and symbols of his reign. – Add to this the degradation of the human species, who in these regions are half deformed or idiotic and all of whom are deprived of anything that can excite interest or admiration. This is a part of the subject more mournful and less sublime; –but such as neither the poet nor the philosopher should disdain.[15]

The logic by which Shelley regards the degradation of the humans in the vicinity as 'more mournful and less sublime' than Buffon's theory that the entire earth will become 'a mass of frost' may not be self-evident. But his central point here is that the deformity and idiocy of the inhabitants of the area are, quite literally, not sublime because such deformity and idiocy merely provide, in human form, a repetition of the mountain's role as pure materiality. Thus, although the mountain has the power to make these people less than human, that very power of oppression sets a limit to itself because it annihilates everything in the human that can understand the mountain's material aspect – with an understanding that Shelley speaks of in the fragment 'On Love'. Throughout *Mont Blanc*, Shelley's attention always moves from images of destructiveness to images of complementarity. In this sense, the poem appears to be almost an endorsement of Kant's remark that nothing in nature is sublime: 'All we can say is that the object is fit for the presentation of a sublimity which can be found in the mind, for no sensible form can contain the sublime properly so-called.'[16]

Shelley here focuses on a central paradox of the sublime – that we should take pleasure in the contemplation of anything that presents a threat to our tendency toward self-preservation. By falling in love with strenuous death, however, Shelley demonstrates the way in which nature's destructiveness is never centrally at issue in the experience of the sublime. Rather, because the human mind can attribute destructiveness to nature, nature needs us for it to be perceived as destructive and to continue to be destructive in any significant way. Thus *Mont Blanc* creates an image of sublimity that continually hypostatises an eternity of human consciousness. Because even the ideas of the destructiveness of nature and the annihilation of mankind require human consciousness to give them their force, they thus are testimony to the necessity of the continuation of the human.

In the poem's first section, 'woods and winds contend' (l. 10); in the second, 'The chainless winds' (l. 22) come to hear the 'old and solemn harmony' (l. 24) that they make with the 'giant brood of pines' (l. 20). The perspective of the mountain, presented in the third section, is the perspective of eternity where 'None can reply – all seems eternal now' (l. 75); and the fourth section offers the inverse of that eternal view – the perspective of mutability and mortality that sees that 'The race / Of man, flies far in dread; his work and dwelling / Vanish ...' (ll. 117–19).

These different sections, although obviously similar, do not offer merely different versions of the same message. If the struggle between 'woods and winds' of the first section does not negate the possibility of seeing these same woods and winds creating a harmony between them, the relationship between the terms of eternity and mutability is even stronger. For it is not just that mutability and eternity are two different ways of conceiving time, but also that it becomes impossible for the poet to imagine eternity except in terms of mutability – the terms of generation in which earthquakes create epochs and broods of little earthquakes – or to image mutability except in the terms of eternity, in the form of a Power that 'dwells apart in its tranquillity' (l. 96).

The poet begins the fifth and final section with a magnificent feat of calculated vagueness and understatement:

> Mont Blanc yet gleams on high:- the power is there,
> The still and solemn power of many sights,
> And many sounds, and much of life and death.
>
> (ll. 127–9)

The understatement registers, among other things, the poet's awareness that his thoughts about the mountain have not changed the universe – or even the mountain. He seems almost to struggle to see the mountain's continued existence as a reason for him to return to his struggle to see it in its materiality. Yet this final section of the poem recapitulates the earlier movement into a language that inexorably begins to treat the mountain landscape as *someone* to be understood not merely through the understanding but through an understanding that operates to complete and magnify its object through an aggrandisement Shelley calls love.

The mountain has 'a voice' to 'repeal / Large codes of fraud and woe' (ll. 80–1) not because 'The secret strength of things / Which governs thought' inhabits it but because the poet is its voice as he finds himself in the process of recognising the impossibility of taking the material as merely material. Just as one can see the letters that go together to make up 'Arve' and 'Ravine of Arve' as an example of the material aspects of language but cannot see them as language without seeing them as implying something more than matter, so one can see the mountain as an example of materiality but cannot see it even as a mountain without seeing it as involving more than matter. The mountain can repeal 'Large codes of fraud and woe' by making it clear that a love of humanity is easy if one can love a mountain that is physically inimical to man. And yet the final irony of the poem is that Shelley can conclude by asking the mountain his most famous question:

> And what were thou, and earth, and stars, and sea,
> If to the human mind's imaginings
> Silence and solitude were vacancy?
>
> (ll. 142–4)

With this question, he reminds the mountain that it needs him. The relationship between man and world has been painted in such a way as to make it clear that complementarity rather than direct communication is at issue in his version of language. But although he reminds the mountain of its need for him, his questions also have all the poignancy of a speech by a lover who still needs to argue his case. He may be a fit anti-type to the mountain, but he is still looking for a mountain who will understand him.

Even though the poem ends with a question directed to the mountain, Shelley's interest in Mont Blanc is, of course, predicated upon the impossibility of the mountain's ever taking any interest in him and answering. The mountain is matter, and its power resides to a very considerable extent in that fact; just as Milton's Eve [Milton's Satan; *Paradise Lost* IX. 465. Ed.] was once 'stupidly good', so matter is, in Shelley's account, 'stupidly powerful', and powerful more because of its stupidity than in spite of it. That is, its power depends upon its never being able to move out of the world of death. Because it can never be alive, it can never be subject to death; because it can never be conscious, it can never experience fear (or love or any other emotion, anticipatory or otherwise).

In light of the poem's final account of the mountain, the first four verse paragraphs might seem to represent a massive epistemological error and a mistake in love as well. For the first two verse paragraphs argue for resemblance between the human and the natural worlds in claiming that the same model can be used for both (the Arve is to the ravine as the 'everlasting universe of things' is to the individual human mind) and in presenting the similarity between the two with a lover's air of pleasure in the discovery of himself in another. In this manner, Shelley addresses the ravine as if it were a version of himself:

> Dizzy Ravine, and when I gaze on thee
> I seem as in a trance sublime and strange
> To muse on my own separate phantasy,
> My own, my human mind....
> (ll. 34–7)

The reversion from thoughts of the ravine to thoughts of his own mind does not betoken any inappropriate narcissism but indicates, rather, the translation of the material to the human that is involved in any effort at making the scene intelligible. As both the formal analogy and the poet's familiar address to the scene argue for the equivalence between the material and the human, Shelley pursues this thinking by analogy down its fallacious course as he attributes sublimity to the mountain in making it appear to transcend itself. Thus he speaks of the 'Power in likeness of the Arve' as not like water but more than water as it comes 'Bursting through these dark mountains like the flame / Of lightning through the tempest' (ll. 16–19) and of those 'earthly rainbows stretched across the sweep / Of the etherial waterfall' (ll. 25–6) that refuse to occupy any single element or place; the transfer of attributes from one element to another lends each an all-inclusiveness that none would have individually.

Of course, the phenomena that are presented as more than themselves because of the transfer of attributes *are* palpably more than themselves, in that the rainbow, while being an interaction of water and air, is made 'earthly' whereas the waterfall produced by the passage of the water over the rocky earth is made 'etherial'. The distinct limit to the self-transcendence of these physical elements is, however, implicit in the conspicuous omission (for the moment) of the fire that emblemises the animation of the elements. Although the water and the air, like the water and the earth, act together to produce a mutual self-transcendence of each, the crucial difference between these mutual magnifications and any real instance of sublime self-transcendence lies in the fact that these elements provide instances of action without representing agency.

If the apparent threat involved in any landscape that might be provocative of a sublime experience is that man (and mind) might be reduced to mere matter, the correspondent activity that occurs is that the poet's sublime account of Mont Blanc and the entire scene around it never allows matter to remain material but rather co-opts it or transmogrifies it by continually mistaking the activity of the material world for agency, by taking it to be as intentional as any human activity might be. Shelley insists virtually throughout the poem upon this confusion between activity and agency as he continually treats the mountain as a person (albeit a particularly large and powerful one). This programmatic confusion discloses a fundamental insight into the nature of sublime experience: in treating natural objects as occasions for sublime experience, one imputes agency (and therefore a moving spirit) to them. Although such imputation would, in other hands, perhaps be the basis for seeing the designedness of nature as an argument for the existence of God, for Shelley it instead identifies the sublime as the aesthetic operation through which one makes an implicit argument for the transcendent existence of man – not because man is able to survive the threat posed by the power of the material world but because he is able to domesticate the material world for the purposes of aesthetics by converting such a massive example of the power of the material world as Mont Blanc from an object into a found object. For what the sublime does for nature is to annex all that is material to the human by appropriating it for aesthetics. In this sense, Shelley in *Mont Blanc* discovers the same assertion of human power that Kant did when he distinguished between the sublime and the beautiful on the grounds that 'we must seek a ground external to ourselves for the beautiful of nature, but seek it for the sublime merely in ourselves and in our attitude of thought, which introduces sublimity into the representation of nature'.[17] At Mont Blanc, in the assertion of human power that any sublime experience represents, Shelley thus revamps the argument from design to redound to the credit of the human observer who converts the object into a found object, not merely matter but matter designed by its perceiver.

Moreover, in treating the sublime experience of Mont Blanc as not merely adapting the material to the purposes of the human and the supersensible (or spiritual) but as a discovery of the human in nature, Shelley collapses Kant's account of the 'purposiveness without purpose' that we discover in aesthetic objects as he speaks of Mont Blanc as if it had purposes in relation to humans. Thus it is that the language of the poem continually moves from epistemological questions, questions of the poet's understanding, to love language in which all the questions are of his being understood.

From *Romanticism and Language*, ed. Arden Reed (London, 1984), pp. 202–14.

NOTES

[Shelley's *Mont Blanc* (1816) is a notoriously difficult poem which explores the relationship of the human mind to the natural world by a contemplation of the sublimity of the mountain. Frances Ferguson's essay reads the poem in poststructuralist terms, arguing that it is concerned with the process of signification. She moves away from some previous readings which have argued that the poem ironically exposes the lack of identity between the *signifier* (the material linguistic form of the sign, i.e. 'Mont Blanc') and the *signified* (the conceptual aspects of the sign, i.e. the mental construct that the sign implies), and she posits instead that the language of the poem is part of a web of linguistic relationships. Ferguson's essay makes particular use of theories of 'intertextuality' discussed in the endnote to Andrew Bennett's essay (8). She also comments on the 'paronomastic' or punning relationship of words in the poem before placing *Mont Blanc* in the context of Shelley's essay 'On Love' where the human mind continually searches for resemblances (or 'anti-types') of itself in the natural world. What Ferguson's essay offers us, in simple terms, is a perceptive and ingenious reading of the ways in which meaning is created and problematised in Shelley's philosophically complex poem. The essay is printed complete. Ed.]

1. The best brief survey of the various debates about the poem appears in the notes to the poem in *Shelley's Poetry and Prose*, ed. Donald H. Reiman and Sharon B. Powers (New York, 1977), pp. 89–93.

2. Richard Holmes, *Shelley: The Pursuit* (London, 1976), p. 342.

3. See Holmes's account, ibid., pp. 339–43.

4. Harold Bloom, *Shelley's Mythmaking* (Ithaca, NY, 1969), p. 20. See also Bloom, *The Visionary Company* (Ithaca, NY, 1971), p. 293.

5. Earl R. Wasserman, *Shelley: A Critical Reading* (Baltimore, MD, 1971), pp. 221–38. Wasserman's reading remains, to my mind, the most impressive account of the poem.

6. Ibid., p. 224.

7. Ibid.

8. Ibid.

9. Bloom, *Shelley's Mythmaking*, p. 23.

10. *Shelley's Prose, or the Trumpet of a Prophecy*, ed. David Lee Clark (Albuquerque, 1954), p. 171.

11. Ibid., p. 170.

12. Ibid.

13. Edmund Burke, *A Philosophical Enquiry in to the Origin of Our Ideas of the Sublime and the Beautiful*, ed. James T. Boulton (Notre Dame, IN, 1958), pp. 43, 71.

14. *Shelley's Poetry and Prose*, p. 170.

15. *Letters of Shelley*, ed. F. L. Jones, 2 vols (Oxford, 1964), I. 499. Quoted in Bloom, *Shelley's Mythmaking*, p. 19, and in Holmes, *Shelley*, p. 340.

16. Immanuel Kant, *Critique of Judgment*, trans J. H. Bernard (New York, 1966), pp. 83–4.

17. Ibid., p. 84.

9

'Mechanism of a kind yet unattempted': The Dramatic Action of *Prometheus Unbound*

KELVIN EVEREST

In a letter to Thomas Love Peacock of 6 April 1819, Shelley wrote from Rome mentioning amongst many other matters the progress of his current poetic project: 'My Prometheus Unbound is just finished & in a month or two I shall send it. It is a drama, with characters & mechanism of a kind yet unattempted; & I think the execution is better than any of my former attempts.'[1] The 'month or two' was presumably to allow for copying,[2] but its vagueness points to a larger irresolution on Shelley's part, which continued for most of 1819, as to whether or when the poem was indeed exactly to be thought of as finished: Shelley seems to have been a long time deciding what 'finished' might mean in relation to *Prometheus Unbound*.

Shelley had, for him, an unusually high opinion of the artistic merits of *Prometheus Unbound*, and this opinion has been generally shared by his admirers, including the many academic admirers he has attracted since the Second World War. For those many readers, on the other hand, who find bad habits and bad influences in Shelley's poetry, *Prometheus Unbound* has plenty of faults. These might include an exceptionally high level of surface difficulty, the effect of the poem's sustained complex abstraction, and also of its combination of pace and facility in versification with long syntactic structures and demanding, constantly shifting formal variety. I do not myself think such qualities constitute in themselves a serious problem in Shelley's poetry; on the contrary, I greatly admire his poetry, in its deployment of these very qualities amongst others. But, paradoxically, I do now find myself dissatisfied with *Prometheus Unbound*, although not for the usual anti-Shelleyan reasons. But the causes of my dissatisfaction do open up areas of difficulty in the poetry which are worrying.

Mary Shelley's long note to the poem in her edition of 1839 makes some judgements and comments which are worth rehearsing, even if they are very familiar. There is, firstly, her insistence that the poem does offer a special kind of difficulty for what she calls 'the ordinary reader':

> It requires a mind as subtle and penetrating as his own to understand the mystic meanings scattered throughout the poem. They elude the ordinary reader by their abstraction and delicacy of distinction, but they are far from vague.[3]

Two things here call for comment. There is first the oddly casual assumption of intellectual superiority, which could in Shelley's case shade with such apparent ease into social superiority. One recalls the implicit social distinctions of the formulation in the Preface to *Prometheus Unbound*, where Shelley speaks of his purpose in the poem as directed to the 'refined' imaginations of the 'more select classes' of poetical readers. These attitudes require, of course, a real effort of historical imagination, and they are very easy to mishear; but they do strike an unsettling note for the modern reader.[4] The other striking point in the passage from Mary Shelley's note is the confident definiteness of its last clause: those elusive 'mystic meanings' may be obscure to the ordinary reader, but they are far from vague. The impression of something very specific in mind is borne out elsewhere in the note, for example in the eloquent assertion that 'Shelley loved to idealise the real – to gift the mechanism of the material universe with a soul and a voice, and to bestow such also on the most delicate and abstract emotions and thoughts of the mind'.[5]

I want to pursue some possible implications of these assertions, and to explore the extent to which Shelley's efforts in the poem to 'gift the mechanism of the material universe with a soul and a voice' are at once central to the very workings of the dramatic action in the poem, and yet also so demanding to the attention and capacities of readers as to constitute a serious problem, and even a serious flaw in conception.

There is one further, very well-known passage in the 1839 note which has proved profoundly unhelpful in its impact on subsequent commentary:

> Shelley believed that mankind had only to will that there should be no evil, and there would be none. It is not my part in these notes to notice the arguments that have been urged against this opinion, but to mention the fact that he entertained it, and was indeed attached to it with fervent enthusiasm. That man could be so perfectionised as to be able to expel evil from his own nature, and from the greater part of creation, was the cardinal point of his system.[6]

This is a seriously misleading statement. It is inherently unlikely that a man of Shelley's intellectual background and commitments would have held such a self-evidently fatuous conception of the problem of evil. Mary's judgement appears coloured by her own mature conservatism, and also perhaps by the less than perfect intellectual accord she enjoyed with her husband in the Italian years. Whatever the reason, the statement has nourished both hostile and well-meaning readings of Shelley's work. But it clearly won't do: *Prometheus Unbound* is plainly not representing revolutionary change in history as if it were to be effected simply by an act of human volition, conceived in pure abstraction. The whole poem is in fact massively preoccupied with questions of the relation of individual human agency to great and apparently impersonal processes of change in history. Stuart Sperry has argued in a fine essay that the seminal issue of Prometheus's recalling of his curse is itself a problematic and ambivalent trigger for the action. Many features of the action which flows from this decision point to an understanding of human action as necessarily determined, at least to a significant extent, by prior determinations beyond volitional control (for example, the recall is itself produced by an antecedent period of suffering, leading to transformed understanding).[7] The problem of the poem's action is the problem of the 'Ode to the West Wind', the problem of human agency in history, the extent of its possibility and the nature of its means. The whole of the second act of *Prometheus Unbound* is given over largely to a representation of how human agency can affect or be merged with the impersonal drives underlying historical development and change.

I would like to focus discussion on the third scene of the second act. The reading which follows has grown out of an effort of sustained close commentary.[8] In relation at least to some poems and passages, this effort has not always been a heartening experience. As a project of explanation and guidance for the seriously interested adult reader, it has for example come increasingly to form a contrast in my mind with the brilliantly illuminating effect of G. M. Matthews's extraordinary essay on the geophysical symbolism of *Prometheus Unbound*, 'A Volcano's Voice in Shelley'.[9] Part of the tremendous power of that essay lies in its promise of enabling access to dazzling and encompassing design underlying the whole range of the immense surface difficulties of the poem.

These difficulties have a variety of causes. They are partly textual; the poem has usually been printed in a very corrupt state, the product of a particularly complicated and tangled composition and publication history, even by Shelleyan standards. They are also partly a product of very basic reading problems. It is puzzling even to try to grasp the parameters within which the drama must be conceived to unfold. At what level, or levels, does whatever happens in the play happen? Is it appropriate or necessary to bear in mind any limits whatsoever to the kinds of action possible? Are there chronological constraints, or temporal constraints of any kind? Are there any imagined limits to which, and which kind of, characters may appear and participate? The deliberate cultural and religious syncretism of Shelley's conception makes for real difficulty in this area particularly.

Answers have of course been attempted, although as a matter of fact genuinely encompassing answers, which try hard to take account of everything that goes on, are not at all numerous. The most persuasive, coherence-discovering reading by far is still Earl Wasserman's, which it is proper to take together with its subsequent reinforcements and developments carried out by Stuart Curran.[10] These readings seek to demonstrate that *Prometheus Unbound* is essentially a poetic exposition of a sophisticated system of thought which informs and pervades all of Shelley's work. The great strength and excellence of Wasserman's reading derives from his scrupulous and fiercely intelligent fidelity to Shelley's own writings. The 'system' is in no sense an imposition from some external body of ideas. Stuart Curran, in a much more broadly-based and bibliographically adventurous study, endorses Wasserman's view that *Prometheus Unbound* expresses a structured metaphysics, articulated in a learned and eclectic syncretistic idiom. Within this structure, Prometheus stands for 'the One Mind', and in common with all the other characters except Demogorgon, he participates in an action of pure mentality. Shelley, in this view, is a thoroughgoing idealist, dramatising the possible modes of relation between 'Being' and 'the mysterious source of all the energy that appears in the domain of the One Mind as the sequence of events'.[11]

The critical insights yielded by this approach are rich and rewarding. But they are founded on the profoundly debatable premiss that Shelley did have any such 'System' to articulate. The most immediately telling evidence against its existence is the fact that Wasserman is obliged to spend so much time in constructing the system, by inference, by the construction or shaping of links and bridges in argument, and in the carefully explained bringing into coherent relation of apparently disparate passages of writing, often diverse in form and occasion, and often separated in time. Shelley simply did not write as a philosopher; his extended prose essays are occasional in character, and do not work as contributions to a self-consciously unfolding process of systematic exposition. He was after all never more than a very young man, who devoted the great majority of his mental energies to writing poetry, or in reading towards poetic projects, or to coping with the unceasing and taxing demands of his exceptionally complex and dramatic personal life. He was developing constantly. The stasis of mental position implicit in Wasserman's approach is an illusion — though certainly a valuable and very serviceable one – created by academic commentary.

But if that is the case, then what are we to make of *Prometheus Unbound*? An extreme limit of the view that the poem is a fully coherent, expository work, to be understood in a systematic way, is perhaps provided by Stuart Curran's contention that the play's exact centre, counting the lines in the final four-act version, falls at the point of Asia's pivotal speech to Demogorgon in scene four of the second act, which is preceded by 1267 lines, and followed by 1265.[12]

The composition history of the poem argues emphatically against the plausibility of any such assumption of deep meditation in its design.[13] Act One was begun, and probably also mostly completed, in the period from August to October 1818, while the Shelleys were staying at the Villa d'Este near Venice. The death of Clara, the intimacy with Byron and the ongoing wrangle over Allegra, and also the still quite recent Alpine crossing and first entry into Italy, all contribute to the background of Act One. This burst of composition was then interrupted by the journey South to Naples via Rome as Winter drew on. Acts Two and Three were written mostly in Rome in the early months of 1819, after returning from Naples. Act Four appears to be written in a different idiom altogether, at a period when the dominating biographical circumstances, and the physical locations of the writing, are quite transformed. Drafting for Act Four covers approximately late summer 1819 through to December. There is also some backward influence of style at this stage; for example, the second half of Act Two, Scene Four, was added very late, and it decidedly picks up the manner of the new writing then simultaneously taking place for the new fourth act.

The style of Act One is distinctive, something new and impressively confident in Shelley's work up to that moment. Formally it is an artful blend of Hellenic and Hebraic elements. Miltonic and Wordsworthian blank verse, in a manner which takes forward the achievement of the versification of *Alastor*, is alternated with lyric writing in a more contemporary idiom, related to the popular work of Byron and Tom Moore. Essentially Act One is an adaptation of Greek tragedy, in stylistic terms as well as in dramatic conception, and as such could be seen as building on ideas which may date back to the period of Shelley's first intimacy with Byron some two years earlier in Switzerland.

The second act is stylistically very different. Its blank verse is remarkable, wholly original and in startling and beautiful contrast with Act One. But the act is also plotted on different principles from those which govern Act One. The first act is a symbolic representation of the constituents of an international crisis, even dateable in a way,[14] and constantly seeking to integrate an ethical-metaphysical perspective with political analysis. Act Two has a new set of preoccupations, hardly prepared for at all in Act One, and indeed only sketchily developed in the later Acts. These new preoccupations can be traced most directly to the impact on Shelley of his arrival in the area of Naples, and the effects of reading he was led to in connection with that visit.

The main features of these influences are concentrated in the famous exchange between Asia and Demogorgon in Act Two, Scene Four. The dialogue marks Asia's realisation that Demogorgon will tell her nothing she does not work out for herself. His power to illuminate is strictly commensurate with the developed understanding of his interrogator. Asia thus initiates the revolutionary crisis as she grasps her own agency in its processes. Demogorgon has just told her that 'the deep truth is imageless', and to this Asia responds as follows:

> So much I asked before, and my heart gave
> The response thou hast given: and of such truths
> Each to itself must be the oracle. –
>
> (II. iv. 121–3)

Oracles utter prophecy. Notoriously, their prophecies are gnomic, adaptable. They blur in their very form the distinction between a future course of events, and the individual's power to change or influence that course. Asia's use of the word here has been elaborately prepared for in the preceding scenes of Act Two, in ways which very strongly suggest that the course of the play has been influenced, deeply influenced and shaped, by experiences and reactions which intervene between the writing of Act One and the working-out of Act Two. Even the crucial set of volcanic metaphors, which Matthews demonstrated to be essential to an understanding of what is actually supposed to be *happening* at this stage in the drama, is not in any important sense prepared for in Act One. It springs more or less fully-formed, out of almost nowhere, and into the heart of the dramatic action in Act Two.

Shelley clearly had some powerful experiences in Naples. The strange 'Author's Introduction' to Mary Shelley's novel *The Last Man*, published in 1826 but begun soon after her husband's death, more than hints at one such experience. It describes a fanciful origin for the novel in the author's chance discovery, in Naples in 1818 in the company of her 'companion', of the cave of the Cumaean Sibyl.[15] The whole of this introduction evokes the Shelleys' very classically-informed travels around Naples to Baiae, Lake Avernus, Solfatara, Vesuvius, with Capri and the other islands imprisoning the defeated Titans always in view, and the landscapes and landmarks of Virgil's poetry always at hand. These sights, with their literary associations, resonating out from the sixth book of the *Aeneid*, activated in Shelley's literary intelligence a startlingly broad and richly intricate range of existing knowledge and reflection.

The poetic writing that grew from this experience is singularly complex, demanding, and strangely conceived. Take for example the opening lines of Act Two, Scene Three:

Hither the sound has borne us, to the realm
Of Demogorgon, and the mighty portal,
Like a volcano's meteor-breathing chasm,
Whence the oracular vapour is hurled up
Which lonely men drink wandering in their youth
And call truth, virtue, love, genius or joy –
That maddening wine of life, whose dregs they drain
To deep intoxication, and uplift
Like Maenads who cry loud, Evoe! Evoe!
The voice which is contagion to the world.

(II. iii. 1–10)

This passage can only make sense if we grant a meditated character to the striking epithets and details which abound. The density of allusion, and the rapidity and fleeting transitions of thought in the lines, are entirely representative of the Act's manner throughout. We cannot lightly call such a quality a limitation, but it definitely does pose a problem. For it is not simply the density that is arresting – that after all is a quality which is pervasive in, say, *Paradise Lost* – but also the undeclared and almost wholly implicit nature of what is nevertheless central to the action at this point. The 'oracular vapour' which is described as issuing from the mouth of Demogorgon's cave participates in an elaborate network of interconnecting motifs and developing strands within the drama. This network is present in many aspects even within this one short passage. The passing mention that 'lonely men' are the ones who drink in the vapour and call its effects after the great libertarian watchwords, hints at a connection between personal failure and a visionary political commitment (feeding on idealism is a compensation for more ordinary lacks). The Maenads suggest a connection with Dionysus and the central oracular shrine to Dionysus at Delphi. The fact that the lines begin by asserting that the 'sound' has borne Asia and Panthea to this place connects up with the use in the preceding two scenes of 'Echoes' which in fact contribute their own music (that is to say, they do more than repeat back the words of the characters). This dramatises the increasingly momentous merging within the characters at this stage of an inner drive to find an historical destiny, and an outer compulsion, sweet but commanding, and bound up with the physical presence of nature, which drives its subjects to a destiny they cannot choose to escape.

The 'oracular vapour' itself implies a very informed awareness in the poem of how classical oracles were thought to work. Shelley would have been long familiar with classical accounts, for instance from the detailed descriptions and discussions in Plutarch and Lucan, both favoured authors of his almost from boyhood. A great many varieties of divination are attested in classical sources; indeed the practice was deeply integral to Hellenistic culture. Almost anything could be read for signs, from the fall of knuckle-bones and the flight of birds, to entrails, sneezes, and twitches. And of course dreams. Dreams as a form of prophecy are deployed explicitly in the opening scene of Act Two of *Prometheus Unbound*, where they are joined with other Sibylline prophetic forms. This scene, like the entire Act, depends in its action on classical accounts of divination, dreams, and the reading of signs in nature, as when Asia and Panthea are exhorted to 'follow' to their destiny by messages stamped on leaves, and signalled in the shadows of clouds on a hillside, and by low sweet sounds in the air.

Oracular prophecy was often described in terms of a frenzied possession, as if under the influence of drugs or inebriation. Shelley in late 1818 would have read very recently of such possessed prophecy, in Barthelemy's *Travels of Anacharsis*, and also in one of his basic reference guide books during his early Italian journeys, Eustace's *Classical Tour through Italy*.[16] The opening of Act Two, Scene Three imagines Asia and Panthea approaching an oracular cavern of the sort associated with possessed prophecy. Both the classical sources, and commentators in the Romantic period, speculated on the possible natural causes of oracular possession in the prophetesses. They were known to have uttered their prophecies from a tripod often placed over an opening in a hillside, and in the mountainous volcanic territory which was usually the setting for shrines there was assumed to be a connection between this practice and the presence of natural intoxicating gases. The oracles were thought possibly to be the result of inhaling such vapours. The Shelleys visited local sights during their stay at Naples which included displays of just such phenomena, for example the 'Grotto del Cane', which produced gases potent enough to make dogs pass out for the benefit of tourists.[17]

Under the influence of gases given off from the depths of the earth, the oracles appeared to give understanding of the underlying purpose in local events. They offered insight into the relation of individual lives and circumstances to history, to the larger unfolding destiny of communities. It is important to bear in mind the very un-Christian nature of Greek thought in such matters. There is no sense of the Christian distinction between free will and necessity in Greek religious experience, but rather a merging of individual agency with what the gods have destined. The Greek model serves very well Shelley's general purpose in *Prometheus Unbound* of representing the individual agent's dialectical and profoundly ambivalent relation to revolutionary change. And the artistic texture of this representation is enriched by the connections between classical oracular lore and practice, and the complex web of volcanic references, whose central role in the dramatic action of the second act has long been acknowledged. The grounding of prophecy in natural properties of the earth also suits well with the sceptical, syncretistic and culturally relativist orientation of the drama's outlook and materials. It enables Shelley to engage with religious questions and varieties of experience, while avoiding allegiance to any received forms of spiritual transcendence. The phenomena of the poem's action all spring from the earth.

At the point reached by the action at the beginning of Act Two, Scene Three, we are still in a pre-revolutionary world, so the vapour emitted by the earth prompts in fact to very mixed kinds of insight, and has effects which mingle desirable and destructive elements. The ideals nurtured in 'lonely men' by the vapour are 'truth, virtue, love, genius, or joy', or so they call them in their partial pre-revolutionary perception of these things. But these ideals act for the present time as a 'maddening wine', and their advocates drain the dregs of this wine to 'deep intoxication', to produce messages which are a 'contagion'. 'Contagion', and also 'intoxication', are very context-dependent in Shelley's usage generally, and can suggest a pestilential madness at one extreme, or at the other an irresistibly fast-spreading and liberatingly uncontrollable bursting of limits. Their implicit duality in this speech suggests that idealism can lead to undesirable consequences given the pre-revolutionary mess of human affairs, but that these same ideals will in their proper time and context work in wholly beneficial, if perhaps as yet not fully imaginable ways.

The combination of metaphysical-political, geophysical, and oracular elements in the plotting of the poem's second act is so deftly worked out, and incorporated at such a deep level of structure, that readers have been very slow to realise its presence. It is no exaggeration to say that these aspects of at least this part of the poem went virtually unnoticed for almost 150 years after the poem's first publication. Certainly, this would seem to bear out Shelley's own assertion that the poem was aimed at a very 'select' class of readers; but in

truth a classically-educated reader, disposed to credit Shelley with a
carefully thought-through scheme of action and ideas, ought not to
find these aspects of the poem's procedures unreasonably inaccess-
ible. That is to say, we can agree that the long obscurity in which
some central aspects of *Prometheus Unbound* were allowed to lie
unacknowledged is mainly the fault of the poem's readers.

But I am not convinced that this could plausibly be agreed in
relation to the obscurity of *all* of the poem's important aspects. As
Act Two, Scene Three proceeds, various specific features of the
writing prompt us to enquire, with Carl Grabo, as to what, exactly,
it is that Asia and Panthea are inhaling.[18] It is plain enough that
Shelley has imagined a volcanic cave which emits 'mephitic'
vapours – that is, the sometimes noxious, stinking and poisonous
gases given off in volcanic sites, which were also capable of intoxi-
cant effects – and that his characters, in oracular fashion, are about
to transform their powers of perception under the influence of an
inhalation. Indeed, Asia seems perfectly aware of what she is doing.
As she contemplates the mountain scenery before her (in a spectacu-
larly un-Christian wondering scepticism), she warns her sister to
take in the scene quickly:

> Even now my heart adoreth. Wonderful!
> Look Sister, ere the vapour dim thy brain;
> Beneath is a wide plain of billowy mist...
> (ll. iii. 17–19)

This warning, 'ere the vapour dim thy brain', can only indicate
Asia's consciousness that the sisters are about to be affected by
inhaling the vapour issuing from the cavern. Thirty lines later the
action of the scene reaches a critical point, at least at this oracular
level of its operation where the volcanic/political/metaphysical
dimensions are subordinated to a dominant concern with oracular
prophecy and its mechanisms. Panthea says:

> Look, how the gusty sea of mist is breaking
> In crimson foam, even at our feet! it rises
> As Ocean at the enchantment of the moon
> Round foodless men wrecked on some oozy isle.

To which Asia responds:

> The fragments of the cloud are scattered up –
> The wind that lifts them disentwines my hair –

Its billows now sweep o'er mine eyes – my brain
Grows dizzy – see'st thou shapes within the mist?
(ll. iii. 43–50)

The confrontation with Demogorgon, that is to follow this scene, is thus prepared for in a sequence which presents that meeting as akin to the knowledge offered in oracular prophecy, which itself here stands in the poem as a dramatic form for the relation of apparently free human action to unanswerable imperatives of historical necessity. It is clear that Shelley is deliberately aiming in the writing here at an effect of growing disorientation and intellectual confusion; for example the dashes in the passage as quoted (though omitted in most texts) are a striking feature in the Bodleian fair copy manuscript. We gather that the shapes from which Asia is about to receive enlightenment are a function of her gas-altered state of mind. But why is the intoxicating oracular gas described by Panthea as a *crimson* foam?

As Grabo long ago indicated, Shelley must in this detail be thinking of then current rational explanations of oracular vapour.[19] The knockout gas in the Grotto del Cane was, and still is, Carbon Dioxide; a seriously harmful gas, without beneficial effects of any sort for human life. But Sir Humphry Davy had early in the nineteenth century isolated and named a more ambivalent and intriguing gas, which he called 'Laughing Gas'. This was Nitrous Oxide, N_2O, a stable, colourless gas with powerful anaesthetic possibilities, described by Davy in his *Elements of Chemical Philosophy*.[20] In early experiments Davy had managed to produce Nitrous Oxide only in conjunction with Nitrogen Peroxide, NO_2, a poisonous orange-red gas. Shelley may also, or alternatively, have had in mind Erasmus Darwin's description in his *Economy of Vegetation* of how Nitrogen ('azotic gas') produces 'crimson clouds' on contact with 'virgin air' (i.e. Oxygen, also then known as 'vital air').[21] In short, Shelley is deploying recent or contemporary scientific accounts of newly-discovered gases known to mix anaesthetic and poisonous properties, but mixed in ways which held out the promise of a means of separating out the effects and controlling them to the benefit of humanity.

He does this in a very specific manner indeed, which in fact leads him to introduce a good deal of detail in the writing which can hardly bear any consistent meaning at all except this exact one. That is a real problem for even attentive and sympathetic readers, because this dimension of the poem's rhetoric is extraordinarily difficult to grasp; more than that, it is in practical terms just about impossible to grasp without the assistance of detailed academic commentary. And yet it is extremely important in the scheme of the poem, and also, once grasped, an arresting and engaging feature of the general aesthetic experience.

The idea of an earth-emitted vapour, which holds the promise of beneficial effects for humanity, but which is partly noxious in the constrained understanding of pre-revolutionary minds and hearts, is returned to towards the end of Act Three. Here too the reader is confronted by a welter of detail which is at once striking and yet virtually incomprehensible except in the exact context of the poem's moral/scientific complex. The Earth describes, in a morally and politically redeemed world, how the effects of the oracular vapour have been transformed within the larger revolutionary transformation:

> There is a Cavern where my spirit
> Was panted forth in anguish whilst thy pain
> Made my heart mad, and those who did inhale it
> Became mad too, and built a temple there
> And spoke and were oracular, and lured
> The erring nations round to mutual war
> And faithless faith, such as Jove kept with thee;
> Which breath now rises as among tall weeds
> A violet's exhalation, and it fills
> With a serener light and crimson air
> Intense yet soft the rocks and woods around;
> It feeds the quick growth of the serpent vine
> And the dark linked ivy tangling wild
> And budding, blown, or odour-faded blooms
> Which star the winds with points of coloured light
> As they rain through them, and bright, golden globes
> Of fruit, suspended in their own green heaven;
> And, through their veined leaves and amber stems,
> The flowers whose purple and translucid bowls
> Stand ever mantling with aerial dew,
> The drink of spirits; and it circles round
> Like the soft waving wings of noonday dreams,
> Inspiring calm and happy thoughts, like mine
> Now thou art thus restored... This cave is thine.
> (lll. iii. 124–47)

This is of course a richly complicated passage, and it raises many questions. Is this Cavern, for example, the very same one described in

Act Two, Scene Three? And when, in historical or cultural terms, are we to situate the temple mentioned in the fourth line? It is a memorable quality of *Prometheus Unbound* that the reader is not only constantly obliged to attend to a host of such questions; the problem is that some of these questions have crucially important answers, whether easily discoverable or not, whilst others, at least to contemporary criticism, continue to elude definitive or even tentative resolution. But there are elements, so to speak, which are perceptible in the speech. What was once a maddening exhalation is now a wholly growth-nourishing part of a beautiful natural order. It is still a 'crimson air', but what used to prompt 'oracular' utterance, in the mixed sense of the second act, now inspires only 'calm and happy thoughts'. Shelley appears to be thinking of Nitrogen, now separated out from its oxide forms, and working only in its recently discovered function as the main ingredient of natural growth.

Shelley's imaginative conception of the dramatic action of *Prometheus Unbound* is marvellously original. When it works, and can be understood to be working, the reading experience, given the density and amazing technical variety of the writing itself, is quite extraordinary, at once exhilarating and intellectually rewarding. But the special nature of Shelley's achievement in the poem is limited by the demands it chooses to make of its reader. It remains in some important respects the work of a writer who has slipped out of touch with the sense of an audience. It is brilliant, but brilliant at a level which is partially defeating, like the brilliance of Joyce's *Finnegans Wake*, or like Blake's illuminated prophecies after *The Book of Urizen*. *Prometheus Unbound* also bears the marks of its composition history. The Acts are less integrated, at certain important levels, than they seem. Significant aspects of the poem's overall organisation are in fact rather disjointed, suggesting a series of creative bursts producing sustained passages of relatively freestanding action and verse which have then been articulated together. This increases the problems posed by the poem's difficulty, for while much of this difficulty is inherent in and integral with the imaginative conception, some of it is the obscurity, or the unsatisfying untidiness, of mixed artistic goals, a shifting focus of argument, and a lack of control in the introduction of sources and materials. It might even prove a more productive way forward for critical commentary if readers sympathetic to Shelley could accept these limitations in *Prometheus Unbound*, and see it for the blend of greatness and obscurity that it really is.

From *Durham University Journal,* 85 (1993), 237–45.

NOTES

[Kelvin Everest's essay seeks to explicate certain aspects of Shelley's rich and complex lyrical drama *Prometheus Unbound* which dramatises the plight and release of the Titan (Prometheus, punished for his gift of knowledge to humanity), followed by the fall of the tyrant Jupiter, and the succeeding political and moral regeneration of the earth. Everest's approach combines traditional scholarship with the insights of recent historicist criticism. He defends Shelley's work against some ingrained critical notions (chiefly created by Matthew Arnold and F. R. Leavis) that his work is too intellectually abstract and that his poetic style is too vague, obscure and fleeting to be taken seriously. More problematic for Everest is the *real* difficulty of Shelley's writing which, at times, demands the sustained attention of academic commentary to make itself understood, and which mitigates the revolutionary impact of the poetry (which Everest also values highly). Everest presents a sustained close-reading of the third scene of Act Two of the drama, contextualising images of oracular prophecy in terms of Shelley's classical and scientific reading. Ed.]

1. *The Letters of Percy Bysshe Shelley,* ed. F. L. Jones, 2 vols (Oxford, 1964), II, 94.

2. For an excellent detailed account of the composition history of *Prometheus Unbound,* see Neil Fraistat (ed.), *The Prometheus Unbound Notebooks* (*The Bodleian Shelley Manuscripts,* vol. ix) (New York and London, 1991), pp. lxiii–lxxxiv.

3. *Poetical Works of Percy Bysshe Shelley,* ed. Mary Shelley, 4 vols (London, 1839), II, 135.

4. I have discussed this issue in 'Shelley's Doubles: An Approach to Julian and Maddalo', in *Shelley Revalued: Selected Essays from the Gregynog Conference,* ed. K. Everest (Leicester, 1983), pp. 63–88; see also Richard Cronin, *Shelley's Poetic Thoughts* (London, 1981).

5. *Poetical Works,* II, 136.

6. Ibid., II, 133.

7. Stuart Sperry, 'Necessity and the Role of the Hero in Shelley's *Prometheus Unbound'*, *PMLA,* 96 (1981), pp. 242–54.

8. I am currently working on the Longman Annotated English Poets edition of Shelley's complete poetry.

9. G. M. Matthews, 'A Volcano's Voice in Shelley', *ELH,* 24 (1957), 191–228.

10. Earl R. Wasserman, *Shelley's Prometheus Unbound: A Critical Reading* (Baltimore, MD, 1965); Stuart Curran, *Shelley's Annus Mirabilis: The Maturing of an Epic Vision* (San Marino, CA, 1975).

11. Wasserman, *Shelley's Prometheus Unbound*, p. 144.

12. Sperry, *Shelley's Annus Mirabilis*, p. 264.

13. In the account which follows I concur with Fraistat (note 2 above) in all particulars relevant to the present discussion.

14. There are reasons for supposing that the poem is set in 1816; see the forthcoming second volume of the Longman Shelley.

15. Mary Shelley, *The Last Man* (London, 1826), introd. Brian Aldiss (1985), pp. 1–3.

16. Abbé Barthelemy, *Travels of Anacharsis the Younger in Greece*, trans. W. Beaumont, 7 vols (4th edn 1806), II, 391–2 and note xx: J. C. Eustace, *A Classical Tour Through Italy* (London, 1813), ch. II.

17. See e.g. Eustace, *Classical Tour*, p. 452.

18. Carl Grabo, *A Newton Among Poets* (Chapel Hill, NC, 1930), p. 186.

19. Grabo's study broke important new ground in the understanding of science in Shelley's poetry, his commentary is however much stronger on sources than on Shelley's purposes in deploying his sources. See *Newton Among Poets*, ch. 11.

20. Sir Humphry Davy, *Elements of Chemical Philosophy* (1811), pp. 399ff.

21. Erasmus Darwin, *Economy of Vegetation* (1791), note to II, 143.

10

Adonais and the Death of Poetry

WILLIAM A. ULMER

'Here lieth One whose name was writ on water.'
   But, ere the breath that could erase it blew,
Death, in remorse for that fell slaughter,
   Death, the immortalizing winter, flew
Athwart the stream, – and time's printless torrent grew
A scroll of crystal, blazoning the name
   Of Adonais!
             (Shelley, 'Fragment on Keats')[1]

Poetry and memory comprise one of literary history's most venerable alliances. Their connection enjoys both mythic sanction, as in the genealogy of the Muses, and critical approval, as in T. S. Eliot's comment that 'not only the best, but the most original parts of [a poet's] work may be those in which the dead poets, his ancestors, assert their immortality most vigorously'.[2] Such celebrations of the past's presence can seem unproblematic enough: we all understand that intertextuality [the poststructuralist notion that a text is not a repository of intentional meaning but an infinite storehouse of citations, repetitions, echoes and references. Ed.] is an element of every text. Still, Eliot's defence of imaginative retrospection harbours a disquieting ambivalence, and not just because we also understand that the past can impose burdensome anxieties. The disquietude follows from Eliot's use of prosopopeia to figure tradition's power as a return of the dead. For, 'by making

202

the dead speak', Paul de Man comments, 'the symmetrical structure of the trope implies, by the same token, that the living are
struck dumb, frozen in their own death.'[3] 'Life to him would be
death to me', Keats said of Milton, and thereby implied similarly
that the connection between poetry and memory involves, at one
remove, a connection between poetry and death.[4] Theorists of the
romantic period occasionally decreed death the mother of imagination. Wordsworth, for instance, traced poetry's lineage to fune-
real inscriptions.[5] But that genealogy merely underscores problems
implicit in all traditional accounts of the imagination's eternalising
office. For if poems arise in a defensive recoil from mortality, as
poets conventionally claim, then 'immortality' becomes a mediat-
ing term in the derivation of poetry from death. Representation
always speaks of something that is gone, always presupposes loss
and absence, and such a presupposition inscribes death in representation as an irreducible element of poetic meaning. The more
self-consciously retrospective the text, the more it risks outright
confrontation with its Thanatopic subtext. Shelley stages just such
a confrontation with the apocalyptic conclusion of *Adonais*, his
richly retrospective elegy for Keats.

Critical disagreement about the conclusion of *Adonais* has made
it 'in some sense the exemplary crux of Shelley's poetry', in Stuart
Curran's phrase, a great divide where Shelleyans declare for life or
death.[6] Death has had its champions. Ross Woodman called
Adonais a 'metaphysical defence of suicide', and many readers similarly stress the poem's apocalyptic scorn of mediation, its progressively revealed commitment to transcendence.[7] By dialectical recoil,
this insistence on aesthetic reflexivity and visionary solitude has led
other readers to champion the worldliness of *Adonais*: its politics,
its traditionalism, and (of late) its rhetorical engagement of an audience.[8] Critics inevitably grant that Shelley's attitudes towards death
and life are interrelated – each other's mutually conditioning reflex
– but lose the logic of their interrelation in emphasising their incom-
patibility. Apocalyptic approaches to *Adonais* typically link isolation with disillusionment in a pessimistic reading of Shelley's
conclusion. As a result, worldliness has usually been appropriated
by critics wedded to the elegy's humanistic optimism, as in Curran's
recent description of *Adonais* as a 'poem of exhilarating, mature
joy' (Curran, p. 180). While such joyfulness can seem an unavoidable legacy of the text's mundanity, it is a legacy we should reject.
Readings of *Adonais* which reconstruct its social contexts or its

solicitation of an audience make an important contribution. Yet they remain strangely, almost wilfully unresponsive to the text's solicitation of death. We must reclaim the apocalypse of *Adonais* for culture, reading it historically, without disclaiming what remains most powerful emotionally in the elegy's final vision: its 'triumph of human despair' (Bloom, *Visionary Company*, p. 349).

My reading of *Adonais* will endorse the apocalyptic position while providing a different rationale for it. I want to explore the poem's turn deathward in the light of its concomitant turn to the past. For *Adonais* abounds in Orphic glances backward. It is a remarkably self-conscious text, invoking elegiac conventions and poetic history in a continual acknowledgement of its own historicity. Critics often attribute the range and prominence of cultural reference in Shelley's poetry to his syncretistic search for the archetype behind our culturally dispersed myths.[9] With *Adonais*, we must adjust these emphases – which tend to make history a barrier to be overcome, a problem rather than a solution – and view Shelleyan allusiveness as a historicist technique. Shelley devotes *Adonais* to a project of historical reconstruction, a project ceding immortality to the preservative power of a cultural inheritance. But his displacement of immortality as literary tradition undergoes a further displacement which refers tradition to rhetoric, so that questions of poetic history defer to the question of a poetics of history. This poetics – dramatised in Shelley's 'pardlike Spirit', the elegist's supplemental mask – ends by subverting the text's vision of historical order. In *Adonais*, history's collapse illustrates a figural logic and testifies to a deathliness inherent in poetic representation. Unveiling this deathliness, the elegy functions less as a cultural archive than as a crypt for unquiet powers personifying the poet's vocational alliance with death. The apocalyptic conclusion of *Adonais* follows, then, from Shelley's determination to explore the cultural and figural aspects of the death of poetry.

I

Recent approaches to Shelley's elegy have been sceptical in premise. While sceptical readings of *Adonais* can prove misleading, they have at least problematised the association of Shelleyan immortality with actual ontological transcendence.[10] Admittedly, Shelley complicates his text's rejection of atemporal redemption by providing a superabundance of immortalities: at times he depicts eternalisation as assimilation by the primal energies of the cosmos ('the burning fountain'), as an undecidable question ('He wakes or sleeps with the enduring dead'), and as the individual personality's transmortality, as when Lucan, Sidney, and Chatterton rise from their thrones to welcome the deceased Keats to the sphere reserved for him.[11] Yet the identities of these welcoming spirits clarify the ultimate nature of Shelleyan consolation. 'In Shelley's Heaven only the poets are to be found', Woodman points out (Woodman, p. 176), because in *Adonais* immortality figures the collective memory of artistic tradition. The elegy seeks an 'artificial poetic eternity' in which 'the poet lives on through the survival of poetry', through his works as they are 'read creatively by succeeding generations'.[12] The problems of cultural canonisation are primarily historiographical for Shelley. *Adonais* accepts the traditional notion of inherent aesthetic quality, inherent canonicity. Shelley understands poetry's cultural preservation as the direct reflex of its imaginative value, ascribing artistic fame to a process recognising rather than producing the text's canonical status. Although liable to political circumvention – by the institutions of publishing and reviewing, economic trends and practices, governmental regulation, and so on – this process is teleologically underwritten by the continuities of literary history, which Shelley links (quite conventionally) to the progress of liberty, and which allow for a historical adjudication of questions of greatness. The immortalising case *Adonais* prosecutes is historicist in aim and assumption.

The question of historical value ramified throughout the polemical contexts which shaped *Adonais*: Shelley's relations with Southey, Byron, and Peacock, and his vocational disillusionment in 1821. Shelley's changing attitude towards Southey has been charted by Kenneth Neill Cameron, who shows that in *Adonais* and its preface Shelley 'had Southey in mind as the critic whom he singles out for especial attack'.[13] His association of Southey with vicious reviewing emerged in his mythologising of the death of Keats. Those associations lend Keats's victimisation an obvious political resonance in that Southey, 'as Laureate, was the foremost literary supporter of the Tory administration' (Cameron, 'Shelley vs Southey', p. 508). But for Shelley, the political apostasy of the first romantic generation also implied a failure of historical understanding. *The Revolt of Islam* had referred the older romantics' conservative quietism to the disappointment of unrealistic hopes for the

French Revolution – that is, to a certain naïveté about the dynamics of historical progression. Revolutionaries who understand the inevitable triumph of liberty, like Shelley's Laon and Cythna, would have disdained the despondency Shelley anatomises in his Preface:

> on the first reverses of hope in the progress of French liberty, the sanguine eagerness for good overleaped the solution of these questions. ... Thus, many of the most ardent and tender-hearted of the worshippers of public good have been morally ruined by what a partial glimpse of the events they deplored appeared to show as the melancholy desolation of all their cherished hopes.
>
> (*Poetical Works*, p. 33)

Corrupt reviewing practices, the example of Southey suggested, bespoke misunderstanding of the libertarian teleology celebrated (nearer the time of *Adonais*) in both the 'Ode to Liberty' and *Hellas*. Disenchanted republicans such as Southey had underrated the resilience and continuity of the progressive spirit of the age.

If the mythmaking of *Adonais* casts Southey as 'the unpastured dragon', it casts Byron as 'the Pythian of the age', a poetic hero undaunted by critical calumny (ll. 238, 250). The portrait of Byron in *Adonais* reveals Shelley trying to enlist Byron in the defence of Keats – an endeavour dubious enough that 'when Shelley sent Byron a copy of *Adonais* on 16 July, he still felt uncomfortable about presuming upon Byron's opinion of Keats'.[14] Shelley had always been troubled by Byron's doubts about social betterment – in part, by his historical pessimism – and implicit in the two poets' disagreement over Keats were divergent historical agendas. These concerned literary history in particular. Byron's annoyance with Keats arose from the vilification of Pope in 'Sleep and Poetry', and thereby from a conception of poetry's progress at odds with the injunction, 'Thou shalt believe in Milton, Dryden, Pope' (*Don Juan* I. 205). James Chandler has shown that this genealogy signifies Byron's verdict not only on Pope but on the competing claims of national and international literary canons.[15] Anti-Gallicist sentiment had reactivated interest in a distinctly English poetic canon in the years following 1819, one inflected by the superiority of the national character and hence, given the French associations of neo-classicist artifice, one which would marginalise the oeuvre of Pope. The contrary liberal perspective, whatever its final assessment of Pope, gravitated toward aesthetic cosmopolitanism. That political logic accounts for what Marilyn Butler calls 'the cult of the South'

among the younger romantic generation: their use of Greek mythology and Italian literature, especially Dante, as foils to the national-
ist orthodoxies of Wordsworth and Coleridge.[16]

Byron's advocacy of Pope represented a similar attack on British
cultural insularity and the conservative retrenchment underlying it.
Yet, as Chandler notes, Byron and his ally Isaac D'Israeli defend
Pope without accepting the universalist criteria of Pope's classicism:

> In elevating the national canon over the classical one, Bowles, Keats,
> and the Lakers insist on the universality of their critical principles.
> Seeing in this move a glorification of provincialism in the name of
> nature, Byron and D'Israeli insist upon a universalised canon of
> classics but surrender the notion that this canon embodies universally
> applicable principles... . Genius finds its merit not in fidelity to a
> changeless Nature but rather in its adaptability to the mutations of
> society and the concomitant variations of culture.
>
> (Chandler, p. 504)

The *Essay on Criticism* grounded its aesthetic principles on
'Unerring Nature, still divinely bright, / One clear, unchanged, and
universal light' (70–1). Byron's own position was thoroughly historicist, even incipiently relativist. A historicist bent underwrites the
social commentary of the *Defence of Poetry*, but Byron's view
would have disheartened Shelley for several reasons: its evaluations
of individual reputations, the respect it lavished on didactic and
satirical writing, and above all the attenuated relevance it accorded
monuments of literary tradition. Byron's rejection of universal standards, his insistence on the applicability of artistic principles only
within their own cultural context, severed past and present. For
Byron, 'Pope's poetic temple ... is to be admired but not imitated',
Chandler remarks; 'Byron saves Pope not for the history of the
future but only for the history of the past' (Chandler, p. 505).

The interrelation of past and present was also a central issue in
Shelley's response to Peacock, whose 'The Four Ages of Poetry',
which Shelley read shortly before beginning *Adonais*, is another
romantic exercise in 'the historical method'.[17] 'The Four Ages' challenged Shelley's reverence for the literary tradition through
Peacock's patronising interpretation of romantic cultural nostalgia.
For Peacock, the inverse relation of historical consciousness and
poetic achievement – 'the maturity of poetry may be considered the
infancy of history' ('Four Ages', p. 8) – had made versified anti-
quarianism too fashionable. Aware of his banishment from the

primeval sources of poetic grandeur, the poet of Peacock's second bronze age spends his time

> wallowing in the rubbish of departed ignorance, and raking up the ashes of dead savages to find gewgaws and rattles for the grown babies of the age... . He lives in the days that are past. His ideas, thoughts, feelings, associations, are all with barbarous manners, obsolete customs, and exploded superstitions. The march of his intellect is like that of a crab, backward.
>
> ('Four Ages', pp. 16, 17)

The consequences of this backward march are formal and cultural fragmentation. To Peacock, the romantic poem is typically 'a modern-antique compound of frippery and barbarism, in which the puling sentimentality of the present time is grafted on the misrepresented ruggedness of the past into a heterogeneous congeries of unamalgamating manners' ('Four Ages', p. 17). 'The Four Ages' dismayed Shelley even more with its claim that the modern historical sense was at once unavoidable and creatively vitiating – that past and present were artistically irreconcilable, rendered essentially irrelevant to each other by their temporal disjunction. Shelley feared the tendency of romantic historicism to conceive every historical epoch as a self-enclosed frame of reference, a source of values legitimate only within their transitory cultural moment. He feared the isolationism latent in historicist analysis.

Those fears gained in strength as Shelley's personal sense of artistic isolation deepened during his last two years. This conviction tolls through the letters from 1821–2: 'I write nothing, and probably shall write no more. It offends me to see my name classed among those who have no name'; 'I wish I had something better to do than furnish this jingling food for the hunger of oblivion, called *verse*'; 'I write little now. It is impossible to compose except under the strong excitement of an assurance of finding sympathy in what you write' (*Letters*, II. 331, 374, 436). Shelley's late texts also manifest his sense of artistic alienation by showing his struggle against it, his compensatory recourse to the dead past for a cultural communality denied him in the present. Like poets ranging from Spenser to Milton, Arnold to Eliot, Shelley had always written a conspicuously derivative poetry. But in the poems of his Italian exile, especially the more ambitious projects of 1821–2, Shelly cultivated a truly intensive literariness. The stylistic re-creation of a Dantean and Petrarchan erotic ethos in *Epipsychidion*, for instance, clearly justifies Timothy Webb's claim that, for Shelley in 1821, 'the combined influences of Dante, Petrarch, Boccaccio, Cavalcanti, and Latini, the process of writing and translating in Italian, and the physical experience of the Italian landscape all fused together ... to produce a literary world of extraordinary potency'.[18] However impressive, the re-creation of early Renaissance Italian culture in *Epipsychidion* is no more obvious – its revaluative traditionalism and literary self-consciousness no greater, finally – than the use of classical models in *Hellas*, the evocation of elegiac tradition in *Adonais*, or the medley of literary influences, models, and figures in *The Triumph of Life*.

Shelleyan literariness was not antiquarian or escapist, however, but culturally syncretistic. The capacious allusiveness of texts such as *Adonais* creates a dialogue of past and present. Shelley's allusions, each one a cultural reference, serve a project of historical reconstruction which conceives the text as a transcultural archive, a forum for the integration of temporally disparate traditions or for the reaffirmation of extant but historically obscured connections. This poetics reflected Shelley's belief – unlike Byron and Peacock – in the essential continuity of different artistic eras:

> The sacred links of that chain have never been entirely disjoined, which descending through the minds of many men is attached to those great minds, whence as from a magnet the invisible effluence is sent forth, which at once connects, animates and sustains the life of all... . [Individual texts are] episodes to that great poem, which all poets, like the co-operating thoughts of one great mind, have built up since the beginning of the world.
>
> (*A Defence of Poetry*, p. 493)

A similar cultural genealogy underwrote the immortalising project of *Adonais*. The elegy's poetic borrowings look not to an Ur-myth construed as the antithesis of historicity, the form taken by history's transcendence, but to mundane traditions verbally reconsolidated by those borrowings. Shelley's commitment to forging historical connections in *Adonais* explains his choice of a Muse, Urania, with classical, Miltonic, and Wordsworthian associations; his distribution of epic achievement among ancient Greece, medieval Florence, and Renaissance England; his Platonic epigraph; his adroit deployment of elegiac conventions; his depiction of contemporary poets; his dependence on Dante; his urbane echoings of Keats's poetry; and even his unprecedented allusion to his own previous work, as when the final stanza of *Adonais* glances back at 'Ode to the West

Wind'.[19] This densely allusive fabric serves as a self-legitimising strategy. It makes *Adonais* a historicist elegy in which Shelley's culturally interrelative allusions re-enact the vision of historical order which underlies the poem as its enabling condition.

What we must recognise at this point are the conceptual alliances Shelley inherited in declining the radical, culturally discontinuous historicism of Byron and Peacock. It is not coincidental that the enhanced historicity of Shelley's late poetry accompanies a resurgent idealism, a renewed interest in the transcendent One. Alan Liu has recently argued against any 'parting of the sea' between 'the representation of history and the apocalyptic or visionary imagination' in romanticism, and the example of Shelley's late work strengthens his case.[20] In *Adonais* historicism and idealism presuppose and complete each other. More specifically, the poem places history and spirit in metaphorical relation, envisioning a negotiation of *zeit* and *geist* as complementary facets of a providential design:

> the one Spirit's plastic stress
> Sweeps through the dull dense world, compelling there,
> All new successions to the forms they wear;
> Torturing th' unwilling dross that checks its flight
> To its own likeness, as each may bear.
>
> (ll. 381–5)

Materiality remains the derivative antitype of a spiritual energy it can only temporarily impede, acting as vehicle to tenor ('likeness') within the compass of a metaphorical idealism. The governing role of metaphor explains why 'Shelley's own relation to the world of his poem is the same as the relation which, in *Adonais*, he attributes to the One Spirit and the material world', and why the creative activity of Shelley's 'plastic stress' 'parallels the activity of the idealist poet struggling to adapt language' to spiritual truth (Wasserman, *Shelley*, p. 487; Cronin, *Poetic Thoughts*, p. 195). With this metaphorical logic Shelley can present eternity as the soul's postmortal translation to an ideal realm – as when the spirits of Chatterton, Sidney, and Lucan appear – and still concentrate on eternity as a trope for the commemorative function of culture. The poem redefines immortality as cultural greatness only after gracing culture with the traditional prerogatives of immortality. In *Adonais* ideas of universality and indestructibility, however historically instantiated, presuppose and require a metaphysical ordinance. They retain their worldly provenance only when legitimised by agencies beyond worldly vicissitudes: for, without those agencies, what guarantees that poetic tradition will not forget Adonais in death just as viperish criticism mistreated him while alive?

Yet the historical vision of *Adonais* recurrently calls those guarantees into question. Given the cultural project of Shelley's elegy, there is a real contradiction in the heavenly celebration of Adonais' ascension including poets 'whose names on Earth are dark' (l. 406). This same possibility – the possibility of oblivion, of tradition's failure to grant fame – is the elegiac occasion of *Adonais*, which unfolds as the plea for an immortality uncertain enough to require the elegist's intervention. If every original poet, as Wordsworth claimed, 'has had the task of *creating* the taste by which he is to be enjoyed', every traditional poet has the task of reconstituting the history which constitutes him a poet.[21] Traditions can become moribund; 'the genre within which Shelley writes *Adonais* died with *Lycidas*', in Richard Cronin's opinion (Cronin, *Poetic Thoughts*, p. 169). In fact, when *Adonais* begins with the inanimate body of Keats, on the one hand, and with so determined a commemoration of past literature, on the other, Shelley correlates the project of resurrecting Adonais with the difficult task of reviving a dying tradition. As we saw, this task accommodates past to present by formulating a genealogy. But as with all texts, the genealogies of *Adonais* are inevitably reconstructive. Ignoring innumerable elegies to invoke the ones he most admired, Shelley selectively makes the history that makes poets live by discriminating, like Odysseus, among the ghosts clamouring to speak. In 1817 he had observed of contemporaneous writers that, although 'they cannot escape from subjection to a common influence', the spirit of the age, 'each is in a degree the author of the very influence by which his being is thus pervaded' ('Preface to *The Revolt of Islam*', *Poetical Works*, p. 35). So too with influence across the ages: tradition empowers individual talent, bestowing immortality, only when reaffirmed by poets whose celebratory powers it reflexively authorises.

Such reflexivity threatens the elegiac enterprise of *Adonais*. Shelley's metaphorical idealism projects historicity as the derivative form of a prior ideality. The idea of history as a retrospective construction of the very poet who looks to it for order destabilises cultural continuity. It raises the radically historicist possibility that principles of artistic value 'mean nothing more than the predilection of a particular age' and that poets' reputations do not 'depend upon their merits, but upon the ordinary vicissitudes of human opinions'.[22] The universalist historicism of *Adonais* opposes itself to these claims. It illustrates a 'Romanticist historical thought … conceived as an attempt to rethink the problem of historical knowledge in the mode of Metaphor and the problem of the historical process in terms of the will of the individual conceived as the sole agent of causal efficacy in that process.'[23] The historical project of *Adonais* seeks resemblance, the common threads interconnecting disparate cultures as links in a sacred chain. Because *Adonais* idealises history as a metaphorical dynamic, the vagaries of the historical process emerge with the progressive disfiguration of Shelleyan metaphor. This disfigurative process attains its greatest clarity with Shelley's elegiac persona, the 'pardlike Spirit'.

II

Adonais thematises the death of Keats as the prospective death of poetry, conventionally reading in it a deathliness endangering the elegist himself. Faced with that threat, Shelley must vindicate the high claims of imagination by writing a poem which, in its greatness, will accord the unheralded, prematurely dead Keats an immortality arising in truth as the reflex of the elegist's immortalising art – less Keats's accomplishment than Shelley's. The elegiac plot of *Adonais* thereby engenders an auto-elegiac subplot focused more on mourner than victim.[24] 'The great pastoral elegies', Harold Bloom reminds us, always turned from the deceased to 'centre upon their composers' own creative anxieties'.[25] Still, those anxieties intensified with the course of history and bequeathed post-Enlightenment elegies a truly pronounced auto-elegiac reflexivity. *Lycidas* discovers consolation in an orthodox transvaluation of life and death: 'So Lycidas, sunk low, [mounts] high, / Through the dear might of him that walk'd the waves.' Secularisation problematised the dynamics of consolation for later poets in the English tradition. After Milton, elegists had to struggle to formulate a creditable consolation and – as we see in *In Memoriam* and *Thyrsis*, for example, as well as *Adonais* – that struggle thrust the elegist to centre stage. When the elegy becomes modern and historicist in assumption, and immortality a figure for cultural canonisation, the elegist increasingly enters the plot of his poem. For then the surviving poet indisputably wields the eternalising power at issue.

Shelley intrudes into *Adonais* in the guise of the 'pardlike Spirit, beautiful and swift' (l. 280). With the entry of this character, the elegiac drama of *Adonais* assumes metaphorical form: the eternity-bestowing Shelley will transmit his greatness to Keats through a chameleon-like act of sympathy, wresting *Adonais* to himself as 'the one Spirit's plastic stress' assimilates materiality. When Shelley's pardlike mourner, the elegist's persona, plays one 'Who in another's fate now wept his own' (l. 300), Shelley projects himself at one remove into Keats's fate. Whatever its biographical rationale, this identification forges a metaphorical union between the two poets, making each the other's surrogate – so that the 'oneness of the dead Keats and the living Shelley [becomes] the axis on which the poem strains towards the infinite'.[26] While figuring the elegist, Shelley's pardlike Spirit shares characteristics of Adonais: the Spirit's tremulous debility, floral drapery, and branded brow recall the fragile poet ('a pale flower by some sad maiden cherished') who was nature's worshipper and society's victim. The mourning Spirit is at once like Shelley and like Keats. He thereby makes them like each other, acting as a trope they cohabit, a metaphor they jointly construct. As a figure of reconciliation, he also serves as an idealisation of poetic influence, illustrating the cooperative exchange between monumental tradition and the living imagination. For Shelley's portrait of the Spirit is at once highly personalised – the intrusion of a misplaced self-pity for many readers – and highly formal. This formality surrounds the Spirit with mythological and biblical associations because, in his classical and Christian affiliations, he personifies cultural tradition. Elegist and elegiac subject, past and present, tradition and individual talent, spirit and history – all are redemptively mediated by an analogical design epitomised in Shelley's pardlike Spirit, and based on the reconciling power of similitude, the power of metaphor.

Yet the substitutive exchanges linking *Adonais* and the pardlike Spirit necessarily involve the differential similitude inherent in metaphor. If the pardlike Spirit functions as 'a means of bringing Keats and Shelley to coincide' (Wasserman, *Shelley*, p. 502), he nonetheless threatens the very coincidence he constitutes. To succeed, the metaphorical plot of *Adonais* must carefully circumscribe the subversive force of difference. Struggling against that force, *Adonais* discloses Shelley 'both identifying with and yet objectifying and distancing himself from' creative error, death, Keats, and the attributes his text accords Keats (Sacks, 'Last Clouds', p. 392). The disclaimed attribute has been variously defined – as regressive longing for the mother, as artistic egocentrism, as enervated delicacy – but variations in the objectified element leave the poem's strategy of objectification structurally unaltered.[27] *Adonais* redistributes the likeness-in-difference fundamental to metaphor into discrete phases of attachment, purgation, and detachment. Shelley's pardlike Spirit initially confirms Keats's death by reading it proleptically as a figure of his own. The elegist's subsequent swerve from death is empowered by his identification with Adonais – motivated by it, of course, but also enabled by the (somewhat uncharitable) metaphorical exchanges organising that identification. Through his elegiac alter-ego, Shelley presumes upon the likeness of self and other to bestow undesired attributes (death as fearful) on Adonais while attracting desirable ones (genius as supreme fame) from Adonais to himself. This figural economy revitalises him through both catharsis and appropriation. Once he refigures Adonais as a repository of negative values, the elegist can presume upon the difference of self and other, and lament in Keats a misfortune from which his sublime art has thankfully liberated him. The climactic immortalisation follows, but as a gesture of noblesse oblige. By this selective reallocation of strength and weakness, Shelley's work of mourning sustains itself in the face of difference. In that way, his idealisation of metaphor as an integrative trope can continue to govern his pursuit of an abundant recompense for death.

The moral vision of *Adonais* therefore remains deeply implicated in Shelley's actual figural practice. Elsewhere I have argued that Shelleyan metaphor typically yields to a progressive disfiguration, producing a figural series linking evanescence and self-reflexivity in a cycle which, first approximating and then recoiling from its object, emerges as the rhetorical corollary of the coherence/collapse rhythm first described by Daniel Hughes.[28] In *Epipsychidion* and *Prometheus Unbound*, Hughes discerns a cyclical economy, a process building from potentiality toward a hypostasis which, as soon as attained, or nearly attained, exhausts itself and reverts to potentiality. This same pattern shapes *Adonais*. In fact, *Adonais* gives it one of its most succinct definitions:

> Who mourns for Adonais? oh, come forth
> Fond wretch! and know thyself and him aright.
> Clasp with thy panting soul the pendulous Earth;
> As from a centre, dart thy spirit's light

> Beyond all worlds, until its spacious might
> Satiate the void circumference: then shrink
> Even to a point within our day and night;
> And keep thy heart light lest it make thee sink
> When hope has kindled hope, and lured thee to the brink.
>
> (ll. 415–23)

These lines indicate the necessity of both worldly and otherworldly perspectives – by implication, of history and spirit – in the elegiac enterprise of knowing Adonais aright. Such knowing moves from the world to a void momentarily filled by the imagination, and then back to the world in a temporalised return, a diastole accompanied by the acknowledgement of 'day and night'. The tidal emerging and lapsing of power in this stanza characterises the overall movement of *Adonais*. Shelley's elegy begins in despair, surges upward to a hypostatised Platonism – a momentary conviction that the 'One remains, the many change and pass' (l. 460) – and ebbs back into dark fearfulness. Coherence and collapse appear again, their figural form more manifest, in Shelley's description of the pardlike Spirit. For this portrait, as Bloom remarks, Shelley 'has caught for us, imperishably, the basis of his style' (*Visionary Company*, p. 346).

Shelley introduces his elegiac persona in stanza 31. Even in this introductory description, the Spirit's self-subversive reflexivity appears unmistakably:

> Midst other of less note, came one frail Form,
> A phantom among men; companionless
> As the last cloud of an expiring storm
> Whose thunder is its knell; he, as I guess,
> Had gazed on Nature's naked loveliness,
> Actaeon-like, and now he fled astray
> With feeble steps o'er the world's wilderness,
> And his own thoughts, along that rugged way,
> Pursued, like raging hounds, their father and their prey.
>
> (ll. 271–9)

In his likeness to Actaeon, this poet personifies an imagination organised as its own origin and self-subversive end. He turned his mind outward to the world until led beyond nature to 'Nature's naked loveliness', an epiphanic vision of divinity. This momentary contact transposes the trajectories of consciousness. What results is a pattern of emanation and return, a retracing of steps. Once reached, the ideal grants Shelley's 'frail Form' a predatory self-consciousness in which his thoughts cyclically relapse upon their own matrices, thereby reconstituting 'their father ... their prey'. Thanatopic in its regressiveness, this reversion binds the poet to death. It refashions him as a phantom, an expiring storm's death knell. Shelley may subsequently garb his poet-figure in Dionysian regalia (ll. 289–93) principally because Orpheus, who ventured into death, also worshipped Dionysius. Yet *Adonais* accommodates its invocations of Orpheus and Dionysius to the same self-reflexive pattern. For 'if a poet is dressed like a Maenad', Scrivener observes, 'the implication seems clear enough: the poet calls into existence his own destruction' (Scrivener, *Radical Shelley*, p. 278), his voice conjuring up the violence that rebounds upon it. Shelley links reflexivity and destructiveness, Actaeon and Dionysius, when the dionysian stanza ends by calling the poet 'A herd-abandoned deer'.

A similar emphasis on self-cancelling evanescence recurs in stanza 32, the passage Bloom finds so quintessentially Shelleyan:

> A pardlike Spirit beautiful and swift –
> A Love in desolation masked; – a Power
> Girt round with weakness; – it can scarce uplift
> The weight of the superincumbent hour;
> It is a dying lamp, a falling shower,
> A breaking billow; – even whilst we speak
> Is it not broken? On the withering flower
> The killing sun smiles brightly: on a cheek
> The life can be burn in blood, even while the heart may break.
> (ll. 280–8)

Many of these images describe a cyclical process in which origin becomes end: rainfall revitalises the hydrogen cycle, waves crest upward from the ocean only to ebb back into it, and the killing sun reclaims a life it fostered. The passage is most Shelleyan, however, in its associative speed, and in the rationale of such rapid change. For Leighton, these images 'seem to present that process of cumulative insufficiency and failure which characterises the language of the sublime'; if 'they are a characteristic metaphorical statement about the very nature of poetry', as she believes, that is because they clarify poetry's vitally metaphorical nature (Leighton, *Shelley and the Sublime*, p. 143). Shelley's lines unfold as an attempt to represent his 'one frail Form' through comparison. In forming a series they extend their framing analogy – the mourner is like 'A pardlike Spirit beautiful and swift' – through substitutive alternatives which are impelled and anchored by the initiating comparison (even as they acknowledge its inadequacy), but which progressively warp it through their own displacements. Shelley's elegiac persona is an oxymoron on the wing. He begins as an animalistic Spirit energised and even predatory in his panther-like vitality. Yet that trope, its representational power exhausted, seems to exhaust itself temporally; it dies into replacement engendered by its original through the decentring restlessness of language. So an abstraction encased in materiality becomes 'A Love in desolation masked' – similar abstractness, similar emphasis on essence and vesture, but a radical metamorphosis of beautiful swiftness into 'desolation'. The next term further disfigures 'desolation' as 'weakness'. By this point the stanza has also eroded the authority of Shelley's supposedly controlling tenor. The passage from a being to abstractions, from a 'Spirit' to 'Love' to 'Power', gains depersonalising momentum with the imminent shift to a lamp, shower, and billow. There is an associative logic to every new troping. It still remains difficult to quarrel with Cronin's description of the stanza as 'a series of phrases linked weakly by apposition' (Cronin, *Poetic Thoughts*, p. 191).

These self-dislocating figural series comprise a rhetoric of temporality: 'even whilst we speak / Is it not broken', Shelley asks of his breaking billow as a figure of figuration. When his tropings of tropes displace an initiating tenor, to which they look back, and when the pardlike Spirit comes surrounded by reflexive figures, the temporality inscribed in Shelley's rhetoric reveals its metaleptic organisation. [Metalepsis: where one image is substituted for another and the substitution is of a far-fetched or remote nature – Ed.] The Shelleyan imagination, Hogle notes, 'always starts as a process reconfiguring vestiges of a dead or dying past' (Hogle, *Shelley's Process*, p. 307), a process seeking to reconfigure a fading origin from its vestigial debris. The historicism of *Adonais* merely provides such metalepses their cultural analogues. It is therefore odd that Shelley's recourse to metalepsis as a governing trope problematises the idea of cultural inheritance, as the pardlike Spirit clearly illustrates. As the elegist's delegate, Shelley's Dionysian mourner encapsulates the history-making project of *Adonais*. Yet he arrives on the scene 'last, neglected and apart', an alienated stranger who speaks 'in the accents of an unknown land' and seemingly totters on the brink of death (ll. 296, 301). The Spirit's traditional trappings may not cause his enervation, but they certainly proclaim it, the vibrations of his thyrsis acting as signs of an unsteady heart and grasp. Furthermore, he surely ranks among the most unsuitably attired guests in all romantic literature. The garish costume he wears, almost parodic in excess, and the histrionic attitude of mourning he strikes are equally mannered and overdone, remnants of once-authentic tradition now unsuited to the occasion. In the pardlike Spirit *Adonais* correlates reflexive figuration with the suggestion of tradition's obsolescence. Shelley's rhetoric of temporality, as it gives rise to metalepsis, apparently produces a temporality in conflict with the poem's historical sense.

The rationale of that conflict lies with the challenge Shelley's reflexive figurings pose to idealist notions of origination. Dedicated to cultural canonisation as a surrogate transcendence, *Adonais* seeks a closed, monumental past in which canonical greatness can be permanently enshrined. As I suggested above, this cultural idealisation conceives retrospection as retrieval rather than construction of the past. A retrospectively constructed historicity would remain open to the various contingencies of the present. Shelley's universalist historicism therefore cannot accept metalepsis as the master trope of cultural canonisation. Instead, *Adonais* correlates tenor with origin and vehicle with end by projecting figuration as an originary Meaning's search for derivative variants of itself. Closure occurs as the prodigal vehicle's reunion with its initiating tenor, 'the burning fountain whence it came' (l. 339). This primal source operates as a totalising metaphor, assimilating each 'spirit' as a synecdochic 'portion of the Eternal' but reconstituting eternal unity on the basis of likeness: 'Dust to the dust', spirit to spirit (ll. 337–9). [Synechdoche: a figure where a whole is described in terms of a part – Ed.] Shelley's speaker agrees that the representational closure of tenor and vehicle remains problematic – 'Flowers, ruins, statues, music, words, are weak / The glory they transfuse with fitting truth to speak' (ll. 467–8) – but the signifier's weakness cannot undo the sublimity of the signified: it survives as a 'glory'. The system of hierarchical analogues created by Shelley's metaphorical idealism allows, almost mechanically, for endless sublimations of this sort.

The pardlike Spirit figures both metalepsis and the failure of tradition, then, because the figural reflexivity he exemplifies disrupts the historical model of Shelleyan canonisation. Metalepsis determines the circular orbits traced by tradition and individual talent whenever their interdependence is subjected to genealogical analysis, interrogated for its origins by an elegist who needs certain origins, who ascribes the imagination's power over death to a recovery of origins. Thus the contradictions writ large in the substitutive exchanges of Shelley's work of mourning. He makes cultural canonisation the source of immortality by associating Spirit with tradition, as in the heavenly pantheon where the great abide. He then associates the elegist too with these privileged values, presenting him as a poet whose adroit orchestration of elegiac conventions marks him as a master of the historical sense. Within this controlling fiction, Adonais serves as a candidate for fame, a secondary, slightly patronised character in a meditation on death which cedes originary power to the elegiac voice intoning the poem. Yet Shelley's two characters easily exchange roles. For the dead Adonais also connotes tradition and greatness. Well before his ascension to 'the kingless sphere' that has awaited him, Shelley identifies him, by his very name, with elegiac conventions and declares him a nursling of the same Urania who inspired Homer, Dante, and Milton (ll. 47, 28–36). This change recasts Shelley's speaker as the aspirant to greatness, as an unassured character who envies Adonais' artistic ascension – possibilities narratively realised in the poem's final stanza. As a metonymy for poetic history, Adonais acts as a precondition of the historicist eternalisation which, supposedly, reverts to him through the intercessions of a power isolated in the speaker. [Metonymy: a figure where a whole (i.e. poetic history) is described by reference to that which is associated with it (the poet Adonais) – Ed.]

The oscillation of 'history' from elegist to Adonais denies traditional meanings a stable locus. Each character's replacement as the figure of tradition thrusts him, as an immediate effect of that replacement, into his alternative role as the figure of individual talent. With this complementary transference, what had been the sphere of a monumental historicity becomes the sphere of the individual subject. The implication is that history cannot be disengaged from subjectivity, that memory is recreative and the past always partly a reflexive construct of the present. Romantic representations of the past, whether autobiographical or cultural, succumb to the perspectivist dilemma depicted in Wordsworth's figure of the rememberer 'As one who hangs down-bending from the side / Of a slow-moving boat', and cannot separate his vision of the bottom from the reflection 'Of his own image' (*The Prelude*, IV, 256, 268). These representations can recapture the past from its present vestiges only by postulating a continuous genealogy. Urania must be a mother, for as a historicist Muse she signifies tradition's genealogical power to give the poet his life. *Adonais* contends that history alone bestows and confirms artistic stature: originality occurs only as 'dead poets' invade the text to 'assert their immortality'. But historical meanings require a greeting of the spirit from the poet; they are born from that greeting as the constructions of a retrospective imagination: the child is the father of the man. Hogle has declared metalepsis the governing trope of the process of cultural production in *Adonais*, the figural form of historical meaning as revisionary transference (Hogle, *Shelley's Process*, pp. 302–7). I would argue that *Adonais* never fully accepts the transferential inter-involvement of creation and destabilisation, never fully disclaims its metaphysical nostalgia and desire for permanent truths and values. By obligating the past to the present, metalepsis renders the past an endlessly reconstructible pawn of contemporary ideologies, with their power to distort the historical record, to forget what deserves remembering. Shelley's reflexive figurations leave cultural continuity unanchored in certain truth. As a result, *Adonais* testifies to a romanticism that so 'disrupts the linearity of the temporal process', in de Man's phrase, 'that no sequence of events or no particular subject' – not even the death of Keats – 'could ever acquire, by itself, full historical meaning'.[29]

Shelley projects this potential meaninglessness as the death of poetry, the cultural erosion of a traditionally encoded artistic greatness. If he freely grants the commonplace that tradition and individual talent are unthinkable apart, he also worries over their reciprocity, over the contradiction of artistic fame as both a derivation and source, an 'echo and a light' (l. 8). In this case it is not 'an idle inquiry to demand which gave and which received the light' (*A Defence of Poetry*, p. 489). When the historicist premises of *Adonais* force Shelley 'to write the literary history within which he places his poem' (Cronin, *Poetic Thoughts*, p. 223), the poem's cultural idealisations lose their centring ground. Who or what will ensure poetry's historical endurance? For Shelley the question was far from academic. He lived its uncertainty, in his aesthetic disagreements with close friends (Byron and Peacock) who might have proven allies and in his own embittered feeling of cultural alienation, his sense of his poems as offerings for 'the hunger of oblivion'. The *Defence of Poetry* mentions lost texts – those of Ennius, Varro, Pacuvius, and Accius (p. 494) – even as *Adonais* postulates poets both great and forgotten, artists 'whose names on Earth are dark' (l. 406). Certainly, the writings of Shelley's final period bear witness to a resilient cultural optimism: at times Shelley no doubt envisioned 'history as a progressive evolution of Spirit that bends time's circle into a spiral reaching ever closer to absolute perfection', as Wasserman writes of *Hellas* (Wasserman, *Shelley*, p. 413). At other times, however, he anticipated Joyce's Stephen Dedalus in envisioning history as a nightmare from which he sought to awake, as *The Triumph of Life* suggests, and as *Hellas* also shows: 'The world is weary of the past, / O might it die or rest at last!' (ll. 1100–1). The achievement of *Adonais* lies largely in its interweaving of Shelley's hope and disillusionment, in its revelation, in fact, of their structural interinvolvement. But the poem's achievement lies also with an extremism – *Adonais*, Sacks comments, 'marks an extremity that no later elegy would reach' (Sacks, 'Last Clouds', p. 400) – which projects the death of history as desire's fulfilment.

From *Studies in Romanticism*, 32 (Fall 1993), 425–51.

NOTES

[In this complex and sophisticated essay William A. Ulmer discusses Shelley's lament for the death of John Keats in the elegy *Adonais*. In this poem, as is generally the case with the elegy, the poet explores notions of literary immortality as well as his own problematic relationship to both a contemporary audience and his sense of a literary tradition. Ulmer's critical approach is deconstructive and his essay revolves around the problems Shelley has in representing immortality: 'Representation always speaks of something that is gone, always presupposes loss and absence, and such a presupposition inscribes death in representation as an irreducible element of poetic meaning.' Ulmer's essay explores Shelley's concern with the past and with death. He argues that Shelley's work is organised by the governing power of metaphor which sees likeness in things different. In Shelley's representation of himself as mourner at the funeral of Adonais (stanzas 31–2), however, Ulmer argues that the the governing trope of the poem becomes metalepsis, that is where a series of images occur as substitutions for one another where the point of their similarity is rather far-fetched or remote. Ultimately, it is this rhetorical figure which organises the literary tradition which Shelley desires to be metaphorically based. Ulmer departs from some previous sceptical and deconstructive readings of Shelley in arguing that the poet never fully disclaimed the idealistic and metaphysical nostalgia with its desire for permanent truth and value. Ulmer's essay is original and interesting in taking the poststructuralist commonplace that the writing of poetry involves absence and invokes death, and then rigorously subjecting this to the case of Shelley's elegy, coming up with fresh interpretations of familiar passages. Only the final section of Ulmer's article which applies the deconstructive notion of supplementarity to death in *Adonais* has been omitted. Ed.]

1. Cited from *Shelley: Poetical Works*, ed. Thomas Hutchinson, rev. G. M. Matthews (London, 1970); hereafter *Poetical Works*. Unless otherwise noted, Shelley's texts are cited from *Shelley's Poetry and Prose*, ed. Donald H. Reiman and Sharon B. Powers (New York, 1977). Shelley's letters are cited from *The Letters of Percy Bysshe Shelley*, ed. Frederick L. Jones, 2 vols (Oxford, 1964), abbreviated *Letters*.

2. 'Tradition and the Individual Talent', in *Selected Prose of T. S. Eliot*, ed. Frank Kermode (New York, 1975), p. 38.

3. Paul de Man, 'Autobiography as De-Facement', in *The Rhetoric of Romanticism* (New York, 1984), p. 78.

4. Letter of 24 September 1819 to George and Georgiana Keats, in *The Letters of John Keats*, ed. H. E. Rollins, 2 vols (Cambridge, MA, 1958), II, 212.

5. Wordsworth remarked that 'as soon as nations had learned the use of letters, epitaphs were inscribed upon' funeral monuments, in the first *Essay upon Epitaphs*, in *William Wordsworth: Selected Prose*, ed. John O. Hayden (Harmondsworth, 1988), p. 323.

6. Stuart Curran, 'Adonais in Context', in *Shelley Revalued: Essays from the Gregynog Conference*, ed. Kelvin Everest (Leicester, 1983), p. 166.

7. Ross Woodman, *The Apocalyptic Vision in the Poetry of Shelley* (Toronto, 1964), p. 172. Besides older, Platonising readers, critics stressing the poem's turn from the world include Harold Bloom, *The Visionary Company: A Reading of English Romantic Poetry* (Ithaca, NY, 1961), pp. 342–50; Earl R. Wasserman, *Shelley: A Critical Reading* (Baltimore, MD, 1971), pp. 462–502; and Peter Sacks, who stresses the text's rejection of interpositional veils, in 'Last Clouds: A Reading of Adonais', *Studies in Romanticism*, 23 (1984), 379–400. Despite prevailing similarities, these readings (unsurprisingly) are not in complete accord; Wasserman, in a pointed allusion to Woodman, states for example that 'the conclusion of the elegy is not the poet's weak prayer for suicide' (p. 484).

8. This viewpoint includes the interpretations of social and political historians, most notably the reading offered by Kenneth Neil Cameron, in *Shelley: The Golden Years* (Cambridge, MA, 1974), pp. 422–44; but also biographically contextualising readings such as James A. W. Heffernan's 'Adonais: Shelley's Consumption of Keats', *Studies in Romanticism*, 23 (1984), 295–315. Ronald Tetreault presents Shelley as 'a public poet ... directing his discourse outward', and his poetry as a process 'which

reaches its fulfilment in the audience', in *The Poetry of Life: Shelley and Literary Form* (Toronto, 1987), pp. 11, 17; for Tetreault, *Adonais* is a dramatic lyric which employs 'the tradition of the pastoral elegy to instruct its audience in their responses and to govern their expectations' (p. 221). Stephen C. Behrendt similarly stresses Shelley's rhetorical orchestration of audience response, his strategies for socially positioning his text, in *Shelley and His Audiences* (Lincoln, NE, 1989), pp. 245–63. To these books one might add Jerrold E. Hogle's *Shelley's Process: Radical Transference and the Development of his Major Works* (New York, 1988) which, given its openendedness, necessarily extends into the process of the text's continual reconfiguration by readers.

9. See Wasserman's influential account of Shelleyan mythmaking, a syncretistic strategy signalled in *Adonais*, Wasserman argues, by Shelley's conflation of Adonis and Adonai in the poem's title (*Shelley*, pp. 269–75, 464–5).

10. On the issues of Shelley's idealism, the reflexive 'allegorising' to which Shelleyan metaphor typically succumbs, and the prominence of death in Shelley's poetry, this essay draws on William A. Ulmer, *Shelleyan Eros: The Rhetoric of Romantic Love* (Princeton, NJ, 1990).

11. See Richard Cronin, *Shelley's Poetic Thoughts* (New York, 1981), pp. 193–8, on the surplus of mutually competitive images of immortality in *Adonais*.

12. The first quoted phrase is Jean Hall, *The Transforming Image: A Study of Shelley's Major Poetry* (Urbana, IL, 1980), p. 129; and the next two from Michael Henry Scrivener, *Radical Shelley: The Philosophical Anarchism and Utopian Thought of Percy Bysshe Shelley* (Princeton, NJ, 1982), pp. 278–9, 280.

13. Kenneth Neil Cameron, 'Shelley vs Southey: New Light on an Old Quarrel', *PMLA*, 57 (1942), 506.

14. Charles E. Robinson's comments, from *Shelley and Byron: The Snake and the Eagle Wreathed in Flight* (Baltimore, MD, 1976), p. 167.

15. James Chandler, 'The Pope Controversy: Romantic Poets and the English Canon', *Critical Inquiry*, 10 (1984), 504. For the politics of canon formation and English literary history in the Romantic period, see also Lawrence Lipking, *The Ordering of the Arts in Eighteenth-Century England* (Princeton, NJ, 1970), pp. 329–34.

16. Marilyn Butler, *Romantics, Rebels and Reactionaries* (Oxford, 1982), pp. 113–37. Butler attributes Dante's prestige among the second romantic generation to J. L. Sisimondi's account of him in *The Rise of the Italian Republics*, to which one might add the availability of the Cary translation. Of course, the influence of Italian poetry on the development of English literature had been commonly acknowledged from the time of Chaucer.

17. James Mulvihill's phrase, from ' "The Four Ages of Poetry": Peacock and the Historical Method', *Keats-Shelley Journal*, 33 (1984), 130–47. Peacock's position, as Mulvihill reconstructs it, is that, since 'the arts, and in particular poetry, are inseparable from the social and economic context of an age', then 'critical opinion must be historically conditioned' as well; consequently, the conclusions of 'The Four Ages' 'are the result of a carefully considered historical perspective' (p. 137). My understanding of Peacock's historicism also relies on Bruce Haley's 'Shelley, Peacock, and the Reading of History', *Studies in Romanticism*, 29 (1990), 439–61, particularly Haley's argument that Shelley viewed poets as 'unacknowledged historians', and that the Shelleyan poet acts as 'the synthesiser of past and present cultural history' (458, 446). I cite 'The Four Ages of Poetry' from *A Defence of Poetry, The Four Ages of Poetry*, ed. John E. Jordan (Indianapolis, 1965).

18. Timothy Webb, *The Violet in the Crucible: Shelley and Translation* (Oxford, 1976), p. 309.

19. Nearly every writer on *Adonais* acknowledges the text's extraordinary traditionalism.

20. Alan Liu, *Wordsworth: The Sense of History* (Stanford, CA, 1989), p. 32. *Adonais* has always resisted determinedly sceptical readings. Faced with that resistance, critics wedded to scepticism typically appropriate *Adonais* for secular humanism by claiming that in the text's manifestly Platonic locutions Shelley is only 'speaking metaphorically' (Cameron, *Shelley: The Golden Years*, p. 438). In *Adonais*, according to such readings, 'immortality' signifies not literally but tropically, as a false surmise, a mere figure for something else: therefore the poem is not idealist. Recent theoretical perspectives have discredited such interpretations by showing that traditional, humanistic conceptions of value and language are variations of the same logocentrism that underlies more overtly idealist doctrines – so that the phenomenon of a poet naturalising the supernatural or 'speaking metaphorically' of the One, however significant, does not thrust the poem beyond idealism. Nor does it (in the case of sceptical readings of Shelley) sunder the text's allegiances to truth: while *Adonais* acknowledges the unavailability of final truth, the poem agonises over that uncertainty instead of embracing it as a touchstone of enlightenment. For an overview of theoretical arguments in the context of *Adonais*, see Angela Leighton's 'Deconstruction criticism and Shelley's *Adonais*', in Everest (ed.), *Shelley Revalued*, pp. 147–64. Hogle's work provides a sophisticated account of Shelleyan idealist locution as always transferentially structured. See, for instance, his treatment of the One in *Shelley's Process*, pp. 263–66, and following; for the limitations of Hogle's approach, see Tilottama Rajan's review of *Shelley's Process* in the *Keats-Shelley Journal*, 39 (1990), 182–5, and Ulmer, *Shelleyan Eros*, pp. 16–18.

21. Wordsworth, 'Essay, Supplementary to the Preface', in Hayden (ed.), *William Wordsworth Selected Prose*, p. 408.

22. Byron, *Letter to Murray* in *The Works of Lord Byron*, ed. Rowland E. Prothero and E. H. Coleridge, 13 vols (rpt. New York, 1966), *Letters and Journals*, V, 553–4, n.

23. Hayden White, *Metahistory: The Historical Imagination in Nineteenth-Century Europe* (Baltimore, MD, 1973), p. 80.

24. Ronald E. Becht argues that '*Adonais* is "about" the speaker and his state of mind', in 'Shelley's *Adonais*: Formal Design and the Lyric Speaker's Crisis of Imagination', *Studies in Philology*, 78 (1981), 194–210; quotation, 194.

25. Bloom, *The Anxiety of Influence*, p. 151.

26. Curran, '*Adonais* in Context', in Everest (ed.), *Shelley Revalued*, p. 174. The metaphorical identity of the 'pardlike Spirit' and Adonais is commonly acknowledged, as line 300 of *Adonais* virtually requires. Some critics deny an identity of Shelley and Adonais by insisting that the 'pardlike Spirit' is not a Shelleyan self-portrait but rather an impersonal figure of literary tradition or imagination – 'a composite of all artists' whose idealism victimises them (Behrendt, *Shelley and His Audience*, p. 252), or a dramatisation of an aesthetic process' (Angela Leighton, *Shelley and the Sublime* [Cambridge, 1984], p. 142). Other critics – those discussed in the following note – stress the disjunctive role of the mourning Spirit by viewing him as a personification of Shelleyan traits from which Shelley wishes to distance himself and, therefore, as a proleptic figure of the eventual dissociation of speaker and Adonais.

27. These attributes are discussed, respectively, by Sacks, 'Last Clouds: A Reading of Adonais', pp. 389–96, Hall, *The Transforming Image*, pp. 133–4, and Heffernan, '*Adonais*, Shelley's Consumption of Keats', pp. 301–11. In concluding his discussion of objectification and disengagement in *Adonais*, Sacks adds that 'a further misrepresentation of Keats in Shelley's adaptation of Adonais to his own ideal likeness, is his implicit negation of Keats's espousal of empathy, unobtrusiveness, and negative capability' (Sacks, 'Last Clouds', p. 396). I am indebted to Heffernan's emphasis on the aggressiveness with which *Adonais* 'consumes' Keats, divesting him of an epic or heroic identity as it transforms him into the pastoral dallier necessary for Shelley's dramatic purposes.

28. Ulmer, *Shelleyan Eros*, pp. 85–92, 132–40, 165–76. See Daniel Hughes, 'Coherence and Collapse in Shelley, with Particular Reference to *Epipsychidion*', *ELH*, 28 (1961), 260–83; and 'Potentiality in *Prometheus Unbound*', *Studies in Romanticism*, 2 (1963), 107–26.

29. Paul de Man, *Allegories of Reading: Figural Language in Rousseau, Nietzsche, Rilke, and Proust* (New Haven, CT, 1979), p. 81.

Further Reading

The reading list below attempts to introduce readers of Coleridge, Keats and Shelley, and indeed, students of Romanticism, to some of the key editions and works which will be of most help to them. I should, however, sound one note of warning. Romantic studies has historically been a very contentious area where many of the important literary-critical battles have been and are being fought out, and as a result there is in existence a substantial and even daunting body of criticism. This work, for a new reader, is often difficult and, at worst, can be alienating. Many of the books and articles on the literature of the period are written to engage in a very specific debate and, as a consequence, they are as specialised and technical as, for example, a work on astrophysics might seem to readers unacquainted with scientific theory and language. So in many ways it is helpful to start with a sound, traditional work of literary criticism to get an overview of the period before becoming more adventurous. An excellent starting point is J. R. Watson's recent study *English Poetry of the Romantic Period 1789–1830* (1985; 2nd edn, 1992). Of course, the reading of criticism can never act as a substitute for reading and thinking about the poetry itself. What it can do, however, is to open up possible ways of approaching the texts, enlarging our understanding of the relationship between the works and their background, both literary and historical.

COLLECTIONS

There are a number of collections and anthologies of Romantic period verse which contain the major canonical works and, recently, collections have included writing by non-canonical male and female writers. Below are some of the most recent and up-to-date in their critical approaches.

Jerome J. McGann (ed.), *The New Oxford Book of Romantic Period Verse* (Oxford: Oxford University Press, 1993). This collection contains a range of verse published between 1785 and 1832, including poetry by women. Arranged by year of publication rather than by author, it omits Wordsworth's *The Prelude* (published 1850). Duncan Wu (ed.), *Romanticism: An Anthology* (Oxford: Blackwell, 1994) contains generous selections of the work of Coleridge, Keats, and Shelley along with the complete 1805 *Prelude* by Wordsworth. Women Romantic poets and non-canonical male poets are also well represented and the anthology contains extracts from the prose writing of the poets and other Romantic essayists. Two selections of Romantic critical essays are useful: David Bromwich (ed.), *Romantic Critical Essays* (Cambridge: Cambridge University Press, 1987) and Peter J. Kitson (ed.), *Romantic Criticism 1800–1825* (London: Batsford, 1989). The latter contains selections from Coleridge's *Biographia Literaria* (1817), Keats's letters, and Shelley's *Defense of Poetry* (1821; published 1840).

THE LITERARY CONTEXT

There are many studies of the relationship of the poetry to the ideas of the time. These are some of the most useful and interesting: Marilyn Butler (ed.), *Burke, Paine, Godwin, and the Revolution Controversy* (Cambridge: Cambridge University Press, 1984), contains extracts from the political writers of the period with an excellent introduction, as does Stephen Prickett (ed.), *England and the French Revolution* (London: Macmillan, 1989). Marilyn Butler's *Romantics, Rebels and Reactionaries* (Oxford: Oxford University Press, 1981) is a challenging study of Romantic writers which places the literature in the context of the times and which criticises the notion of 'Romanticism'. Raymond Williams's *The Country and the City* (London: Chatto & Windus, 1973), challenges simple notions about nature and the countryside in English poetry. Other useful studies include: Kelvin Everest, *English Romantic Poetry* (Milton Keynes: Open University Press, 1990); Boris Ford (ed.), *The Romantic Age in Britain*, Cambridge Cultural History, Vol. 6 (Cambridge: Cambridge University Press, 1989, reprint 1992); A. D. Harvey, *English Poetry in a Changing Society 1780–1830* (London: Macmillan, 1980); and Stephen Prickett (ed.), *The Romantics: The Contexts of English Literature* (London: Methuen, 1981). For studies of the ways the poets were received by contemporary reviewers, see Theodore Redpath, *The Young Romantics and Critical Opinion: 1807–1824* (London: Harrap, 1973) which contains substantial extracts from the reviews. There are also individual *Critical Heritage* (London: Routledge) volumes on all the canonical Romantic poets except Wordsworth, and several on the non-canonical poets (such as Southey, Scott, Clare, etc.): J. R. de J. Jackson (*Coleridge*), J. E. Barcus (*Shelley*), and G. M. Matthews (*Keats*). The definitive edition of contemporary reviews of the Romantics is Donald H. Reiman's *The Romantics Reviewed: Contemporary Reviews of British Romantic Writers* (New York and London: Garland, 1972) which is a nine-volume compilation containing facsimiles of all known contemporaneous reviews of the major poets. For further material on the reception of, and audience for, Romantic poetry, see Richard D. Altick, *The English Common Reader: A Social History of the Mass Reading Public 1800–1900* (Chicago: University of Chicago Press, 1957) and Jon P. Klancher's important study, *The Making of English Reading Audiences, 1790–1832* (Wisconsin: University of Wisconsin Press, 1987).

GENERAL STUDIES OF ROMANTICISM

One of the best ways of approaching the literature of the period and its criticism is to look at a collection of essays on Romanticism. Several of these are current and easily available. Stuart Curran's *The Cambridge Companion to British Romanticism* (Cambridge: Cambridge University Press, 1993) contains excellent chapters on many aspects of the Romantic period and its literature (politics, language, gender, and criticism). Also very useful, and more focused on individual poets and poems, is Duncan Wu's *Romanticism: A Critical Reader* (Oxford: Blackwell, 1995). A more advanced and theoretical collection of essays is Cynthia Chase's

Romanticism (Harlow: Longman, 1993) which contains several important contemporary essays in the development of Romantic studies. This is true also of Kenneth R. Johnston et al.'s collection of essays, *Romantic Revolutions: Criticism and Theory* (Bloomington: Indiana University Press, 1990) which focuses on the recent critical debates surrounding British and American theories of Romanticism. Two other collections of essays are especially valuable. M. H. Abrams' *English Romantic Poets: Modern Essays in Criticism* (London & New York: Oxford University Press, 1960) includes classic essays, such as A. O. Lovejoy's 'On the Discrimination of Romanticisms' and Jack Stillinger's 'The Hoodwinking of Madeleine'. Arden Reed's *Romanticism and Language* (London: Methuen, 1984) by contrast contains predominantly deconstructive essays by leading critics of the present generation of Romantic scholars. Useful for reference is the *Encyclopedia of Romanticism: Culture in Britain, 1780s–1830s*, ed. Laura Dabundo (London and New York: Routledge, 1992).

Traditional literary studies of the Romantic movement include the following, several of which have been discussed in the Introduction: M. H. Abrams' *The Mirror and the Lamp* (New York: Oxford University Press, 1953) and *Natural Supernaturalism* (New York: Oxford University Press, 1971) are important studies of the ideas of the poets which argue for the notion of a Romantic movement united by shared ideas and concepts. Harold Bloom's *The Visionary Company: A Reading of English Poetry* (Ithaca, NY: Cornell University Press, 2nd edn, 1970) is a study of the major Romantic poets written before the author developed his theories of the anxiety of influence discussed in the Introduction. Two important works by René Wellek arguing for the coherence of a European Romantic movement are: 'The Concept of Romanticism in Literary Scholarship', in *Concepts of Criticism* (New Haven, CT: Yale University Press, 1963) and, *A History of Modern Criticism: 1750–1950*; Vol. 2, *The Romantic Age* (London: Jonathan Cape, 1955–   ). A very useful, recent study of the ideas of the period is Marilyn Gaull's *English Romanticism: The Human Context* (New York: W. W. Norton, 1990). Several general accounts of the poetry of the period will also be helpful. Stuart Curran's *Poetic Form and British Romanticism* (Oxford: Oxford University Press, 1986) is excellent on the forms of Romanticism, including such neglected subjects as the hymn. Thomas McFarland's important work *Romanticism and the Forms of Ruin* (Princeton, NJ: Princeton University Press, 1981), deals with the Romantic preoccupation with the unfinished and fragmentary. Anne K. Mellor's *English Romantic Irony* (Cambridge, MA: Harvard University Press, 1988) is a sceptical reading of Romantic poetry utilising the German critic Friedrich Schlegel's theories of Romantic Irony. David Simpson's *Irony and Authority in Romantic Poetry* (London: Macmillan, 1979), also deals with the relationship between poet and reader. J. R. Watson's *English Poetry of the Romantic Period 1789–1830* (Harlow: Longman, 1985, 2nd edn, 1992) is an excellent overview of the period and its poetry.

In addition to the books and essays mentioned in the Introduction a number of studies of the period have commented in the light of poststructuralist thought and attempted to get away from notions of Romanticism. Stephen Copley and John Whale (eds), *Beyond Romanticism* (London:

Routledge, 1992) contains a series of essays which attempt to do this from a mainly historicist perspective. Marilyn Butler's *Romantics, Rebels and Reactionaries* (Oxford: Oxford University Press, 1981) and Jerome J. McGann's two studies *The Romantic Ideology* (Chicago: University of Chicago Press, 1983) and *The Beauty of Inflections* (Oxford: Clarendon, 1985) are discussed in the Introduction. Tillottama Rajan's *Dark Interpreter: The Discourse of Romanticism* (Ithaca, NY: Cornell University Press, 1980) and *The Supplement of Reading: Figures of Understanding in Romantic Theory and Practice* (Ithaca, NY: Cornell University Press, 1990) contain ingenious deconstructive readings of Romantic poetry.

WOMEN AND ROMANTICISM

It is no longer possible to read the poetry of the canonical Romantic poets in isolation from the work of the female writers of the time. Helpful books on the subject which an interested reader might wish to consult include the following. First the texts: two good collections of the poetry of female writers are easily available: Jennifer Breen (ed.), *Women Romantic Poets 1785–1832* (London: Dent, 1992) which regrettably contains little of Felicia Hemans's poetry, and Andrew Ashfield (ed.), *Women Romantic Poets: An Anthology* (Manchester: Manchester University Press, 1995) which has a larger selection. A reader approaching the subject for the first time would probably be well advised to start with Stuart Curran's 'Women Readers, Women Writers' in the *Cambridge Companion to British Romanticism*, ed. Stuart Curran (Cambridge: Cambridge University Press, 1993) and also to consult Curran's ground-breaking essay 'The "I" Altered', in Anne K. Mellor's important collection of essays on the subject, *Romanticism and Feminism* (Bloomington: Indiana University Press, 1988). The most current and accessible study of the area at the time of the writing of this book is Anne K. Mellor's *Romanticism and Gender* (London: Routledge, 1993) which postulates the notion of a 'masculine' and 'feminine' Romanticism in the period. These books are discussed in the Introduction. Two other important works are Mary Jacobus's *Romanticism, Writing and Sexual Difference* (Oxford: Oxford University Press, 1990) which is mainly concerned with the Wordsworth circle, and Margaret Homans's *Bearing the Word: Language and Female Experience in Nineteenth-Century Women's Writing* (Chicago: University of Chicago University Press, 1986) which discusses the work of Dorothy Wordsworth, Mary Shelley and Emily Brontë. An important new collection of essays by leading critics in the area of Romanticism and gender is *Re-Visioning Romanticism: British Women Writers, 1776–1837*, ed. Carol Shiner Wilson and Joel Hafner (Philadelphia: University of Pennsylvania Press, 1995) which has essays on some of the most significant women writers of the period.

STUDIES OF INDIVIDUAL POETS

Samuel Taylor Coleridge

The most convenient edition of Coleridge's *Poems* is that by John Beer for Everyman Press (London: Dent, 1974; revised, 1993). This contains the complete poems, including a parallel text of the 1798 and 1828 versions of

The Rime of the Ancient Mariner as well as the earlier form of 'Dejection: An Ode', the 'Letter to Sara Hutchinson'. The scholarly edition of the *Poems*, ed. by J. C. C. Mays in *The Collected Works of Samuel Taylor Coleridge* (Princeton, NJ: Princeton University Press, 1969–in progress) is forthcoming.

The authoritative biography of Coleridge has not yet been written, but Richard Holmes's *Coleridge: Early Visions* (Harmondsworth: Penguin, 1989) provides an attractive and interesting account of the poet's life until his departure to Malta in 1804. A much darker view is conveyed by Norman Fruman's controversial exercise in reverse hagiography, *Coleridge: The Damaged Archangel* (London: Allen & Unwin, 1972) which looks at the life from a Freudian perspective. Fruman regards the poet as a neurotic who was pathologically given to appropriating the work of others. Some useful traditional studies of Coleridge' s work include the following: John Beer's *Coleridge The Visionary* (London: Chatto & Windus, 1959) and his *Coleridge's Poetic Intelligence* (London: Macmillan, 1977) are both excellent examples of traditional literary scholarship tracking down Coleridge's reading and doing justice to his interest in poetic and philosophical subjects. J. A. Appleyard, *Coleridge's Philosophy of Literature* (Cambridge, MA: Harvard University Press, 1965) is a sound study of the critical ideas of the poet. Coleridge's philosophical interests are notoriously recondite and obscure. The best, and most scholarly, account of the subject is Thomas McFarland's magisterial *Coleridge and the Pantheist Tradition* (Oxford: Oxford University Press, 1969) and Raimondo Modiano's *Coleridge and the Concept of Nature* (London: Macmillan, 1985) is also very helpful in dealing with the influence of the German philosophers that Coleridge read.

Some other helpful traditional literary studies of Coleridge's poetry include: Humphry House, *Coleridge* (London: Rupert Hart-Davis, 1953); Stephen Prickett, *Coleridge and Wordsworth: The Poetry of Growth* (Cambridge: Cambridge University Press, 1970) which is good on both poets and on their language and symbols; and George Watson, *Coleridge the Poet* (London: Routledge & Kegan Paul, 1966). Other excellent studies of Coleridge's relationship with Wordsworth include Lucy Newlyn's *Coleridge, Wordsworth, and the Language of Allusion* (Oxford: Oxford University Press, 1986), Paul Magnuson' s *Wordsworth and Coleridge: A Lyrical Dialogue* (Princeton, NJ: Princeton University Press, 1988) and Susan Eilenberg's *Strange Power of Speech* (essay 2, this volume). Kathleen M. Wheeler's, *The Creative Mind in Coleridge's Poetry* (London: Heinemann, 1981) deals with the process of reading a Coleridge poem and is very good on the poet's use of notes, prefaces, and glosses in his poetry. Tim Fulford's *Coleridge's Visionary Language* (London: Macmillan, 1991) concerns Coleridge's lifelong preoccupation with figurative language and includes discussions of *The Ancient Mariner* and 'Frost at Midnight'.

There are two excellent historicist studies of Coleridge's work. Nicholas Roe's *Wordsworth and Coleridge: The Radical Years* (Oxford: Clarendon, 1988) and Kelvin Everest's *Coleridge's Secret Ministry : The Context of the Conversation Poems* (Sussex: Harvester, 1979) both deal with the poet's relationship to the French Revolution, providing the reader with a political and historical context for the 'Conversation Poems'.

There are several collections of essays on Coleridge's work which give the reader some sense of the range of his achievements as well as of the variety of critical approaches to his work. R. L. Brett (ed.), *S. T. Coleridge* (London: Bell & Hyman, 1971), includes essays on the range of Coleridge's interests as does Kathleen Coburn (ed.), *Coleridge: A Collection of Critical Essays* (Englewood Cliffs, NJ: Prentice-Hall, 1967). Leonard Orr (ed.), *Critical Essays on Samuel Taylor Coleridge* (Boston: G. K. Hall, 1994) includes some excellent essays on the poetry and the prose, including Anne K. Mellor's very useful discussion ' "This Lime-Tree Bower My Prison" and the Categories of English Landscape Description'. Harold Bloom (ed.), *Samuel Taylor Coleridge* (London: Chelsea House, 1986) has a range of essays from different critical perspectives on Coleridge's poetry and prose writings. There are a couple of good collections of essays on *The Rime of the Ancient Mariner*. Alan R. Jones and William Tydeman (eds), *The Ancient Mariner and Other Poems* (London: Macmillan, 1973) has some important articles, including E. E. Bostetter's 'The Nightmare World of *The Ancient Mariner*' and Harold Bloom (ed.), *The Ancient Mariner: Modern Interpretations* (London: Chelsea House, 1986) contains a more recent collection of writing on the poem by mainly American critics. This collection includes William Empson's famous essay *The Ancient Mariner*. Jerome McGann's highly influential new historicist essay, 'The Meaning of the Ancient Mariner', is included in an important collection of historicist studies of Romantic poetry, *Spirits of Fire*, ed. G. A. Rosso and Daniel P. Watkins (London: Fairleigh Dickinson, 1981). Patrick J. Keane's *Coleridge's Submerged Politics* (Missouri: University of Missouri Press, 1994) is very detailed commentary on the background to *The Ancient Mariner*. A good brief discussion of modern interpretations of the poem can be found in Patrick Campbell, *Wordsworth and Coleridge, Lyrical Ballads: Critical Perspectives* (London: Macmillan, 1991).

John Keats

Several editions of Keats's poetry are available. M. Allott (ed.), *The Poems of John Keats* (London: Longman, 1970) is an excellent edition with good notes. John Barnard (ed.), *John Keats, the Complete Poems* (Harmondsworth: Penguin, 1973) is also well and comprehensively annotated. Jack Stillinger (ed.), *The Poems of John Keats* (London: Heinemann, 1978) is a very accurate edition by one of Keats's most knowledgeable and careful scholars. *The Oxford Authors: John Keats*, ed. E. Cook (Oxford: Oxford University Press, 1990) contains a good selection of the letters as well as the majority of the poems. The most recent edition of the poems is *Selected Poems of John Keats*, ed. Nicholas Roe (London: Dent, 1995). The standard edition of Keats's letters is *The Letters of John Keats, 1841–21*, ed. Hyder E. Rollins, 2 vols (Cambridge, MA: Harvard University Press, 1958). There is a substantial, one-volume, selected edition by Robert Gittings, *The Letters of John Keats: A Selection* (Oxford: Oxford University Press, 1970).

Keats seems to attract more literary biographers than the other Romantic poets. In particular W. J. Bate's *John Keats* (Cambridge, MA: Harvard University Press, 1963) is an excellent and thorough study of the life, and equally fine is Robert Gittings's *John Keats* (Oxford: Oxford University Press, 1968).

New readers to Keats will find Brian Stone's *The Poetry of Keats* (Harmondsworth: Penguin, 1992) an accessible introduction to the life and poetry. Other useful introductory studies include: Douglas Bush, *John Keats: His Life and Writings* (London: Weidenfield & Nicholson, 1966), and William Walsh, *Introduction to Keats* (London: Methuen, 1981). By critical consensus the best single book on Keats is Stuart Sperry's *Keats the Poet* (Princeton, NJ: Princeton University Press, 1973: reprinted 1991). Some useful collections of essays on Keats include: W. J. Bate (ed.), *Keats: A Collection of Critical Essays* (Englewood Cliffs, NJ: Prentice-Hall, 1964); Jack Stillinger (ed.), *Twentieth Century Interpretations of Keats's Odes* (Englewood Cliffs, NJ: Prentice-Hall, 1968); K. Muir (ed.), *John Keats: A Reassessment* (Liverpool: Liverpool University Press, 1958), and most up-to-date and current is Hermione de Almeida (ed.), *Critical Essays on John Keats* (Boston: G. K. Hall, 1990) which gives the reader a good sense of the state of Keats studies. M. H. Abrams' *English Romantic Poets: Modern Essays in Criticism* (New York: Oxford University Press, 1960) includes several classic essays on Keats's poetry, such as W. Jackson Bate's, 'Keats's Style: Evolution Toward Qualities of Permanent Value', Jack Stillinger's ironic and anti-Romantic 'The Hoodwinking of Madeline: Skepticism in "The Eve of St Agnes"', and Arnold Davenport on Keats's 'To Autumn'.

It is probably fair to say that Keats criticism has been the more traditional and literary in its scope and method, at least until fairly recently, and that critics have tended to concentrate on matters of style and artistic purpose. Studies of the poetry from this perspective include: John Barnard, *John Keats* (Cambridge: Cambridge University Press, 1987); B. Blackstone, *The Consecrated Urn* (Harlow: Longman, 1959); Morris Dickstein, *Keats and his Poetry* (Chicago: University of Chicago Press, 1971); Ian Jack, *Keats and the Mirror of Art* (Oxford: Clarendon, 1967); J. Jones, *John Keats's Dream of Truth* (London: 1969); Christopher Ricks, *Keats and Embarrassment* (Oxford: Clarendon, 1974); M. R. Ridley, *Keats's Craftsmanship* (Oxford: Clarendon, 1933); Helen Vendler, *The Odes of John Keats* (Cambridge, MA: Harvard University Press, 1983); Earl R. Wasserman, *The Finer Tone: Keats's Major Poems* (Baltimore and London: Johns Hopkins University Press, 1953; revised, 1967). Andrew J. Bennett's *Keats, Narrative and Audience* (Cambridge: Cambridge University Press, 1994) is concerned with the reader's response to the poetry (essay 7, this volume).

Historicist studies of Keats have recently begun to appear. Jerome McGann's essay 'Keats and the Historical Method in Literary Criticism' of 1979, reprinted in *The Beauty of Inflections* (see Introduction) pioneered the application of historicist methods to Keats's texts. Marilyn Butler's *Rebels, Romantics and Reactionaries* (see Introduction) likewise placed Keats's poetry in its historical context and the Summer number of *Studies in*

Romanticism, 24 (1986), 'Keats and Politics: A Forum', ed. Susan Wolfson, opened up the issue to more general discussion. Two further studies adopted a Marxist approach to Keats's work: Marjorie Levinson, *Keats's Life of Allegory: The Origins of a Style* (Oxford: Blackwell, 1988) and Daniel P. Watkins, *Keats's Poetry and the Politics of the Imagination* (London and Toronto: University of Toronto Press, 1989). Kelvin Everest, *English Romantic Poetry* (Milton Keynes: Open University Press, 1990), A. W. Phinney's 'Keats in the Museum' (essay 6, this volume) and Nicholas Roe's 'Keats's Lisping Sedition' (essay 5, this volume) both discuss the political implications of Keats's style. The most recent collection of essays on Keats's work, Nicholas Roe (ed.), *Keats and History* (Cambridge: Cambridge University Press, 1995) contains essays by major Romantic scholars on the relationship between Keats's texts and their historical context.

Keats has also proved a fertile ground for recent feminist studies. After Susan Wolfson's pioneering 'Feminising Keats' (essay 4, this volume), a number of studies have appeared. A new reader of Keats will find Margaret Homans's 'Keats Reading Women, Women Reading Keats', *Studies in Romanticism*, 29 (1990), 341–70 and Anne K. Mellor's *Romanticism and Gender* (London: Routledge, 1993) particularly useful. Alan J. Bewell's brilliant essay 'Keats's "Realm of Flora"', *Studies in Romanticism*, 31 (1992), 71–98 is also good on the gender implications of Keats's use of language.

Percy Bysshe Shelley

There are a number of editions of Shelley's poetry available. Timothy Webb's *Percy Bysshe Shelley: Selected Poems* (London: Dent, 1977) is a very useful edition with good notes, and Alastair D. F. Macrae's *Percy Bysshe Shelley: Selected Poetry and Prose* (London: Routledge, 1991) has a good critical commentary and includes some important prose writings. Donald H. Reiman and Sharon Powers, *Shelley's Poetry and Prose* (New York: W. W. Norton, 1977) is the standard edition. Geoffrey Matthews and Kelvin Everest have edited the first volume (1804–17) of *The Poems of Shelley* (Harlow: Longman, 1989) and a further two volumes (edited by Everest) are projected.

Two excellent biographies of the poet are available: Michael O'Neill's *Percy Bysshe Shelley: A Literary Life* (London: Macmillan, 1989) is helpful to undergraduate readers of Shelley and Richard Holmes' *Shelley: The Pursuit* (Harmondsworth: Penguin, 1974) is the authoritative work. Also helpful is Claire Tomalin's *Shelley and his World* (London: Thames & Hudson, 1963).

To arrive at an overview of the development of Shelley criticism, new readers can consult Patrick Swinden's casebook collection of mainly traditional literary criticism, *Shelley: Shorter Poems and Lyrics* (London: Macmillan, 1976) and Michael O' Neill's excellent collection of essays from differing critical viewpoints, *Shelley* (Harlow: Longman, 1993), which includes a fine introduction and helpful commentaries. Other good collections of essays are: Miriam Allott (ed.), *Essays on Shelley* (Liverpool: Liverpool University Press, 1982); G. Kim Blank (ed.), *The New Shelley:*

Later Twentieth-Century Views (London: Macmillan, 1991) and Kelvin Everest, *Shelley Revalued: Essays from the Gregynog Conference* (Leicester: Leicester University Press, 1983).

For a reader unfamiliar to Shelley's work Timothy Webb's *Shelley: A Voice Not Understood* (Manchester: Manchester University Press, 1977) is an ideal introduction to the poet's ideas and poetry. There are several good new critical or formalist studies of Shelley's poetry, including the following: Richard Cronin, *Shelley's Poetic Thoughts* (London: Macmillan, 1981); William Keach, *Shelley's Style* (London: Methuen, 1984), F. R. Leavis, *Revaluation: Tradition and Development in English Poetry* (Harmondsworth: Penguin, 1972); Angela Leighton, *Shelley and the Sublime* (Cambridge: Cambridge University Press, 1984); and Michael O' Neill, *The Human Mind's Imaginings: Conflict and Achievement in Shelley's Poetry* (Oxford: Clarendon, 1989).

Shelley has also attracted the attention of a number of historicist and contextualist studies. As well as Marilyn Butler's *Romantics, Rebels and Reactionaries* and Jerome J. McGann's *The Romantic Ideology* (discussed in the Introduction) the following are useful: Timothy Clark, *Embodying Revolution: The Figure of the Poet in Shelley* (Oxford: Clarendon, 1989); Stuart Curran, *Shelley's Annus Mirabilis: The Maturing of an Epic Vision* (San Marino, CA: Huntington Library, 1975); P. M. S. Dawson, *The Unacknowledged Legislator: Shelley and Politics* (Oxford: Clarendon, 1980); Terence Hoagwood, *Skepticism and Ideology: Shelley's Political Prose and Its Philosophical Context* (Iowa City: University of Iowa Press, 1988); Marjorie Levinson, *The Romantic Fragment Poem: A Critique of a Form* (Chapel Hill, NC: University of North Carolina Press, 1986); and Michael Henry Scrivener, *Radical Shelley: The Philosophical Anarchism and Utopian Thought of Percy Bysshe Shelley* (Princeton, NJ: Princeton University Press, 1982).

Shelley studies has attracted a number of poststructuralist and deconstructive readings, including Paul de Man's 'Shelley Disfigured' (discussed in the Introduction) and Frances Ferguson's 'Shelley's *Mont Blanc*: What the Mountain Said' (essay 8, this volume). Other such readings include: Jerrold E. Hogle, *Shelley's Process: Radical Transference and the Development of His Major Works* (New York: Oxford University Press, 1988); J. Hillis Miller, *The Linguistic Moment: From Wordsworth to Stevens* (Princeton, NJ: Princeton University Press, 1985); Tillotama Rajan, *Dark Interpreter: The Discourse of Romanticism* (Ithaca, NY: Cornell University Press, 1980); Ronald Tetreault, *The Poetry of Life: Shelley and Literary Form* (Toronto: University of Toronto Press, 1987); and William A. Ulmer, *Shelleyan Eros: The Rhetoric of Romantic Love* (Princeton, NJ: Princeton University Press, 1990). Two good psychoanalytical studies of the poet are: Christine Gallant, *Shelley's Ambivalence* (London: Macmillan, 1989) and Stuart M. Sperry, *Shelley's Major Verse: The Narrative and Dramatic Poetry* (Cambridge, MA: Harvard University Press, 1988).

Feminist studies of Shelley are not as prominent as those of Keats, but in addition to the general studies mentioned above, Nathaniel Brown, *Sexuality and Feminism in Shelley* (Cambridge, MA: Harvard University

Press, 1979) makes out a case for Shelley's importance in the development of feminist and androgynous ideals, and Barbara Charlesworth Gelpi, *Shelley's Goddess: Maternity, Language, Subjectivity* (New York: Oxford University Press, 1992) uses Lacanian ideas to explore Shelley's concerns with maternity, creativity and language.

Notes on Contributors

Andrew Bennett is a Lecturer in English at the University of Bristol. He has taught at the universities of Tampere in Finland and Aalborg in Denmark. In addition to his *Keats, Narrative and Audience* (Cambridge, 1995), he is the co-author of two books (both with Nicholas Royle): *Elizabeth Bowen and the Dissolution of the Novel: Still Lives* (London, 1995); and *Literature, Criticism and Theory: Key Critical Concepts* (Sussex, 1995). He is the editor of *Readers and Reading* (London, 1995).

Susan Eilenberg is Associate Professor of English at State University of New York. She is the author of *Strange Power of Speech: Wordsworth, Coleridge & Literary Possession* (Oxford and New York, 1992).

Kelvin Everest A. C. is Bradley Professor of Modern Literature at the University of Liverpool. He is the author of various books and articles on Romantic topics, including *Coleridge's Secret Ministry: The Context of the Conversation Poems* (Sussex, 1979) and *English Romantic Poetry* (Milton Keynes, 1990). He has also edited *Shelley Revalued: Essays from the Gregynog Conference* (Leicester, 1983); (with G. M. Matthews), *The Poems of Shelley*, vol. 1 1804–17 (London, 1989); *Revolution in Writing* (London, 1991); *Essays and Studies on Percy Bysshe Shelley* (London, 1992) and (with Alison Yarrington) *Reflections on Revolution* (London, 1993).

Frances Ferguson is Professor of English and the Humanities at Johns Hopkins University. She is the author of *Wordsworth: Language as Counter-Spirit* (New Haven, CT, 1977) and *Solitude and the Sublime* (London, 1992).

A. W. Phinney was formerly Assistant Professor of English at Harvard University. Currently an attorney practising in Boston, Massachusetts, he has also served on the staff of Senator Edward M. Kennedy as counsel to the US Senate Committee on Labor and Human Resources in Washington, DC. He holds degrees from Yale University, the Université de Paris III, Princeton University, and Harvard Law School.

Nicholas Roe is Reader in English at the University of St Andrews. He is author of *Wordsworth and Coleridge: The Radical Years* (Oxford, 1988) and *The Politics of Nature* (London, 1992), and the editor of *Keats and History* (Cambridge, 1995), *William Wordsworth Selected Poems* (Harmondsworth, 1992) and *Selected Poems of John Keats* (London, 1995).

Karen Swann teaches at Williams College, Williamstown, Massachusetts. Her publications are in the area of feminist and psychoanalytical readings of Wordsworth, Coleridge and Keats, and their reception. She is presently working on a new book called *Lives of the Dead Poets,* concerning death and poetic identity in the Romantic period.

William A. Ulmer is Professor of English at the University of Alabama. He is the author of *Shelleyan Eros: The Rhetoric of Romantic Love* (Princeton, NJ, 1990).

Kathleen M. Wheeler is a Lecturer in the English Faculty of the University of Cambridge. She has published widely on English and German Romanticism and is the author of *Sources, Processes, and Methods in Coleridge's 'Biographia Literaria'* (Cambridge, 1980), *The Creative Mind in Coleridge's Poetry* (London, 1981), *Romanticism, Pragmatism, and Deconstruction* (Oxford, 1993), and *Modernist Women Writers and Narrative Art* (forthcoming).

Susan J. Wolfson is Professor of English at Princeton University. She is the author of numerous essays on Romantic-age literature as well as *The Questioning Presence: Wordsworth, Keats, and the Interrogative Mode in Romantic Poetry* (New York, 1986), and *Formal Charges: The Shaping of Poetry in English Romanticism* (forthcoming). Her essay on Keats (reprinted above) is part of a book in development, *Figures on the Margin: Romanticism and Questions of Gender*.

Index